DECOUPAGE

This Italian secretary features an arched panel in each of the top doors. Marbleizing frames the top, middle and writing section, base and legs. Warm earth tones are contrasted against the green trees in the prints cut out for the front. Background details have been laid in mottled clouds.

Patricia Nimocks

DECOUPAGE

CHARLES SCRIBNER'S SONS

NEW YORK

Contents

INTRODUCTION

The History and Origins of Découpage 11

Understanding the Materials You Work With 49

Preparing Furniture for Découpage, Painting, Etc.

Découpage Procedures   67

Projects to Try 134

Conclusion 160

DECOUPAGE

INTRODUCTION

The History and Origins of Découpage

Découpage is the art of decorating surfaces with applied paper cutouts, according to Webster's International Dictionary. It comes from the French découpage, from *découper*—to cut up, cut out. Webster uses an excerpt by Leo Lerman, "(She) would coil up on the frayed needlepoint of a rosewood sofa and spend her time making découpage." Even in such a brief excerpt one can sense the antique and elegant environs of découpage.

Découpage is the name of a style of work and is preceded usually by a preposition—in découpage or with découpage—being synonymous with cutouts. One who does découpage is a découpeur—not a découpager. One who is cutting is découping—not découpaging. Work finished is done with découpage—not découpaged. Découpage is always spelled as one word.

This is a skillful art in which one achieves a dimensional quality by cutting an irregular edge. This serrated edge blends optically and is more easily applied to a surface. Découpage is an art of elegance. Work produced in this manner should reflect an exquisite quality. It is easy to identify immediately as découpage and doesn't look like any other art. There is a crisp refinement about découpage that distinguishes this work the moment you see it. The stylish appearance is uncommon, mellow and usually antique in character. Découpage is always an individual creation. It can be identified as an extension of one's own personality. The pieces one creates will reflect one's own love of beauty, choice of subject, and care of finishing that is typical of one's own character.

There are three main types of découpage:

The 18th Century découpage—true découpage—classic in feeling, is made of originals or reproductions of hand-colored 18th century prints.

11

19th century scrapbook pages, using German embossed and die-cut designs. Although intended for the scrapbook, they became ornaments for boxes, screens, panels, valentines, and furniture.

This is done in the character of the antique work. Trompe l'oeil (fool the eye) was done in this manner; however, it can be done also in Victorian or Modern découpage.

The Victorian découpage is done with precolored and cutout embossed scrapbook pictures and gold paper braid. During this period, the gay home-loving Victorians made use of these cutouts on practically everything. This is the introduction to découpage for many who are shy about coloring or cutting.

The Modern or Contemporary découpage makes use of currently printed papers—such as calendars, gift cards, magazines, and wrapping papers. This is another form of découpage for the beginner who has a favorite illustration or some greeting cards that would do very well for a first project.

18TH CENTURY DÉCOUPAGE

The découpage work in which we are most interested today relates closely to the "arte povero" of 18th century Italy. It was given the name because "arte povero", *the poor man's art*, was an imitation of the fine lacquer work brought in from China and Japan. The English succeeded in making the closest replicas of the lacquer furniture. The Italian work, however, became such an imaginative and colorful form of decorating that this technique was copied and local designs, as well as styles, came into being all over Europe and the British Commonwealth.

The French découpage was done in the most intricate and lacy cutting. The subjects used were dainty flowers, butterflies, birds, cherubs, musical

A page from a late 18th century scrapbook from England. The center engraving is hand colored. The surrounding cut-out designs are freehand drawings, which are water colored.

instruments, garlands and traditional little trophies. Their découpage was in the stylish character of the 18th century furniture—quite fanciful and ornate.

The German découpage, as well as some Austrian, was a little heavier following the character of Biedermeier furniture. The scrapbook pictures of embossed flowers, birds and all types of tiny miniature embossed tradespeople, children, cherubs, ribbons and so on decorate work by the Germans. They preferred solidly pasted together geometric forms—medallions, octagonals, diamonds, circles and squares. Their colorful work with the embossed scrapbook material has never been surpassed. The embossed printed and precut motifs were invented by the Germans, so their supply was accessible. Caroline Duer—a distinguished editor of Paris *Vogue* magazine—was a noted designer of découpage, using the embossed paper scrapbook flowers, hanging baskets, and gold paper braid on her furniture and little boxes. Cooper Union Museum in New York acquired one of her original chest-cabinet creations.

The English découpage is feathery, beautifully and intricately cut. Much of their work was done on various colored fine papers. Their large screens, which were used in so many places, were lavish and decorative. They were particularly active découpeurs during the early 19th century with this delicate work. At the middle and toward the end of the 19th century, the English turned to the use of embossed paper scrapbook pictures. Queen Victoria was one of the most famed of the collectors of découpage. Her extensive collection included miniature architectural works of castles, palaces, cathedrals and historical buildings. These were reminiscent of the intricate fold-out valentines—and may have been the forerunners. This type of cutting and mounting to give the illusion of depth is called vue d'optique, whether it is framed or in a deep box.

About 160 years ago an invalid by the name of Amelia Blackburn created garlands of flowers and birds so exquisite, original and so unique, that the paper cuttings she did were called "Amelias." For many years after her death they were still called by this name. The craftmanship she displayed was quite phenomenal. The feathers of the birds were each cut with such deftness that close inspection reveals no less realistic a feather. The ordinary white paper that she used for the cuttings was drawn very carefully, cut accurately and colored to closely resemble nature. The feathers and tufts on the birds were no thicker than a hair. Pin pricks were used on the bodies where scissors could not get the desired effects. Her remarkable delicacy of cutting and accuracy of detail must have taken indomitable patience. When one considers her personal handicap, it seems these cuttings were a triumph of the talented and persistent Amelia Blackburn.

This rare and fine George II black lacquer bureau bookcase was done in raised motifs to resemble the oriental work. The modelling, gilding, and superb crafts-manship of this piece is typical of the best work of the period, 1725. The side handles indicate the bureau may have been made as campaign furniture, in three sections.

The exquisite Venetian secretary is ornamented in the best style of "arte povera." The background is hand-painted, with cutout figures, flowers and animals. The center door panel is painted to resemble a vue d'optique.

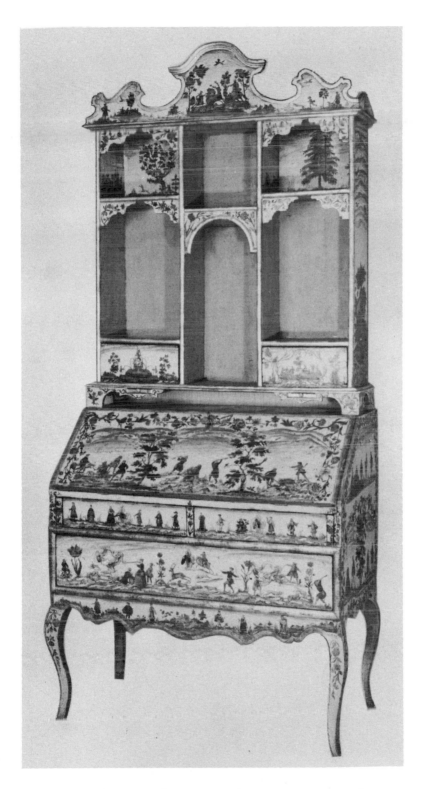

A very attractive variation on the more traditional secretary is the writing-desk cabinet. Rare porcelains were kept in the niches. Hunting scenes decorate this piece. The horses, leaping deer, dogs and hunters create an active atmosphere. Apron border and sides depict bucolic splendor.

This antique Italian cradle could prove to be an inspiration in contemporary use of découpage prints. Hand-painted stems connect the roses. Inside scallop detail is done freehand.

The kneehole desk has been a classic since the 18th century. The scrolled cartouche surrounds springs of country flowers on the drawers. The side reveals a country house with people in the foreground. Soft apricot, pale yellow and earthy greens would be colors very much in keeping with this Italian Provincial desk.

A museum in Nordscia has examples of découpage which appear to have been colored or tinted with watercolor, producing a dim glow. The work was serene in its rich coloring.

Portuguese découpage is as brilliant and dazzling as a tinsel-strewn Christmas tree. Brightly colored paper is used for their cutout work. They have traditional designs interpreted in skillfully cutout foil and tinsel paper. Provincial patterns used are similar to Pennsylvania Dutch; however, much more delicately done. The effect of the rich colors and tinsel foil is reminiscent of the late afternoon sunlight shining through a stained glass window.

Polish découpage craftsmen have been doing cutouts for generations. Their work is usually done in colored papers superimposed to make exacting designs, immediately recognized as cut paper motifs. Most of this work is provincial and it is done in bisymmetric patterns.

Mexican découpage is bright, colorful and used as ornamental motifs at the many holiday festivals. Mexican artists have been very adept in the use of papier mâché in recent years and more and more découpage can be expected from this artistic country.

Belgian découpage was usually cut with a knife and done in the manner of silhouette cutting except for pierced work and reverse cutting. Little information is available on their découpage which was done at the turn of the 18th century. The tiny cutouts look like faded threads and are unbelievably delicate.

Découpage has always been a craft to share. If you could imagine the great undertaking of a journey in 18th century France or England, you know why the families who got together prolonged their visits. Weeks of being together before they returned home created an opportunity to share many hours. The hostess would plan to use their time imaginatively. Often the guests would bring along new ideas. Fine scissors were a basic tool in every lady's work table so it was only natural to begin cutting pictures for a scrapbook. This time-consuming art was very popular throughout Europe and England. The local printers around London made every attempt to produce prints that would catch these ladies' favor. The small prints were very delicate and they covered every subject.

Robert Sayer collected the works of many artists, Martin Englebrecht, Jean Pillement, and others not signed. He bound his volume of about two-hundred pages and called it *The Ladies' Amusement Book.* I am sure these little inspirations were used as basic design material for more than scrapbook pictures. They lend themselves well to needlework pictures and could be very suitable in repeat patterns for textile design or enlarged for repeats in wallpaper design.

Découpage was beginning in Italy also in the 18th century, but in an entirely different way. The first pieces of paper which were pasted onto a surface in the very earliest works of découpage were done by artists who may have been unable to do a handsome line drawing but could do a very good job of cutting and, therefore, they pasted prints onto their furniture. The backgrounds of these pieces were often done in egg tempera, using cloud effects in many muted tones. In some backgrounds trees and shrubs were painted. The foreground was filled with the cutout figures of people in a typical setting. Of all the Italian work done in cutout ornament, many of the classic examples are desks or secretaries.

The woods which were used in Italian furniture generally were soft because in Italy there are very few hardwood trees. It is also possible that the pieces of lumber imported from nearby countries did not always match and, therefore, the surfaces of these odd pieces of wood were covered with gesso. Gesso is a combination of Spanish whiting similar to chalk and it is bound with rabbit skin glue or perhaps hide glue available in Italy at the time. The entire secretary was covered with this gesso and a smooth ground was laid for the application of prints. These prints were previously hand-colored in a technique resembling our watercolor.

The secretaries were known as arte povero (the poor man's art). The name became a classic designation for the cutout prints. In the books that are available describing the 18th century secretaries, the work is referred to as incised or appliqué. The witty and graceful art of découpage furniture (arte povero) was born in or near Venice. The largest number of beautiful secretaries done in découpage are credited to the Venetian craftsmen. This beautiful city was, of course, the center of a great deal of commercial activity and it was by far the most opulent of the cities in Europe.

The Italians were as active commercially as the Spanish and British in trade with the Far East. The treasures brought from the Orient had a very strong influence on European designers. The original works were rare and extremely expensive; therefore, imitations, adaptations and variations of the Chinese and Japanese pieces were produced according to the limitations of materials or imagination of the artist. The delicate gold line work, latticed design motifs, and other exquisite tracery of the oriental motifs were adapted to furniture used in fashionable homes.

The early Italian secretaries were more than ornamental. They were of great utility value and importance to the master of the house. Such a piece provided storage for fine letterpaper, documents of importance, reference and correspondence. It was always placed prominently as it represented the finest personal furniture possession of the master of the household. A very small percentage of the people were literate and those few who had a good education were highly regarded. Since the secretary identified the educated, it was selected by the bride to take to her new home. The Italians strengthened their political position by intermarriage of the leading families in the neighboring city-states. They also made matrimonial alliances with foreign rulers, and frequently would include the scriban or secretary in the collection of furniture the bride took to the new court. This practice of taking a dowry collection into another country spread the cultural commodities of the Italian courts. They were very enthusiastically received in France by such ladies as Marie Antoinette, Madame DuBarry, Madame Pompadour. Each of them commissioned work done in the exclusive manner of the Italian scriban.

The engravings of Pillement, Watteau, Boucher, Englebrecht

It is quite certain that some prints were cut out before the 18th century. Few have been authenticated for use on furniture or accessory objects before the year 1700. Ever since paper and prints have been available to man, these creative materials have been used as ornaments. How far back the art goes or where it was done and who did it are not nearly as important as what material relates directly to découpage as we know it today.

Until the use of engraving and etching, the only line work for reproduction was block printing done with wood blocks. These were used primarily as illustrations for religious works or for educating in the religious context. Most of this work was done by monks or sponsored by the church. Therefore, we could conclude that the earliest forms of printing were predominantly religious and educational. The earliest ornaments and vignettes were religious symbols since so much relating to the church was transferred from pagan or old worship practice and embraced in the Christian tradition.

The engravings, etchings, stone lithographs, aquatints, mezzotints, and other reproduction methods used in the 18th century provided a wealth of material on many subjects. These prints, highly ornamental and of decorative quality, would provide a great temptation to the découpeur. Engravings were not highly regarded by the collector or the patron. They were widely done as reproductions of masterpieces and paintings of great value. The engravers were a group of highly skilled people whose work was unique. Often a single plate could take up three years of a dedicated engraver's life. The beauty and precision of their work has paid off in the long run, as these works which were earlier scorned are now prized by museums, which have special curators of prints.

The 18th century artists, whose works were copied, scorned the engravers and sought to have them barred from the artists' guild. There were a few artists who did direct etching and engraving of their own and who were far more broad-minded about the profession or art of engraving.

The most notable French engravings were created from the year 1710 to the end of the century. Aging Louis XIV saw a new era of rejuvenation. Watteau was to be a dominant figure throughout the century. In many books on 18th century French engraving there is no mention of Pillement at all. He rarely did his own engraving and much of the work that he designed was engraved by someone else. This designer, who in his own time was not especially noted, has since been recognized as the inspired genius whose work is preferred by the découpeur. Also, there were many crayon and pen sketches from both Jean Pillement and François Boucher. Reproductions of these sketches are highly regarded by those currently engaged in the art of découpage.

In France the flowering of découpage was linked with the prints of the engravers and artists of this 18th century period, who were creating elegant designs suitable for ornamentation of all types in the spirit of the new decor. Jean Pillement was most prolific; he created exotic flowers, birds, cartouches, borders, and small scenic vignettes. Pillement's wonderful world of fantasy was largely designed for repeat uses—such as fabrics, textile design and wall ornamentation, wallpaper, wall panels, bas relief plaster. For this reason, we see his characters climb ladders into the scene above where there are other characters in a balancing act or perhaps fending off a dragon. His ornamental people were for the most part in the Chinese style, called by the French name—chinoiserie. He designed many fantastic insects, butterflies, birds and floral garlands. These flights of the imagination prove his mastery of drawing and his real creative genius. It seems certain that Pillement did not design with the idea of his prints being cut. They were to be inspirations for plaster work for the textile designers and other decorators of the day.

Pillement's chinoiserie is not always popular with those new to découpage. On the contrary, it is rather ignored as the novice "oh's and ah's" at the marvelous drawing Boucher exhibits in his cherubs and well-rounded drawings of Venus. Boucher was an engraver and artist as well. As you become more familiar with découpage you will have a deep and growing appreciation of Pillement's chinoiserie.

Martin Englebrecht's sturdy characters, made to represent the trades, show a humorous collection of people who are constructed from their own wares. A clockmaker and his wife made from clocks and clock parts, a pastry vendor made up of tiers of goodies, and others immediately recognized by symbols of their occupation, were original and popular engravings sought by the collector and now are of permanent importance in découpage.

This beautifully scaled Venetian secretary is quite small in comparison to the secretaries of other pictures. The vivid coloring is truly remarkable considering the age of the piece. Typical of designs of the third quarter of the 18th century, its graceful lines and carefully done scenes distinguish this secretary as a masterpiece.

Both right and left sides are shown with the cabinet closed. The backgrounds and clouds are painted. The figures, animals and ships are "arte povero".

The open doors reveal a burnt orange background with freehand painting done in green tones. The claret-colored brocade lining the cabinet also covers the shelves. A surprisingly modern color scheme results from this color combination. The classic door panel and desk writing panel designs were used from the Renaissance through the 18th century and are in use today on furniture imported from Italy.

Gold tea chest paper is the ground for Pillement's fantasia of flowers, so easily adapted to any surface. The 18th century palette is used for coloring.

Pillement prints are very popular because there is such a wealth of material, light and airy, which combines very easily in decorating any shape or panel. The four chinoiserie prints and three flower prints used are colored in the 18th century palette. Background painted deep golden yellow.

VICTORIAN DÉCOUPAGE

During the latter part of the 19th century, die-cutting and embossing made colored scrapbook pictures easy to use and very popular. About this time gold foil was embossed and die-cut in the same manner. These companion materials were produced in Germany and used extensively there; however, they were produced with the idea of being used in scrapbooks and for other ornamental uses. They were used in Germany on furniture—generally these embossed cutouts were pasted together in geometric shapes—following the contours of the furniture. Biedermeier furniture was the style most frequently used. The English used scrapbook pictures on screens, frequently in a dense concentration of material.

A cameo medallion, used uncolored, is pasted on a turquoise ground and decorated with silver-embossed paper braid. Many coats of varnish create a beautiful finish for this piece of Victorian découpage.

This tabletop screen is 9 inches high and shows panels of the Twelve Days of Christmas. The gold-embossed borders provide attractive ornament. The script is mounted on the back.

A collection of Victorian découpage using gold paper braid for decoration on the tree, tea caddy, wastebasket, stamp holder, flower vase and cruet.

CONTEMPORARY VICTORIAN DÉCOUPAGE

Victorian découpage is identified by the embossed die-cut material that is used. If hand-colored cutouts accompany the scrapbook embossed material, it is still called Victorian because of the predominant use of border designs and fill-in ornaments. If small borders are used in gold paper braid and the majority of the cutout material is from current full color prints, it is called modern découpage because of the large proportion of modern material that is used. When gold paper braid border material is used on a piece which is predominantly a reproduction of

The center shadowbox is a key holder with a tiny metal boat in the foreground. Gold paper braid and embossed scrapbook pictures ornament the other pieces.

The antique balloon print was placed on a rich old gold background. Gold-foil-embossed doves, dragonflies and a delicate border complete this useful and attractive tray.

Mardi Gras tray—decorated with ball invitations and gold-foil-embossed crown, jester, crescent, dwarf and a filigree border. The background is painted deep yellow.

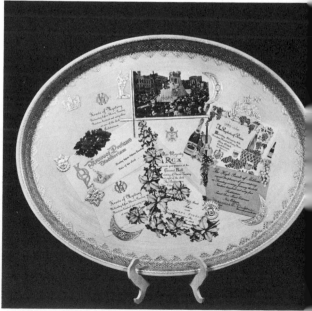

18th and 19th century prints, the work is referred to as 18th century découpage. There are many combinations in which all three kinds of material are used and you would call this simply découpage, and avoid trying to estimate how much of one or another is used and what to call it. Think of the situation in terms of fabric—silk, cotton, and nylon. If you have a predominantly silk costume you will call it silk even though cotton trim is used. If you have a cotton dress with nylon lace it is called a cotton dress. If you have a combination of all three you refer to it by the type of design, such as a daytime costume or an after-five dress. So, in the instance of the use of all three types of découpage refer to it as "a three-panel découpage screen with Chinese motifs," or "a trinket box done in découpage with an apricot background."

In using Victorian scrapbook pictures, they too can be cut apart for better placement—or to make the design less static. They can be cut apart to make an open composition, or to make two pieces about the same size. The gold paper braid is cut apart for greater versatility. A horizontal scroll border can be cut apart and made into a vertical design.

The most important facet of découpage is the idea—which basically begins with the designs you use, how you use color, and the relationship of sides and top in a three-dimensional piece. In the instance of a screen or two-dimensional piece the total design impact is the thing to observe.

Generally, you will use Victorian embossed material for its color and ornamental quality. Many designers of small pieces such as boxes and trays use the gold paper braid to add an embossed texture to the piece on which they are working. A neat beaded or scrolled border, after being glued in place, is painted with two base coats along with the remainder of the box. The whole embossed area is glazed with an antiquing mixture and wiped to give an ornamental effect without the color of the metallic border.

Use borders imaginatively—they will greatly enhance your work. They can be used to alter the appearance of a geometric shape. A rectangular box is not as intriguing until a spandrel shape is placed around the central figure. Spandrels can be used as a completely solid frame or only the oval frame without the triangular corner ornaments. In picture frames for photographs, the oval mat is called a spandrel mat. In framing 18th and 19th century portraits, the wooden oval cut-out was called the spandrel.

On a very long box—3" x 12"—break the surface into three rectangular areas with borders. The larger center rectangle should be horizontal and the two ends vertical. This is almost the effect of a double window with a pair of shutters. When using octagonal boxes it is best to use an oval or octagonal design on the top. A rectangle or a square on an octagonal box is an awkward use of space.

The beautiful designs and lovely cutting on this box are repeated in an interior design plan. A very narrow gold border is used to define the contours of this well-made box. The oriental flowers are quite suited to the box which shows oriental influence. Pale pink ground is used for the natural colored flowers and figure.

Many of the borders will contour in long arcs but it is difficult to make one turn a short curve. If you want to use a narrow border up to a half-inch wide to turn a curve, cut through the border seven-eighths of the way across, just leaving a thin strip to hold the border together. Continue this clipping every quarter of an inch closer or farther apart according to the contour. Now bend gently to the curve. Practice this on a strip of paper.

It is a good idea to use sealer on the back of all embossed work to help keep the contoured motifs crisp. Apply white glue to both surfaces, the box and the border, let set about a minute to become more tacky, then press together. This makes a firmer contact and it dries faster.

A shell pink ground is used for this small octagonal box. The shells are colored in natural tones. Mother-of-pearl is used on the narrow end panels. The varnish has given the entire box a subtle umber tone—the shell pink appears salmon.

Glove box—Knights on a Spanish gold background ornamented with golden scrolls and border. A light glazing of red metallic covers print and scrolls.

This bisque ceramic heart box was sealed and painted shell pink. The cherubs are colored in the Boucher palette. Narrow ribbons were drawn in with pencil, then colored to add a softer, more interesting line to the outside of the cartouche border. These ribbons are easily seen on the lower front, sides and center top. Embossed border and a soft varnished finish complete this piece.

The arresting composition of this screen is well worth studying. A beautiful balance of shapes is evident as well as a careful selection of prints in just the right scale.

Operatic characters, urns and scrolls provide musical motifs. This butterfly grand has only 44 keys. The prints are all black and white. The narrow border is gold. It can be seen on all edges and banding the legs.

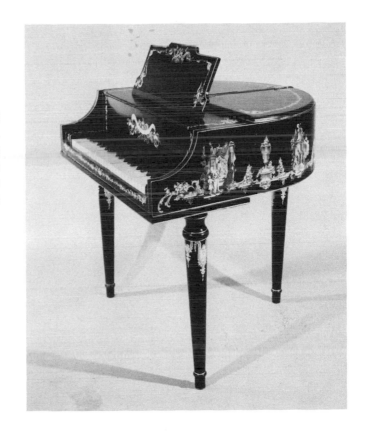

The rear view shows how the scenic episodes are augmented by the urn motifs, scrolls and flowers. This project was done rapidly as all prints used were cut two at a time.

The tray is done with cut-out Chippendale scrolls which have gold tea paper accenting the center cut-out. A Pillement print in the center of the tray is a choice subject for this charming black and white accessory. The foreground box is dark red, featuring the same center print but using cartouche borders. Note the feather cutting on the trees, right and left front.

This reproduction of an old New England wooden tub is painted black and has a colored fruit print for decoration.

Boucher's cupids are colored in delicate skin tones and placed against a ground of French blue, a simple and effective treatment completed with gold paper braid border on top and bottom. Lions' heads soldered on either side are accented with gold.

Cherubs and scrolls, very popular and decorative, set the theme on this provincial tray, which would be at home in many settings.

An Italian chest of diminutive proportions has a variety of flowers, fruit, people and animals used very effectively for ornament. The Venetian yellow ground is mellowed with a very subtle mottled antiquing. Top and bottom banding is done in old blue with gold leaf accents.

Both the front and back of this corner chair are accented with delicate flower sprigs. All the prints are 18th century, as is the palette used for coloring. Powder blue is used as a ground. The well-polished varnish mellows the colors on this unusual piece.

QUESTIONS AND ANSWERS

Victorian Découpage: Gold Paper Braid

1. Q. How can I make the gold paper border flat so it does not take so much varnish to cover it?
    A. Use a roller or burnishing tool to press the embossing and flatten it after you paste it into place.

2. Q. What do you use to make the gold turn silver color?
    A. Lacquer thinner or denatured alcohol (Solox) will remove the stain, leaving silver foil exposed.

3. Q. What is the best way to put the narrow gold borders on?
    A. Apply white glue to the surface you are decorating and to the gold braid; allow to dry a little, then press together.

4. Q. How do you soak gold paper braid off when you use white glue?
    A. You can't. White glue is waterproof.

5. Q. What do you use to antique the braid? Can the same be used for brass feet?
    A. You can use artist's oil paints in black and Van Dyke brown, thinned with turpentine. Apply and wipe off. Antiquing glazes are also fine. You can use acrylic or even watercolor for the antiquing stain on any gilded surface and brass accessories. Burnt umber and burnt sienna are also good antiquing colors. Raw umber is favored by many. When using watercolor, protect with acrylic spray.

6. Q. Do the gold paper braids tarnish?
    A. No, they are aluminum foil stained with yellow, which gives the appearance of gold or brass.

7. Q. I have a lot of paper braid in different colors of gold. Will this show under the varnish?
    A. Yes, all the color variations will appear as different after many coats of varnish.

8. Q. How do I make all the gold braid the same color?
    A. Remove all the stain to silver and stain them again with a yellow stain in a lacquer base, or use many coats of orange shellac to obtain the same tone on all the braid.

9. Q. Is the gold paper braid back in style now? How about embossed scrap book pictures like flowers and cherubs?
    A. For a long time Victorian fancy work was scorned. It was not collectible. Antique dealers assured customers they didn't even have a piece of Victorian around. Today, the craft work and the

This unique clock is made from a drawing by the artist who created the découpage ornaments. A cabinetmaker followed her pattern and applied the ornamental scrolls which she collected. The result, complete with a winding clock movement, is an elegant standing clock. Ivory ground, gold scrolls, pre-colored prints.

This stunning headboard of black lacquer is decorated with pre-colored illustrations. By dividing the long horizontal area into three parts, the design plan was made much more interesting.

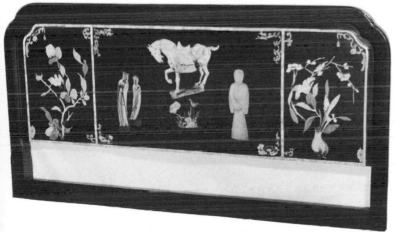

ornaments of this opulent and ornate decorating period is again in style. Regardless of how good or bad a period of design is, history shows that styles do return a generation or two later.

10. Q. Was there much découpage work done in gold braid and embossed paper cutouts?

A. The Austrians and Germans made lovely ornate decorations in tight geometric styles on furniture in the 19th century. Much Biedermeier furniture was done this way. Caroline Duer, once fashion editor of Paris *Vogue,* was the best known modern designer of découpage using this material. Her work was lovely and fashionable—purchased by museums and private collectors alike.

11. Q. How do you prepare the gold braid for Victorian découpage or to use as borders for other things?

A. It is a good idea to spray acrylic over the gold braid when you first get it. Spray it over the foil side first in an even spray—passing over back and forth at a steady moderate pace. The plastic spray will hold the yellow dye in place, which is rather easily removed when you seal over the braid with sealer or shellac. Also, spray the back side of the whole piece. If you always prepare the gold paper braid this way, it will be ready to use with no loss of time preparing it just before you use it.

12. Q. Is gold paper braid called by any other name?

A. Yes. It is given many different names by the many people who sell it, either prepacked or in open stock. It is called Dec-it by Harrower House, Decorets by Taylor House, Fools Gold by East House, and other trade names. It all comes from Germany and Austria.

13. Q. Can the antique material be obtained anywhere?

A. Brandon Memorabilia in New York City has a good selection of antique gold braid and scrapbook pictures.

Marbleized Papers, Tortoise Shell and Gold Tea Chest Paper

1. Q. Where do you use marbleized paper in découpage?

A. Usually, these papers are not used except for lining. They can be used as a background if the pattern is very subtle. Marbleizing is a lot of design competition for cutout pieces.

2. Q. Do you seal this paper before you use it?

A. Use sealer on the front before pasting. Some of the marble colors may be water soluble or may bleed with the use of sealer. Seal the piece before using because it will not stretch when wet with paste. Lacquer or acrylic sprays as well as shellac can be used as a sealer for marbleized paper.

3. Q. How do I prepare gold tea chest paper to use for a découpage background?

    A. Use varnish or acrylic spray on the gold side. Use sealer or shellac on the back. This paper can be very fragile when moist with paste. Also, remember you will have to level the paste underneath—which means you will press the excess paste to get it out.

MODERN DÉCOUPAGE

Modern découpage is distinguished by the use of currently printed flowers, birds, little figures and a whole world of subjects which are printed in full color. The beginners in découpage find this material gets them started without spending the time required to color a print. It opens the door for many who would never do any découpage if they had to color a print. Most of these people do learn to color later and find it wasn't so difficult after all. A most pertinent fact about modern découpage (other than opening the door for the beginner) is that it is very inexpensive. It is possible to find greeting cards to cut out, even gift wrapping papers or pictures from discarded magazines. These materials can be very beautiful and easy to work with; however, there are a few hazards. One important caution is to obtain colored prints which do not bleed under the sealer. The way to test for bleeding is simple and a standard step in preparing your material. Apply sealer. If it doesn't bleed or make a halo of color from the printed area, it is satisfactory. If one sealer doesn't work, try an alternative. First, try the alcohol soluble découpage sealers, or even shellac.

If the print bleeds, there is yet another possibility. Try an acrylic spray. In some instances acrylic sprays make inks bleed but the découpage sealer works well. Try it both ways. If neither prevents the problem, dispose of the print. It just can't be used.

Another caution is to work with papers of the same weight. Heavier and lighter papers rarely work well together and very likely the character of the material is different on the various weights of paper.

A very important caution is that you should not use aluminum spray paint on the back of a print. It may correct the problem of ink showing through but you encounter a greater problem. Rarely does a print hold well if it has aluminum paint on the back. The most frequent problem découpeurs have asked me about is that of the print lifting or having a blister under it. In nearly all these cases they had used aluminum paint. Under the many coats of varnish, much stress is created as the varnish

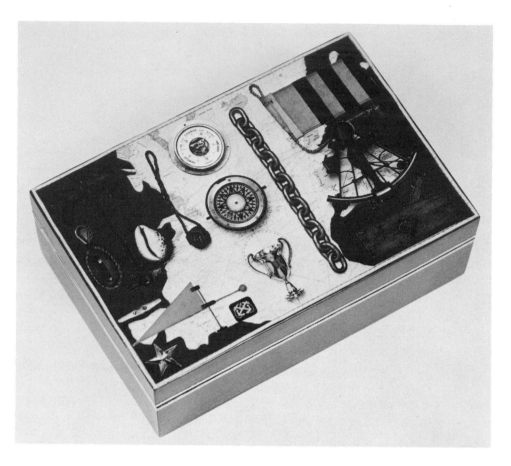

This handsome and easy-to-do box has a red-brown painted background, items cut out of a yachtsman's mail order catalog and a durable varnish finish.

dries and shrinks. This blister may occur as early as three months after being finished or as late as two years.

I am sure many people work out methods of using magazine prints. What works one time may not work the next time. The many types and grades of paper used in modern printing are as different as the varieties of printing inks. Most of the inks are not alcohol soluble or soluble in mineral spirits, which is the vehicle in many acrylic sprays. We're just worrying about the few inks that do bleed and how to control them.

Since the most important material for modern découpage is the print and how to prepare it, I've tried to acquaint you with some problems. Generally, you should not have any problems if you seal the print on the front, let it dry, and cut it out. Apply paste to the surface and press the print in place. After many coats of varnish, you'll have a very lovely piece.

Combine gold paper borders and corner ornaments with motifs cut out of greeting cards which are embossed. This Victorian material helps extend the few designs one can obtain from a greeting card. Very charming little trinket boxes can be made from cutout greeting cards, especially if a message or little poem is placed inside the lid.

Many of the beautiful and very exclusive découpage basket purses are done with modern découpage materials. The loveliest prints from Switzerland, Germany, Austria and England are available in series of Gould's Birds, Redouté's Fruits and Flowers, and Audubon Bird Prints. These are found in inexpensive books or portfolios and are a very good buy. There are also books of Austrian folk costumes and people from many other countries done in a decorative style very suitable for découpage.

Around Christmas time many inexpensive children's books are available in gay colors and charming subjects. The animals are beguiling and are large enough to be very easy cutting. This is wonderful material for some small piece of furniture. Once at an auction we found a sturdy little toy box, which could double as a child's seat. It was in good sound condition so we painted it a teal blue flat enamel, which was a perfect background color for bright animals, birds, and Santa Claus with his ornate sleigh. A fireplace with stockings, bright bricks, and glossy new toys made

The little trunk-shaped box is painted shell pink and has prints from a child's song book.

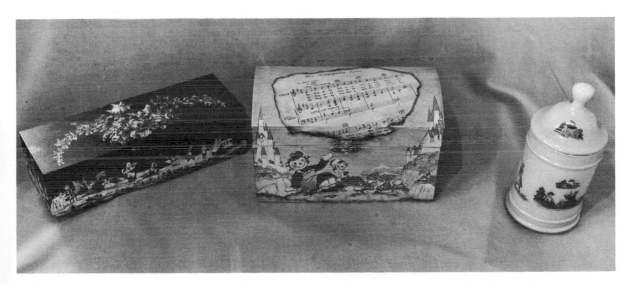

A thriving community of sea ceatures is set against a celadon green background. The color prints are cut out from a children's nature book.

An old footbath is painted yellow ochre and decorated inside with cut-out prints of Audubon's chipmunk, squirrel, and outside with game birds.

Color prints of wildflowers provide related design material to accompany Audubon prints of birds. The black background is a lovely contrast color for this wastebasket.

The French flower prints on the box at the right are in the Provincial Garden palette with a frost green ground. The panel and boxes to the left are in the 18th century palette. Shell pink was used as a ground color on the panel, then Aquamarine Treasure Jewel color was brushed on. Treasure Gold trims all these pieces.

The Chinese flavor of this waterfowl and its surroundings has a graceful movement, kept in motion by the changing reflections of mother-of-pearl placed as water highlights and feather accents.

a good print for the back, which is where we began the design. Santa and his reindeer were on the left side, all the little animals and birds were placed on the front and the right side, so Christmas was not evident from the front. The same toy box could be used through the holiday season as a log box in years to come. It was necessary to buy two books (under a dollar each) to have sufficient material.

The three types of découpage materials are as different as if they were entirely unrelated. In the world of the 18th century prints, the delicate material and fabulous engravings are a real inspiration to work with. Relaxing with a Victorian découpage project is yet another world. It is entirely different from 18th century work to use ornate gold paper motifs cut apart and reassembled to suit your needs. The modern materials are as new as today and offer a truly inspiring selection of prints.

When you use a large print or magazine picture with very little cut out of the center, try to make some small cutouts so the varnish can tack the print down to the surface. This should be helpful in preventing any later release of the print from the surface.

Sometimes you can combine a very attractive print from a magazine with black and white prints in the right scale, which you color to match. If the additional prints are used on the sides and not right next to the colored book prints, the illusion will be that they are all alike.

QUESTIONS AND ANSWERS

Modern Découpage

1. Q. Why don't you recommend wallpaper for découpage?
   A. It is pulpy and coarse. The patterns are never fine. Often the layers of heavier paper will stratify and come loose. It is impossible to cut intricate patterns and it is difficult to cover with varnish. Avoid heavy prints and wallpaper. They weren't made to be covered with layers of varnish.

2. Q. What about using fabrics, real butterflies and flowers? Some people do découpage with these materials.
   A. This is not découpage. Avoid this kind of thing.

3. Q. What do you do with a magazine picture that you want to use, but there is black type on the back?
   A. Erase as much as possible—gently. Place on a medium to dark shade of background. This camouflages the type. If you still see the type, do not use the picture as the varnish will exaggerate the type. After all, you can't use everything you can cut out.

An extravagantly beautiful secretary. The off white background is sumptuously accented with gold across the scrolled top, door frame, base details and legs. A limited palette is used to color the prints which are mostly dressed figures. Rose, medium blue and mauve are used in the free-hand brush work of the borders and center flowers in the doors.

Very pale apricot inside the cabinet is hand-scrolled with slate blue and white, making a subtle transition for the various metal urns, tea pots and lower porcelain figures. The green door frames, seen also inside the writing area, are not seen until the opened doors reveal this striking color accent.

Understanding the Materials You Work With

The materials you work with are really not difficult to understand. There are a few rules to go by but your best teacher may be yourself. You learn the most from your own mistakes. There aren't many that will baffle you. A problem faced by many new to découpage reminds me of a patient who sees many different doctors and only finds out he is more confused than before. Please use one book for reference and bear with the author until you understand the material. Do not quote from many different sources and follow the advice of each person you consult. Everyone is working for the same result but the methods may be a little different. After you understand one approach, then branch into another author's work. Each one will cover something you haven't learned before. But do not mix them all together! Your own keen observation is the answer to your search for knowledge.

Read the labels on everything you buy. Notice the percentages of solids in varnish, get what you pay for. Ask questions of the people who sell you material. Write letters to people who write articles. They expect to answer questions—they can answer yours, too. All paints, varnishes and sealers should have clear labels explaining drying time, solvents, what to clean your brush with, and the number of fluid ounces must be accurate. Read all of this information. Buy only products of reputable manufacturers. Nationally advertised brands are the best buy.

UNDERSTANDING PASTE, GLUE, MUCILAGE, ADHESIVE

The more delicate and intricate cutting is done on lighter weight paper. This fragile cutting should be pasted down with a light découpage paste. It holds very well and is easy to move out from under prints as it sets more slowly than white glue.

Heavier paper, such as is found in hand-made paper of antique prints and other papers used for prints in color, requires heavier paste or glue, such as the white glue—Elmer's, Duratite, and so on. Paste is also used for these heavier prints, but the white glue *is not* used in fine cutting. It is sometimes difficult to remove excess white glue after it is hard and set because it is waterproof. Adhesive is a name generally given to the whole group of paste, glue, cement and other compounds used to adhere materials to each other. It comes from the Latin meaning "to stick." Read all labels. This should tell you what you need to know.

You do not use cements or heavy duty wood and laminating adhesives except for wood repair or some special glass-to-wood use. Do not use paste for heavy repairs—only on papers.

"Adhesium" available at paint and wallpaper stores is widely used on glass before application of a pasted print. A thin coating of this clear material is wiped on clean glass and allowed to dry. After the print is pasted on the surface and is dry, a damp sponge or cloth is used to remove the "Adhesium" and excess paste from the glass surface. If you use tea chest paper over all the background you leave all the "Adhesium" to help the paper adhere to the glass. It is not a paste or glue itself but is used to help prints adhere to glass. This sticky material would be good used on any gloss surface such as a lacquer tray or a prefinished metal.

SEALERS

There are many kinds of sealers. The oldest and most traditional is shellac. Orange shellac is bleached for "white" shellac, which is pale in color. Rectified shellac is an artist grade which is refined to remove certain impurities. Any of these three types has a limited shelf-life, which means the time between manufacture, sitting in a warehouse, on a dealer's shelf, and finally in the customer's possession. The shelf-life of shellac is only about six months under most favorable conditions. If it is not fresh when applied to a surface it becomes gummy and is very slow to dry or even may not dry for weeks. This is very bad because in using solvent alcohol to remove the old shellac you may damage the prints, and surely you will remove stain from the gold paper braid which will turn it silver.

Modern sealers developed for découpage are the result of modern chemistry. They have indefinite shelf-life and always dry as they should. They will require only one caution, do not use them in a moisture-laden atmosphere. Alcohol, which is the solvent for all sealers, attracts moisture, thereby accumulating water in the sealer film and appearing to be a frosty coating.

Découpage sealers are important in preventing dark paint colors from bleeding. It is a good idea to apply sealer to the entire surface of the work you are doing before varnishing. If you know the paint color you have used does not bleed under varnish, it is not necessary to seal before varnishing. You can make a test panel to determine which paints bleed.

Sealers have another advantage. They act as a paint bonding adhesive on glass or other very slick surfaces. Découpage sealers remain slightly plastic and prevent paint chipping from a glossy metal or glass surface.

The découpage sealers are important in penetrating the surface of the paper to change the porous surface into a non-porous surface. A sealed print will not be discolored by varnish. Paper which is sealed is stiffer and easier to cut. Most important, the sealer-saturated paper will not disintegrate when it is wet with paste and moved with the fingers for removal of paste or to flatten the print. Finally, when you clean off excess paste, the print, though delicately cut, will remain intact.

WHAT PAINT TO USE

The flat enamels are by far the most suitable paints to use for découpage. You can easily see any extra paste that is yet to be removed, as it is glossy on a flat paint surface. But the greatest advantage of the dull surface is that varnish adheres to it much better. Semi-gloss paints are used as a second choice. It is wise to avoid rubber base or water base paints. It is possible to obtain flat enamel or flat oil paints everywhere paint is sold. It is not always easy to find the right color, but these can be mixed by the merchant who sells you the paint. If you'd like to experiment in mixtures, it is possible to do this quickly and with no waste of paint. Dip a few drops of paint from one can, a touch from another, and blend on a piece of wax paper or newspaper. This way you can see if the colors you are blending will become the color you hope to obtain.

Paint basically is varnish with colored pigments added. Since you will be working with turpentine or mineral spirits as thinners, do not hesitate to add one or the other if your paint seems too thick. It is very important to have paint level out flat. If it doesn't, you are using too much or it is too thick. The best application procedure in paint and varnish is to apply thin coats, be frugal. You cannot have drips or runs if there is no excess paint build-up.

KNOWING YOUR MATERIALS CHART

Product	Thinner	Drying Time Between Coats	Remove With	Type of Drying	Flammable
Shellac	Alcohol	45 minutes	Alcohol	Evaporates	Yes
Varnish	Turpentine	24 hours	Paint remover	Oxidize	Yes
Acrylic Spray	Mineral Spirits	1 hour	Turpentine	Evaporates	Yes
Lacquer	Lacquer Thinner	4 hours	Lacquer Thinner	Evaporates	Yes
Epoxy Varnish	See Label	8 hours	Not soluble	Polymerize	Yes
Oil Paint Flat	Turpentine or Mineral Spirits	24 hours	Paint remover	Oxidize and Polymerize	Yes
Enamel	Turpentine or Mineral Spirits	24 hours	Paint remover	Oxidize and Polymerize	Yes
Metal Primer	Turpentine or Mineral Spirits	24 hours	Paint remover	Oxidize and Polymerize	Yes

THINGS TO AVOID

Types of material that are difficult to work with:
1. Wallpaper, post cards, photographs
2. Fabrics, printed embossed wrapping paper
3. Wood fiber, crepe paper, tinted tissue paper
4. Natural plant material—leaves, petals, butterflies

Types of material that bleed:
1. Some magazine, calendar and greeting card prints
2. The watercolors which are aniline dyes. These are liquid—ready mixed in small bottles.
3. Some of the *leaves* of color which are soluble in water.
4. Alcohol soluble inks

How to test:

If the alcohol soluble sealer causes these materials to bleed, try an acrylic spray. If no color comes through to the back of the colored print now and no halo of color from the ink, then it can be used. If you still have doubt, brush the varnish on a small test area before you cut. If a print bleeds do not use it.

SILICONE AS A HAZARD

Be sure to notice what is in any spray you use to keep the fabric soil-resistant. If you use a silicone spray you can contaminate a good varnish finish. Silicones in hand creams or anywhere else act as a separator and may prevent adhesion of future coats of varnish. This is a caution measure. If you are going to refinish a piece of furniture which you know has had a furniture polish spray used often, this piece should be checked. If the spray can label reads, "contains silicone," it may not hold a varnish or paint at all once the finish is worked on. There is very little that can be done. See your paint dealer. There is always hope that some product will be available to neutralize this penetrating separator.

WHAT SCISSORS TO USE AND WHY —KNIVES AND BLADES

Découpage scissors: the most popular and best scissors are the fine steel cutlery known also as cuticle scissors. They stay sharp the longest and this is important. These are held with thumb and third finger with the blades resting against the index finger. Usually the blade is held pointing out.

Silhouette scissors are very convenient for cutting fine work or straight lines. Many people prefer these easy-to-use scissors. Generally, the finger hole is larger and suits men better than the découpage scissors.

Embroidery scissors can also be used if they are small, sharp and well adjusted; that is, not too loose. The turn screw can be tightened or loosened to make cutting easier. A tiny amount of oil or vaseline in the hinge and rubbed over the blade is helpful. Never use rusted scissors —or permit them to rust.

Shears and larger scissors are used only for cutting large prints in two or occasionally for long strips of border material. They are heavy and not suited to fine cutting.

Oiling and Adjusting the Scissors: New scissors are rather like new shoes—they look well but they need to be broken in. A good machine oil will keep the blades and hinge in perfect order. If the scissors need to be loosened, the set screw can be released slightly. If, after cutting awhile, the scissors seem to drag or resist cutting, gently touch each of the blades with a tiny amount of oil. Even the tiny amount of natural skin oil on the face is enough to lubricate the blade. After your scissors are broken in, the cutting seems much easier. Natural wear is the best way to break them in. Do a lot of practice cutting.

Knives and razor blades are invaluable for certain types of cutting. If you cut well with a knife or have always used a razor blade, it may be difficult to sell you on the idea of scissors. Take my word for it—much of the cutting done in découpage is easier, more attractive and much less strained with the right scissors.

BURNISHING TOOLS

Special tools to bevel the edges of the print, or press it into the background wood, may save half the effort of burying the print in varnish. The burnishing tool is pressed along the edges of the cutout print after it is pasted in place and dried. In softer wood or on a gesso finish it may be possible to embed the print level with the surface before applying the sealer. Then proceed with the varnish finish.

The steel burnishing tool has a choice of two ends: the spoon-shaped end is for working on a flat surface. The other end is for narrow crevices and right angles such as along the molding at the bottom edge of a box.

The agate burnisher, used for polishing gold leaf, is superb for burnishing the print edge in découpage work. Agate, being a semiprecious stone,

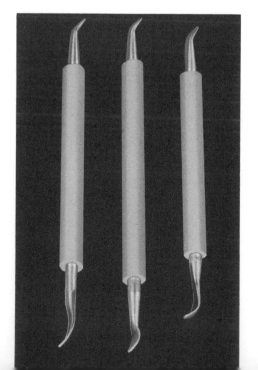

Three burnishing tools are shown. The spoon end is used to press the print edge into the background. The point end is used on embossed border edges.

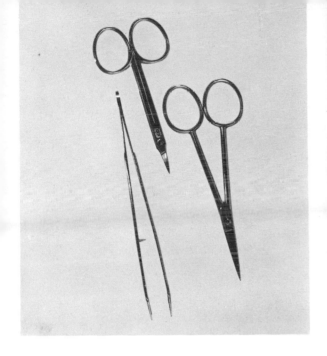

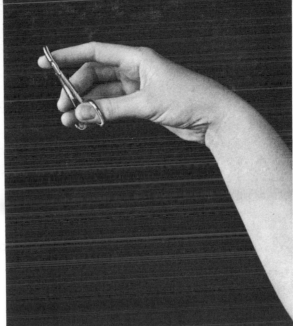

Either the curved découpage scissors, or slender silhouette scissors are essential; tweezers are necessary to handle delicate cuttings.

The scissors are held with thumb and third finger in a very relaxed manner.

when shaped, hand-polished and mounted in a metal ferrule is a very expensive tool. It is possible to use small smooth agates not mounted to accomplish burnishing, but it is tiresome and not as effective.

QUESTIONS AND ANSWERS

Burnishing

1. Q. How can I flatten a print and embed the edges into the wood before varnishing?
    A. Use a steel or agate burnisher. Press the edges gently, then more firmly with increasing pressure until you barely feel the edge.

2. Q. Can this be done right after pasting?
    A. Wait an hour at least. You can burnish *before applying sealer or after.*

3. Q. Will this help flatten wallpaper cutouts?
    A. Yes, but it is a job. Avoid wallpaper.

4. Q. Can I use any other object for burnishing, such as a silver spoon?
    A. Stainless steel is hard and won't wear off. Silver may be soft enough to wear and leave dark marks. Stainless is better. Test the object

you have in mind. A nut pick, used on the back side, may work for you if you don't have a burnisher.

5. Q. Where can I obtain a burnishing tool and what do I ask for?
   A. Art and craft stores have these supplies. Any découpage supply store should have them.

6. Q. Will a burnisher work on metal and glass?
   A. Yes, it will bevel the edges but obviously it can't embed the print. Masonite and other hard dense surfaces come in this category, too.

7. Q. Will a burnisher help embed fabrics cut out for découpage?
   A. Do not use fabric cutouts. This is not découpage.

8. Q. For what is the narrow end of the burnisher used?
   A. Crevices and inside corners, such as along a box with a base molding or narrow contours.

TWEEZERS

This handy tool will prevent damage to your prints. If you have small pieces to place into paste, the tweezers are an invaluable tool. They assist you in lifting a print from the pasted surface, if it is necessary. Curved-nose tweezers are by far the best to buy; however, if you have a pair of the spade-nose tweezers, the kind stamp collectors use, these are useful in handling the prints. Cosmetic tweezers are also useful, but they are much stiffer. A pair of tweezers I enjoy very much are longer and finer than the short curve-nose tweezers. These were purchased at a dental supply house, which I'm sure will sell you if you don't mind spending a little more money for this very fine tool.

BRUSHES

There are many kinds of hair and bristle that are used to make brushes. The small brushes used for little boxes are probably squirrel, ox, pony, camel, sable, or some other soft hair. They should be cleaned in a proper solvent, shampooed, shaped and set aside to dry. The larger brushes, one inch to two inches wide, are ox hair or other combinations, and are more difficult to clean after use. Dip them in their solvent and clean until no more color comes out. Then, wash with detergent and water—a couple of good sudsy shampoos—wrap in a *paper* to make the chisel shape end. Dry the brush, bristle end down, so water will not dry in the ferrule causing rust.

Brushes used in sealer are cleaned thoroughly in alcohol and shaped to dry. If your brush dries a little stiff, it wasn't stored clean. Alcohol will always soften this brush. More sealer used on the brush will dissolve the previous sealer. The same is true of lacquer brushes, cleaned in lacquer thinner.

Varnish brushes are the most tedious to clean because they are used daily during the build-up of a découpage finish. It is very satisfactory to leave the brush in turpentine from day to day until you are finished. This will prevent varnish from drying along the shafts of hair, which is one thing that causes a poor varnish finish. The dried varnish always seems to work out, coat after coat. Don't let it happen to begin with. Use the varnish brush only for varnish. Label the sealer brush and the brush used for paint and don't use them alternately.

PUMICE AND ROTTENSTONE

These are two different materials coming from two very different places. The largest deposits of pumice are in Sicily. Pumice is a volcanic ash, a silicate, and a sharp abrasive used also as scouring powder. It is used with oil as an abrasive to smooth down a varnish finish. Pieces cut from an old felt hat are excellent to be used for a rubbing pad—and re-used for a long time. A pound of pumice costs about thirty cents.

Rottenstone is a clay deposit which is dried, ground into a powder, and also used as a rubbing abrasive. Its cutting action is not as severe as pumice.

The advantage of using pumice or rottenstone is that they are much less expensive than wet or dry sandpaper and will contour more easily when used with a felt pad for rubbing. They are a little less convenient to store and messy to clean up. After all, an abrasive is an abrasive. Use the one which seems to work best for you—or whatever you feel does the job. I am inclined to use the #400 wet or dry sandpaper because there is a wider choice of abrasives in the grades of sandpaper and steel wool.

THE MAGNIFYING GLASS

Sometimes it is difficult to see the work you are doing and you wish to use a magnifying glass in preference to reading glasses. The precision ground glass that hangs from a cord around the neck is very practical and light weight. You may prefer the sand unit—to be placed on a table. Be sure to have a suitable light wherever you do your work.

Preparing Furniture for Découpage, Painting, etc.

The beginner must learn to discriminate between the bad dents and charming irregularities which contribute natural distress and the look of antiquity to a piece. By all means remove ring marks and geometric shapes of accident. Sandpaper must be changed when it fills. The disposable sandpaper is of less value than human energy.

The final coats of paint will show up irregular sanding. Sand in the direction of the grain. When sanding on the edges of painted surfaces, you must be very careful not to rub through the paint. Develop a sense of touch. Use the tips of the fingers to feel the surface lightly, without pressure. If the pressure is heavy you will feel only your own pressure, not the surface texture. It is possible to feel roughness that cannot be seen. Care must be taken to sand absolutely even and level. This makes the ideal surface for découpage.

FILLERS USED FOR FURNITURE WORK

Any repairs that are badly done are obvious. This is as unacceptable as the original damage. Minor repairs are filled with spackling compound —ready mixed or the kind to which you add water; use for cracks, holes, or any gouges. This material can be molded for replacement of broken mouldings. Larger cavities should be laid with glue first so the spackling will remain in the hole. When this material shrinks—and it will with a large hole—it must be brought back up to the surface and allowed to dry again, sanded, and sealed. Plastic wood can also be used for repair of holes. Allow to dry and sand level.

58

Vinyl filler (by various trade names) is made to fill open grain wood. This is wiped across the grain. It will fill small holes and cracks as it surfaces the wood. Sand when dry, and seal with shellac.

GLUE JOINTS OR SWELL WOOD

A good glue should be used to tighten joints or make other repairs before work proceeds. At the time a joint is glued you must apply pressure. It is a good idea to wrap old innertube rubber strips around the piece of furniture. It does not scratch and will contour to the piece on which you are working. A furniture vise should be used on large pieces.

If you have loose joints which can't be glued easily, swell the wood. This is done by a single application of one-half alcohol and one-half glycerin. Mix these and place eye droppers full in the dowel holes. It may take a few days for this to be tight, but it will hold.

SHELLAC—THE ORIGIN OF LAC

In Siam and India the lac trees are host to many small insects which cause the tree to "bleed" or secrete a sticky substance. This substance is the lac flake that is gathered or harvested only at night. After being melted, purified, and finally graded, it is exported. When it arrives in the United States, various manufacturers buy it and "cut it" with alcohol. A four pound cut should be diluted fifty percent with alcohol when you use it. This means you're using a two pound cut. Four pounds of lac, or solids, are added to a gallon of alcohol to make the four pound cut; only two pounds of lac are added to a gallon for the two pound cut.

Shellac deteriorates and is apt to become gummy after six months. It is absolutely necessary to use only fresh shellac. Write the date purchased on the label. Metal containers darken shellac—store it in glass containers. Shellac should be stirred, never shake it—this creates bubbles. In damp weather the alcohol will cause shellac to bloom. Milky shellac is anhydrous and attracts water like salt. If shellac gets cloudy, an application of alcohol should remove the bloom—then let dry. Do not work in a moisture-laden atmosphere when using shellac or varnish. After an hour of drying time, shellac may be coated with paint.

Good studio practice demands a brush used only for the sealer. For boxes and small projects you will need a small brush about one-half to one inch. If you are doing furniture or other large pieces, you will need a one-and-one-half inch to two inch thin bristle brush. A thick brush discharges too much shellac or other sealer. You will be able to do a better job using natural bristle brushes. My feeling is that my own limitations in talent are sufficient. I can't be hampered further by less than the best tools.

How to Apply Shellac to New Wood

Load the brush. Press out the excess on the inside of the container. (Drawing it across the edge of the can creates air bubbles.) Use quick even strokes, being careful not to overlap. The strokes should begin with a full brush in the center of the area to be covered; continue with light strokes across to the outer edge. Follow quickly by stroking from the center to the opposite edge. The brush will generally hold enough shellac to repeat this procedure on the following stroke. When the brush is less full, pressure is needed on the heel of the brush to discharge the remaining shellac. Reload the brush to complete the coverage and repeat the procedure. For carved pieces, use a minimum brush load. Tap the end bristles into the deep places to assure complete coverage. Pick up any runs or excess in the gentle tapping. A fine shellac coat requires precision, quickness, and a deft touch. If the shellac brush should become hardened—and alcohol doesn't do the job—it may be cleaned in a solution of half and half ammonia and water. NEVER SOAP. Shellac is the most used sealer; however, if you use lacquer sealer, sanding sealer, or pigmented sealer, they are to be applied in the same way as shellac.

HOW TO PREPARE THE SURFACE FOR PAINT

Raw Wood

Unpainted furniture fresh from the store or cabinet maker still requires sanding. There are often whiskers of wood or tool dents which should be sanded with 2/0 garnet sandpaper. Sink any nail heads with a nail set and fill with a good wood filler or vinyl filler. Also, fill any joining cracks. These cracks should be sanded. Check for any leftover glue—chip off with razor blade and sand smooth. Dust the piece or clean up with a vacuum cleaner brush, use a tack rag, and then seal. The sealer closes the surface of thirsty raw wood and prevents uneven absorption of the paint. Only raw wood is sealed before painting.

Varnished Wood

Many new products are available for surface preparation of old varnish. These are mostly solvents. These will have names like Prepare-it, Sur-

Three tiny trinket boxes are done on pastel grounds of ivory, powder blue and shell pink. The 18th century palette of colors is used for the prints. Very narrow gold borders are used at the top, bottom, and at the edge where they meet.

facene, or Liquid Sandpaper. They do not do the job of sandpaper but they soften the old surface, which makes it more receptive to paint.

If you have a piece which has raised or blistered veneer, cut a narrow slash with a razor blade, fill with glue and weight the area, using wax paper to prevent sticking to the weight. Edges should be clamped with a C-clamp, using wood blocks. Fill any chips with wood filler, seal the chipped area with shellac and sand. Refer again to the use of fillers, if needed. Your piece is now ready to paint.

Painted Wood

A previously well-painted piece needs little work. It is wise to wash it with turpentine or mineral spirits to remove any grease or old wax. A light sanding assures best adhesion. The surface preparations such as Liquid Sandpaper, Surfacene, or Prepare-it are good insurance that your paint will hold well.

Drips and rollovers (the ridge of paint sometimes seen on the edges) should be chipped and sanded off. Chips in the paint should be carefully feathered out with 2/0 and 6/0 garnet paper. After sanding, wash off remaining residue with alcohol or mineral spirits. If filler is needed for holes, fill and sand. Shellac this area to seal it.

Glass or Glossy Metal Surface

Though you don't often paint over mirrors, glass or glossy metal, such as chrome, it is a good idea to include this information here. A penetrating healer* should be used on these surfaces first, as the sealer will stick tightly to the slick surface and act as an adhesive for the paint. Any sealer labeled as "penetrating" will do this job.

* See supply source

Metal

It is a good idea to use a metal primer as an undercoat on all metal. This specially designed paint will protect the surface and prevent rust. It provides a good surface for the paint. Metal primer must dry overnight. Hardware should be primed before painting. Old painted hardware should be left in a can of lacquer thinner till clean, or use paint remover. You may need a wire brush—a suede cleaning brush is handy. Emery cloth is good for removing rust; also, wet or dry sandpaper can be used. Wash the surface with alcohol, apply a metal primer and dry overnight. Your metal is now ready for painting.

Metal preparation is really easier than wood but it does require some different materials.

OLD METAL—PAINT CHIPPED, DAMAGED, DENTED METAL

Use paint remover to clean metal. Hammer the dents out as smooth as possible. Wash with alcohol. Apply metal primer. Dry overnight and you are ready to paint.

OLD METAL—PAINTED

If the paint is in good over-all condition, you need not remove the paint. Simply wash with alcohol to remove the wax or oils. Sand lightly with very fine sandpaper if the surface is glossy. You are ready to paint.

OLD METAL—NOT PAINTED

Use sandpaper and steel wool if there is rust on the tin. Wash with alcohol and apply one coat of metal primer. Dry overnight and sand lightly. You are now ready to paint.

NEW METAL—GALVANIZED

Wash with a diluted acetic acid or vinegar. Diluted acetic acid is found at drug stores and sometimes paint stores. This etches the surface to cause good adhesion. No primer is necessary. Apply two or three thin coats of paint. A smooth surface is vital. Thin paint flows out easily and makes a level surface. Sand very lightly (just like whisking off fingerprints) between coats. Caution: diluted acetic acid may be dangerous to use. (see label.)

NEW METAL—NOT GALVANIZED

Wash with alcohol and apply metal primer. Sand and apply paint.

NEW METAL—PAINTED

On a tray with screened or lithographed scenes or flowers—use fine sandpaper over all to remove gloss and create a surface for good paint adhesion. Apply three thin coats of paint.

GOLD LEAF—JAPANESE PAPIER MÂCHÉ

Do not sand, but apply four coats of two pound cut of shellac—one hour apart. Alternate coats of shellac—one vertical, one horizontal, or use two coats penetrating sealer, such as Treasure Sealer.

Antique Gesso

The white thick layer on old frames and furniture that looks like plaster is likely gesso. This material was used in Europe to cover the surface of patching and joining odd pieces of wood. The scarcity of cabinet wood and the fact that hardwood was not easily available, brought about the need for an attractive finish. This gesso is made of whiting—a chalk-like powder and glue. It does not shrink, but the wood is likely to. The old pieces in Europe are not prone to cracking and shrinking as they are kept in places cooler and more humid. When these antiques are brought into our heated homes, they dry out and shrink.

The antique tray is ornamented with the prints of Jean Pillement. The 18th century palette is quite authentic for color. The epaulette cask at the right has a ground of palladium leaf and the prints are colored in the grisaille palette.

Delicate cut-outs are carefully placed on this footed box. The brass ring on the front is especially effective because of the ornaments surrounding it. Subtly antiquing the brass fittings makes the whole effect more authentic.

RESTORING ANTIQUE GESSO

Chip off all loose pieces with a knife. Sand and feather out these places down to the wood. There will be some places, such as carvings, where this is not possible and the piece must be filled with a vinyl filler —such as the ready-to-use spackling. It is helpful to use a small artist paint spatula for little filling jobs. The small tool is good for smooth repairs. After filling the holes, sand, and seal with shellac. On such a piece, you will have to decide if an over-all shellacking would be wise. In most instances, the piece should be shellacked all over. It is then ready to receive paint.

Plaster—Marble—Stone and Leather

In order to prepare these materials for paint the surface must be cleaned thoroughly with alcohol.* This will remove old wax and oils. Fill any holes or cracks with a vinyl filler, allow to dry, and sand smooth. You are ready for the shellac. Use a two-pound cut. Apply four thin coats forty-five minutes apart. This will thoroughly seal the surface preparing a perfect base for the paint.

TO REPAIR A TEAR OR HOLE IN LEATHER

When a hole must be repaired in a leather panel of a screen, glue a round patch of fabric on the *back* side of the leather. A synthetic resin

* Alcohol-solvent alcohol, wood alcohol, denatured alcohol, the same as you use in a chafing dish burner.

64

or vinyl glue is used to hold the fabric. Fill the front area of the hole with a vinyl filler for a patch. Stain it with oil color thinned with turpentine—the color you will be using on the front. Seal with shellac when dry. Basically, this procedure would be followed in repairing a hole in a leather covered table top. If the hole was made by a cigarette, the charred portion should be scraped out and underlaid with a thin coating of glue to hold firmly the vinyl filler patch.

Replacing Molded Pieces—Casting in Plaster

A good impression can be obtained usually by pressing modelling clay or kindergarten oil clay against the piece to make a mold. Water will act as a separator. When you have the mold ready, mix a little plaster to fill the cavity and the replacement is made.

TO MIX PLASTER

Use a small plastic bowl or half a rubber ball to mix the plaster. Fill with the amount of water that the finished project will take. You can pour water into the cavity to measure this. Usually, a two part plaster to one part water is a good ratio. Pour plaster into the water until it appears to be saturated; do not stir until all the plaster is in the water. After stirring, the mixture begins to form and thicken in approximately five to ten minutes. As soon as the forming begins, pour the plaster into the mold. After twenty to thirty minutes you can remove the model from the mold. It may take forty-eight hours to dry the plaster—then, seal with shellac.

REMOVE DUST, SANDING RESIDUE OR RUST

This is very important. Your paint job depends on being done over a clean—not dusty—surface. It is also possible to contaminate the rest of the paint in the can if you transfer dust into fresh paint. Use a magnet to pick up steel wool particles. A vacuum cleaner attachment is very good to use on a sanded piece. A tack rag is a valuable "tool" for the painter. They are inexpensive and ready to use, and are available at hardware or paint stores. You may prefer to make a tack rag, using cheese cloth and a little slow drying varnish. Keep this in a glass jar between uses to prevent drying. The ready-made tack rags stay tacky.

Metal

Wastebasket—previously painted:	Sand lightly to create a surface for adhesion of paint. Wash with alcohol, then paint it. Use a contrasting color inside. Make a cardboard bottom board—seal and paint.
Wastebasket—raw metal:	Wash with vinegar. Dry and paint an undercoat of metal primer. Make a cardboard bottom board—seal with shellac and paint. Attach pull ribbon to edge to remove bottom for good cleaning.
Teapot—needs plating:	Wipe off with alcohol and apply paint directly to metal.
Aluminum Pitcher:	Apply penetrating sealer directly to aluminum to create a bonding base for the paint. One even coat is adequate.
Watering Can—raw metal:	Wipe with vinegar. Apply metal primer—one coat, then ready for paint.
Tray—unpainted:	Wipe with alcohol. Apply metal primer. Sand when dry and apply paint.

Ceramic Unglazed—Bisque Ware

Box and Lid:	Apply two generous coats of sealer to close porous surface. Then you are ready to paint. Ceramic stains may be used as a paint.
Picture Frames:	Apply two generous coats of sealer to close porous surface. Apply base color.
Rose Bowl—other bowl shapes:	Apply two generous coats inside and out of sealer to close porous surface. Apply base color.
Vase or Cylinder Urn:	Pour sealer on the inside—roll around to cover all inside surface. Apply two coats to the outside and dry. You are ready now for base color.
Switchplate—Socket Plate:	Apply two coats of sealer and dry. You are ready for base color.

Découpage Procedures

ASSEMBLING THE COMPOSITION

As you lay out your design, there may be too much foliage or other material in one area and a need for some extra material at another place. Cut it from one place and use where it is needed. This redesigning of the print material is unique in découpage and a tremendous design advantage.

For your first design projects, I would suggest cutting a piece of paper the size of your box lid or tray and complete the temporary composition tacked onto this paper. Then, you can pick up the pieces one at a time to paste them into place rapidly before your pasted surface is dry.

It is best to remove all hardware from the box and put the hinges in to fit the finished dimensions of the box. If the hinges fit before the box is decorated and varnished, it is unlikely they will fit perfectly when you reassemble the box. It might be necessary to raise the hinge with a piece of cardboard slipped between the box and the hinge—not noticed when the screws are replaced.

Planning a Focal Point

A good composition emphasizes good design. We have an inborn sense about design and we let this guide us when we place design materials in a harmonious relation to each other. When creating a design, let intuition guide you in the decisions about the placement and arrangement of the cutouts. One has an intuitive feeling that things balance; that colors are harmonious and that the scale is well coordinated. Good design is harmoniously arranged around a point of interest. The balance and rhythm which you create depend on carrying out a well laid plan. Sometimes your plan will be quite simple; although you do not use a great many motifs, the placement of your cutouts emphasizes the focal point and attracts the eye.

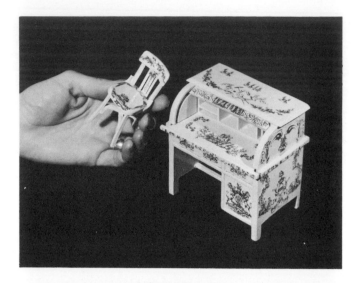

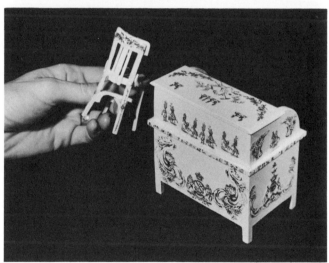

A miniature piece of furniture is a very good project on which to practice design. The prints are cut from a découpage print catalog, assembled, and pasted in place. After this experiment you can order the actual prints and make a full scale desk and chair.

Pasting a scroll border on a lampshade is the last step in completing this accessory. Extra paste is removed with the damp plastic sponge.

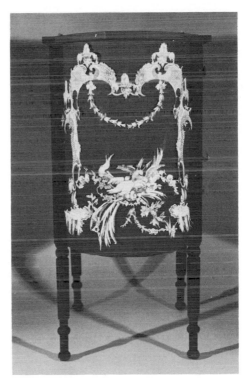

Progressive photographs were made as the various cutouts were laid in place. These parts are held temporarily by the use of a tacky plastic while the design assembly is in progress. The small pieces of plastic are peeled off, and the print is then pasted down.

This series of three progressive steps shows the back panel being tacked in place.

This illustration shows a suggestion for the top design.

An alternate garland is placed on the top and this cutting was used to complete the sewing cabinet.

The ground color for this sewing cabinet is burnt carmine (shown on pencil color plate facing page 80). The black and white prints are left uncolored, and the yellow dye was removed from the narrow embossed gold borders, leaving the trim in a silver color, much more suitable for this piece. The border made the structural panels and legs more attractive.

Some pieces which you plan will not have a point of interest or focal point. This type will have repeat motifs in a balanced relation to one another but they emphasize the importance of the structure of the furniture itself.

In the case of a very plain piece you can build an important scene as a focal point. On an ornate bombé or galbé piece it may be impossible to establish a focal point without detracting from the furniture structure, so the designs will decorate the surface and point up the basic form.

COLORING WITH OIL PENCILS

When you begin to use oil pencils you are forced to observe closely how color blends occur. You will note that even though you always knew leaves of trees and other foliage are green—try coloring a flat green leaf —something is missing. It just doesn't have any character or direction. Now let me help you observe something about the leaf and how to color it. Use a terra cotta #64 pencil softly as an undercoloring. Make the upper farther edge stronger, tapering to a light tone at the lower nearest edge. Now color with #46 grass green. Next, use terra cotta over the deep coloring again—gently but enough to note a deeper tone. Use zinc yellow #1 at the near edge of the leaf. If you hold this drawing out at arm's length, you will see your leaf has direction; it tends to be horizontal instead of vertical. You have control over depth and direction—you must guide color to make it work for you.

Let's try another example of form. Color a peach a nice flat peach color, an even coloring over all. Again, you'll observe a completely flat peach—it has no shape—even though it is the right color. If you add warm colors to ripen it, the peach will still remain flat. Get a peach, an orange, or other round fruit—notice why it has a round appearance. It has a source of light which highlights the surface nearest the source of light. If there is a light directly overhead, the highlights will be nearest to the light—move the light bulb. The source of light and the highlights follow the bulb. Just as the sun hits one side of the earth to make it bright, the opposite side is its darkest in the absence of light. Sometimes a reflection can give underlighting to make a second source of light and enhance the shape—just as sunlight reflecting from the moon lights the dark side of the earth.

Let us color the peach again with an understanding of color—an observation of form. Use terra cotta #64 to make a color foundation darker in the shadow—very pale to no coloring on the highlight. Use #17 pink to establish the apricot color, blending gently from dark to light. Use straw

The pencil is held at an angle and is used following the lines in the engraving. Gentle blending is done so that no pencil mark can be seen.

#58 to blend over the middle tones between light and dark. Use red #17 and burnt carmine #65 to augment the shadow. Zinc yellow #1 is used for the highlight, and last blend a little white #72 over the top half of the peach. This frosting with white can give the illusion of softness like the downy covering many peaches have.

Before you indulge in the delightful experience of coloring trees and buildings, observe them. You will be surprised how flat the forms are on an overcast day and how sculptural the form when the sun is near the horizon. Early in the morning the sun gently molds and shapes form, lighting the landscape from relatively flat forms to rich voluptuous forms. There is no greater thrill than the observation of beauty. It is abundant and around you all the time.

Color has perspective, too. The things nearest you are strongest in color; those at a distance are pastel; at the greatest distance they are muted by the mist in the atmosphere. An important observation in a sunlit scene is that the lightest light, such as the corner of a building, is next to the darkest dark. Using this knowledge, you will gain perspective dimension when you color buildings.

In many of the 18th century prints, the ground around the figures and animals could be very uninteresting if you use only green. The roadways or paths would not be grassy; traffic would have worn the grass down to the earth. Use terra cotta and straw color, as well as pearl gray and burnt carmine, along with three colors of green.

Coloring a Print

Découpage is an art involving a great deal of learning. First, it is necessary for you to master coloring the prints. This phase of découpage is of utmost importance because it is the foundation for so much of the work you will do. Understanding color and using color is more than an exciting experience; the whole world of sight is involved in our response to color.

The 18th century or Classic découpage is done with hand-colored reproductions or with original prints. The antique examples were all hand colored. You will enjoy coloring once you gain courage through a little practice. The beginner is apt to want to use all the colors available on the first print. This is frustrating and not practical. When you color flowers use a book with good color plates for a guide. Encyclopedias have butterflies, shells, flowers, and costumes which you can use. Borrow books from the library to help you when you start coloring. In no time you will be very pleased with your coloring ability, and delighted with the prints you've completed. You will find that you continue to gain confidence and improve your color knowledge with each bit of coloring.

After you have colored quite a few prints you will discover you are just beginning to learn. The art of coloring is not accomplished quickly. If you abandon coloring for a while, it takes a little practice to get back to your previous standard. Do not expect to do one print and be an expert any more than to bake a cake from a mix and feel you are now a pastry cook.

What Color Schemes to Use

These six palettes are suggestions which will help you, but are by no means the limitations of coloring. The beginner or advanced student appreciates color suggestions and these selections should prove to be invaluable. You need not use *all* the colors in the palette. Eventually, you will be able to develop your own color techniques and in some instances abandon the palettes suggested, replacing colors to your taste. My personal philosophy in teaching découpage is to boost your courage, talents and curiosity to the point where you are able to carry on in your own individual way, no longer needing instruction but instead creating freely and with great personal flair.

The 18th Century Palette: Begin coloring your figures, trees and all subject matter with a terra cotta pencil, coloring lightly and *only* in the shadows. With this color as underlay in the shadow area of the print, there is a lovely unity of tone. Use your pencils in the direction of the lines in the engraving. Notice that the shadows actually carry the color and give dimension to your work. Now, very gently add light green to the tops of trees and grasses, blending to darker green. Add touches of blues, pink, red, yellow and straw. Last, accent shadows and make crisp details with the burnt carmine. Have an extra piece of paper beside your print to try out blends with your pencils. When you discover certain tones that especially please you, write down the name or number of your combination so you can do it again. I like to do flesh in a fragile pink and accent the shadows lightly with a yellow green. This results in a blend very near skin tone. Try this on a piece of paper first to see how it works. Sometimes, I like to add, also, a bit of pale blue for cold highlights *over* the yellow green. Look at the back of your hand. Try to identify the many colors that make up real flesh. Use blue over green for some leaves; blend pink over them to subdue the color. Use pink and brown for tree trunks; go over these with yellow ochre. It is possible to erase if it is ever necessary. Use a gentle pencil eraser. The Pink Pearl eraser is recommended. If you have a black and white print with very dark shadows, *erase the dark inky shadows* before you begin, to make it easier to color.

The Toile de Jouy Palette: In France, the Southern region became quite noted for its interpretations of fabrics printed with pictorial line drawings. These repeat motifs were inspired by the engraver's work and were very desirable for casual fabrics. The toiles are done in a single family of colors. In the reds we could use light, medium, and deep colors to capture the essence of the print. A group of three blues or three greens can be used in the same way. Or perhaps the grays would suit you best in three different colors for the *Grisaille Palette.* The Grisaille is usually used to imitate the

75

tones of marble sculpture and its shadows. Therefore, it may be a bit more formal in comparison to the casual monotone of blues, reds, or greens. The colors in the toile de jouy palette are very effective on a background of off-white or a tint of the colors used. The Grisaille Palette is most stunning on black, but it will do equally well on any vivid color background.

The Empire Palette: In the year 1800 Josephine Bonaparte had just acquired the mansion, Malmaison. She was bent on making the gardens there the finest in Europe. Ultimately, this splendid extravagance covered 4,500 acres and was the great triumph the Empress Josephine had hoped for. Her official artist for recording the beauty and variety of every known rose of the time was Pierre Joseph Redouté. This very talented artist had previously enjoyed the patronage of Marie Antoinette. His undying fame was earned by publication of *Les Roses* following a series of eight folios of *Les Liliacées.* The Empire Palette is taken from this period with the Empress Josephine at the center of the fashion scene. Gold and ivory, with apple green, royal blue, and exotic woodtones were predominant on furnishings of the period as accent colors.

The Boucher Palette: If coloring the cherubic designs and prints is your choice, you should learn to handle this palette. It is excellent for the delicate cherubs and flesh tones in François Boucher's drawings and similar subject matter. #16 flesh pink is used in the light areas, terra cotta in heavy shadows. Use pale green for foliage and pale blue for ribbons and other ornaments. This color effect originally was produced by using the sanguine pencil or oil chalk as in a line pastel. A watercolor wash in blue or green was used to accent ornamental features. This delicate coloring accentuates the beauty of the drawing and was a technique employed by many 18th century artists. If your preference is those prints showing cherubs and others which are drawings in an informal mood, this is a palette you will use a great deal and enjoy more as you use it. See Coloring a Boucher Print, next page.

The Pompadour Palette, blue and apricot—This group of colors is inspired by Madame de Pompadour's love for the cool blues, using warm colors as complimentary accents. Though two centuries old, this is still a favorite choice of many of us today. Some of the most stylish furnishings can be accomplished in the Pompadour Palette. A cabinet with two doors above and drawers below could be done with a central panel painted in apricot for background and the cartouche made of cut-out prints using this palette. The background border around the cartouche could be painted a soft pale blue. The varnish finish will mute and relate these colors with a subtle overtone. During Madame de Pompadour's residence at Versailles, her personal suite was decorated in this color scheme.

The Provincial Garden Palette, lavenders and fragile blues, pink, and green—Many of the smaller flowers of the French countryside are in lilac colors, fragile blue, and mingled with the daisy-like marguerites. These colors are in such happy company together, you will see them used often in the daytime fashions of the period. Color the ladies' garden costume frocks in flower tones. The Provincial Garden Palette is a favorite color group when you use a soft pastel background color on furniture or boxes.

Coloring a Boucher Print

The Boucher Palette for coloring cherubs and other prints with flesh tones.

1. Following the lines of your engraving, color with #64 terra cotta all deep shadows on the clouds, people, ribbons, etc. Lightly warm all mid-tones with this pencil—you will have a lovely sanguine coloring when you have completed this step. If there is an area too dark, use an eraser to tone down the shadow.

2. Do not rush, color carefully. Using #16 flesh pink, color all pale skin tones, even up into the hair; however, not all of the hair area. This pale tone will cover a great deal of the ink in case you need to tone down some of the engraving.

3. Subtly blend pink madder lake #17 over the pale flesh at the knees, toes, above the eyes and in the shadows. If you get too much color on these fragile angels, use a Pink Pearl eraser to diminish color.

4. Now, using #58 raw sienna color the hair and wings, also any basket, arrow quiver, or other natural color material. Do not cover up the highlights. Later you can accent these with white. Go over areas of skin to enhance the natural skin tones.

5. Use #47 grass green to go very lightly over the pinks—not the light skin tones—the contrast color will bring a vibrance to the skin. Look at the back of your hand—see the many colors that can be distinguished, particularly the illusion of blue for veins.

6. Terra cotta #64 will add a sculptural quality to the figure when you again go over each shadow area—this time covering any possible ink from the background.

7. Zinc yellow #1 should bring dancing lights to the gold of the hair, if you have not covered the highlights. Blend into the surrounding hair. Do the wings now with the same color. Don't forget the basket and quiver of arrows. The arrow feathers can be #39 turquoise blue.

8. Water green #44 is used heavily on the shadows of all the ribbon and fabric flowing about the cherubs.

9. Pink madder lake #17 is used over the flowers in the basket. Select a few, go over flowers and leaves, also use #39 turquoise blue. Do not blend over the pink but use the blue as little tufts of blue flowers. It must keep its identity. Go over the blue garlands to color the darkest

shadows with #46 emerald green. CAUTION: DO NOT color without regard as to what is happening to your forms. The build-up of color is meant to enhance form as well as local color. Hold the print back a little—turn it upside down to evaluate your work. Hold it to a mirror—this is the test!

10. Emerald green #46 is good for leaves. Color in circles, letting up pressure so the green becomes just a mist of color around the edges. Go over the edges to be sure you do not have a white line on the edge when you cut. Do this with your skin tones, as well. These color run-overs tend to make the shapes softer. Outline makes a hard crisp edge and shape. (Sometimes you need this to distinguish texture. Use it only when you wish to denote crisp shape—out of place in the Boucher cupid setting.) A contrast of light and dark also adds crispness to form. This should be noted in the blue ribbon garlands. It is soft but rather shiny like satin. Use #72 white over white highlights. This shows up later *under the varnish*—not now as you color.

11. Use #34 sky blue to color all cloud forms. Use circular strokes, round and round in small circles, leaving the white *all* white. Do you notice the substance given by the terra cotta which you laid on when you started? This blends and gives depth and richness to the cloud forms. The white in this pale blue mutes the ink and makes the clouds even more misty—or even a little smoky. Keep turning your pencil so it doesn't flatten out too much on one side.

12. Raw sienna #58 should be used in long lines to follow the engraving for sky and background—do a light color application. Go over the pale blue with #58 raw sienna. This will pick up the sky color and make the clouds more interesting.

13. Go back with #17 pink madder lake to pink any toes, fingers, or shadows that need a little more color and warm up the clouds and sky a little.

14. Kingfisher blue #38 should be used on grape and other leaves, over the green you already have on them.

15. A final detail—deepen the quiver and thongs with terra cotta #64 —also, any stems and twigs, even go over skin shadows if there is any ink showing.

16. Burnt carmine #65 can be used very lightly to distinguish certain details on ribbon garland and shadows, but be careful with this strong color.

17. Use #72 white to blend any skin tones which are too warm.

18. My coloring is a little intense in the shadow. I'll erase a little to tone it down. Are you pleased with your coloring? A little practice and you'll be surprised with your ability to make color behave and form come alive.

ABOVE: *Abbé de St. Non basket—see page 80.*

BELOW: *Boucher cherubs—see page 77.*

Coloring a Basket of Flowers

(A Print by Abbé de St. Non)

1. Color *all shadows* lightly with #64 terra cotta.

2. Do all leaves lightly in #46 emerald green. Fill in tiny areas with green, so you do not have to cut them out. Connect leaves with ladders.

3. Color the ribbons #33 light blue, draw in additional ribbon with a pencil and color blue.

4. Color bell flowers #33 light blue, also accent blue ribbon.

5. Large roses—color #58 raw sienna lightly over terra cotta #64; use #17 pink madder lake heavily in the shadows to bring up the color and tone down the engraving. BE SURE TO LEAVE HIGHLIGHTS.

6. Color a balanced group of smaller accent flowers in #15 geranium lake.

7. Go back with #17 pink madder lake, do apples and other fruit which should be a rosy color. Then accent with #15 geranium lake.

8. Color the basket with #58 raw sienna, also, spade and wood the same color.

9. When coloring grapes with #48 May green, make little ovals with the highlight left in.

10. Use #40 turquoise green for small flowers.

11. On the large single flowers partly colored with #5 straw yellow, accent centers and shadows with #64 terra cotta. Go back with #5 straw yellow to do any tiny accents or flowers which should be in this color. Also, go over the previously colored green leaves around the outside to give a sunlight glow.

12. Do fruit in the bottom of the basket with #15 geranium lake. Do flowers with #33 light blue. Go back over all outside leaves with #4 primrose yellow, then strengthen the colors of other leaves with #46 emerald green. This is an opportunity to fill in areas which will be very intricate to cut. Be sure no leaves have white edges. After you finish cutting you may have to go back and color if this step is not done now.

13. Accent highlight on wooden walking stick with #17 pink madder lake; color the remainder of the stick with #64 terra cotta.

14. Last of all, use #65 burnt carmine for your shadow accents, particularly behind leaves and in darkest areas of the garlands and basket.

By now you have fully developed your coloring and the last deep accents bring greater depth and contrast to the coloring. Your print should be a lovely medley of color without anything outstanding—an over-all pleasing effect.

1. Elm Yellow	19. Madder Carmine	37. Oriental Blue	55. Vandyke Brown
2. Lemon Cadmium	20. Crimson Lake	38. Kingfisher Blue	56. Raw Umber
3. Gold	21. Rose Madder Lake	39. Turquoise Blue	57. Brown Ochre
4. Primrose Yellow	22. Magenta	40. Turquoise Green	58. Raw Sienna
5. Straw Yellow	23. Imperial Purple	41. Jade Green	59. Golden Brown
6. Deep Cadmium	24. Red Violet Lake	42. Juniper Green	60. Burnt Yellow Ochre
7. Naples Yellow	25. Dark Violet	43. Bottle Green	61. Copper Beech
8. Middle Chrome	26. Light Violet	44. Water Green	62. Burnt Sienna
9. Deep Chrome	27. Blue Violet Lake	45. Mineral Green	63. Venetian Red
10. Orange Chrome	28. Delft Blue	46. Emerald Green	64. Terra Cotta
11. Spectrum Orange	29. Ultramarine	47. Grass Green	65. Burnt Carmine
12. Scarlet Lake	30. Smalt Blue	48. May Green	66. Chocolate
13. Pale Vermilion	31. Cobalt Blue	49. Sap Green	67. Ivory Black
14. Deep Vermilion	32. Spectrum Blue	50. Cedar Green	68. Blue Grey
15. Geranium Lake	33. Light Blue	51. Olive Green	69. Gunmetal
16. Flesh Pink	34. Sky Blue	52. Bronze	70. French Grey
17. Pink Madder Lake	35. Prussian Blue	53. Sepia	71. Silver Grey
18. Rose Pink	36. Indigo	54. Burnt Umber	72. Chinese White

This series of colors is used in making up the palettes.

Coloring French Chinoiserie

(A Print by Jean Pillement)

The 18th Century Palette plus #22, #41, #58

1. Use #64 terra cotta as a light coloring: the trees, children, rocks; stronger in the deep places as the shadows carry the color. If you find an area too dark to accept color, use an eraser to diminish the ink. Always color in the direction of the lines of the engraving. Leave the lightest areas for highlights—we'll color these white later. When this step is done you should have a sanguine coloring which would be complete as is.

2. Use #46 emerald green to color all leaves and other greenery. Since there is a lot of green to color keep turning your pencil to maintain the point. Make the shadows deeper. Do the distant foliage in circular motions, developing soft green puffs of delicate leaf structures. Fill in areas between branches that would be hard to cut. Go beyond the edges so the color spills into the background. This makes it possible always to have a colored edge when you are cutting. You can color after the sealer has been applied, even after your cutting is done.

3. Use #5 straw yellow to light the background trees with a sunny hue. Color the ground lightly and any flower centers. Some of the Pillement trees are really just outsize flowers in magnificent exaggeration.

4. #58 Raw sienna looks like the color of bamboo poles. Color delicate little fences, ground, and some rock ends with this color.

5. The Children Playing Badminton, print A, and the large flower petals to the left are done with #5 straw yellow. This color easily covers the ink. In print B, Children With a Top, the large flower trees to the left are centered with #5 straw yellow. The flowers themselves should be overlaid with #18 rose pink, especially the shadows. *DO NOT color the highlights yet.* Go over #18 rose pink with the stronger #17 pink madder lake. Use #15 geranium lake to make a fringed outline, nearly around the flower. Back to #17 pink madder lake and color the twigs and highlights on back of trees with this pink.

6. In the Children Playing Badminton, print A, use #17 pink madder lake over the large yellow trees to accent the outline edge in a deep sawtooth. Also, tip the cascades of foliage on the trees to the right with #17. Doing the tops of the crescents will make the tree appear to be in bloom.

7. Coloring the costumes: Make a strong base color of #5 straw yellow on the tunic of the child. Accent neck and armbands with #15 geranium lake.

8. On another child's tunic, color #33 light blue strongly in the

French chinoiserie prints by Jean Pillemont—see page 81.

shadows. Use #40 turquoise green for the rest of the mid-tones, still leaving all highlights. Color the hat to match.

9. Now color the oriental skin; first, with #58 raw sienna, using a little strength on the hands and face. Go over this with #18 rose pink, lightly. Accent the blue costume with #65 burnt carmine; also, identify the eyes and shadows on the figure, making leggings this same color.

10. Use #33 light blue to cool the leaf shadows under the lower frame structure at the bottom of the cartouche. Also, go over cascading leaves of the tree from the underside. The cool shadows make the children seem more animated in their bright warm colors. Work this color in many shadow areas with the dimensional qualities of a shadow on an overcast day. Do not make it too definite.

11. Color rackets #15 geranium lake, badminton bird #33 light blue and #65 burnt carmine. Use #15 geranium lake for sticks for the top spinners.

12. The one remaining child should have his tunic done in #58 raw sienna with a color developed by overlaying #15 geranium lake. Use #64 terra cotta for shoes, as well as #15 geranium lake for the other pair.

13. With #5 straw yellow again, warm the background clusters of trees, also, do tops of the chunky cartouche* structures and some of the tree trunks where a sunlight glow can be seen.

14. With #48 May green subdue the pinks on lower cartouche area; also, the pink on the fences and tree branches.

15. With #64 terra cotta tone the blue shadows on the tree bark, *blending to keep colors from being streaks.* Color in soft little circles or in the direction of the engraving to avoid pronounced coloring.

16. Greatly strengthen the red tunic by blending #17 pink madder lake over all. Then define deeper red with #15 geranium lake.

17. Use #22 magenta for shadows on the blue tunic. Be cautious with this color, use just a little. Gently blend over the red tunics and trousers to relate all these costumes. #41 jade green is used to tone the tree leaves.

18. Last, we'll use #65 burnt carmine to define forms. Use it on the branches next to flower or leaf forms to make the distinction between tree and leaf. This color helps with perspective. It is necessary to prevent these forms from all being in the same plane. Some are near, others fade back. The nearest shapes are more clearly defined. Look out the window to see distant forms hazy, close ones crisp. Pick up the edge accents of the tree flowers, also their stems. Color any sticks, twigs, strings, toys, not already in color. This is the time to draw in any final ladder or attachment to make the composition hold together while cutting.

---

* Cartouche—The stylized frame or border motif enclosing the subject matter.

19. You will note we did not use white at all in this design so far. It can now be used on the skin tones and over the light areas of the tree flower as well as the ground. Having blended these areas, your picture is complete.

The chinoiserie prints are the most difficult to color. If you can handle this coloring, you can master any print. Guidance cannot be underestimated; however, you are the one who renders the coloring and since you can interpret directions into a beautiful picture, one day you will do without this aid and be on your own!

The Limited Palette (Grisaille)

If you would like to enhance and add a sculptured look to the black and white print, it will take just two colored pencils and white. Use terra cotta #64 first in the shadow areas only, color many of the outlines as well. With this completed you have a print which appears to be a sanguine drawing—it has rather an antiqued quality. Use a pale blue #34 pencil on the areas tangent to the terra cotta shadows. The lightly tapered terra cotta coloring blends with the pale blue on some contours. The pale blue gently rounds the scrolls and figures by it self in others On the contours, where you have not used any color, press the white to add highlights. The white is distinct under the varnish but does not seem to be there at all before it is sealed and varnished.

Prints for which we suggest using the limited palette are crests, scrolls, cherubs, architectural, processional groups, sculpture and frieze motifs —often seen in borders. This subtle sculptured color is called grisaille— meaning gray in French. Under the varnish the colors have life and are more beautiful than just black and white.

Other Color Groups

All of the limited palettes will be used in the same way as grisaille. First, color the shadow areas with the darkest pencil, always following the lines in the engraving. Then, gently blend next to it the middle tone, and last, use the lightest tone as a blend toward the highlight or palest area of the contoured form. It is a good idea to use white as color on the highlight. (No color should be under white.) You will not see this colored area show up until after the varnish. In all the things we do at the time of coloring, we must consider the color under varnish, if varnish is to be used. Sealer will also bring the white into focus. The only times you do not use varnish over the print will be when pasting the print under glass or in ribbon découpage when the print is not pasted to anything.

PALETTES

18th Century Palette

#19-5	Straw Yellow	#19-40	Turquoise Green
#19-15	Geranium Lake	#19-46	Emerald Green
#19-17	Pink Madder Lake	#19-48	May Green
#19-18	Rose Pink	#19-64	Terra Cotta
#19-33	Light Blue	#19-65	Burnt Carmine

Suggested background colors: pale blue, apricot, pale green, royal blue, apple green, old gold, Venetian red, pink lake, Venetian yellow, shell pink.

Limited Palettes

PINKS

#19-15 Geranium Lake
#19-17 Pink Madder Lake
#19-18 Rose Pink

GRISAILLE

#19-39 Turquoise Blue
#19-64 Terra Cotta
#19-72 Chinese White

BLUES

#19-36 Indigo
#19-38 Kingfisher Blue
#19-39 Turquoise Blue

YELLOWS

#19-4 Primrose Yellow
#19-3 Gold
#19-7 Naples Yellow

GREENS

#19-41 Jade Green
#19-44 Water Green
#19-47 Grass Green

ORANGES

#19-5 Straw Yellow
#19-10 Orange Chrome
#19-13 Pale Vermilion

Background colors: off white, pale blue or green. For the grays: onyx black, cherry red, apple green, royal blue, old gold or Venetian yellow.

The Provincial Garden Palette

#19-1	Zinc Yellow	#19-39	Turquoise Blue
#19-15	Geranium Lake	#19-40	Turquoise Green
#19-17	Pink Madder Lake	#19-41	Jade Green
#19-22	Magenta	#19-46	Emerald Green
#19-25	Dark Violet	#19-47	Grass Green
#19-26	Light Violet	#19-65	Burnt Carmine

Suggested background colors: Periwinkle blue, pale blue, frost green, antique white, shell pink.

Pompadour Palette

#19-11	Spectrum Orange	#19-34	Sky Blue
#19-13	Pale Vermilion	#19-35	Prussian Blue
#19-16	Flesh Pink	#19-38	Kingfisher Blue
#19-17	Pink Madder Lake	#19-40	Turquoise Green
#19-33	Light Blue	#19-58	Raw Sienna

Suggested background colors: Pale blue, royal blue, apricot, old gold or Venetian yellow.

Boucher Palette

#19-1	Zinc Yellow	#19-46	Emerald Green
#19-16	Flesh Pink	#19-47	Grass Green
#19-17	Pink Madder Lake	#19-48	May Green
#19-18	Rose Pink	#19-58	Raw Sienna
#19-34	Sky Blue	#19-63	Venetian Red
#19-38	Kingfisher Blue	#19-64	Terra Cotta
#19-39	Turquoise Blue	#19-65	Burnt Carmine
#19-44	Water Green	#19-72	Chinese White

Background colors: Apricot, old gold, ivory and an antique white.

Empire Palette

#19-16	Flesh Pink	#19-57	Brown Ochre
#19-29	Ultramarine	#19-60	Burnt Yellow Ochre
#19-30	Smalt Blue	#19-66	Chocolate
#19-46	Emerald Green	#19-70	French Gray
#19-47	Grass Green	#19-72	Chinese White

Suggested background colors: Ivory, antique white or onyx black.

There are numerous suitable ground colors that will occur to you. It would be a long list indeed if all the possible colors were listed. Use your own good judgment and plan within the framework of your chosen color scheme.

QUESTIONS AND ANSWERS

Understanding Color and Coloring

1. Q. What is the difference between oil pencils and water color pencils?

   A. Derwent, Prismacolor, Paradise and Venus are brands of pencils which are not soluble in water. You can't blend or dissolve the color by wiping a wet sponge across the page. Mongol and other water color or water soluble pencils will bleed if you wipe a damp sponge across a page colored with this type pencil. Be sure to seal all coloring with a good sealer. This will prevent their bleeding when in contact with paste and water later.

2. Q. Can water color be used to color prints?

A. Yes, it is faster—perhaps easier for many people and quite controllable. The colors can be more brilliant, but it is not easy to seal them so the color doesn't come off when you paste. This is the only place that you'll have trouble. Seal water color at least two coats, top and one on the back. Test a print in water after you seal, if you're not sure the print is adequately protected. Two coats of découpage sealer or acrylic spray should be used for water colored prints.

3. Q. Can water color and pencils be used on the same print?

A. Yes, but seal with two coats on the top and one coat on the bottom if much water color is used.

4. Q. Will all water colors work equally well?

A. You must test each brand. Water color was not made to have a sealer or varnish brushed over it but you must always seal. Make a test of all your colors on typing or bond paper, and seal. This should be a good test.

5. Q. Are poster colors or tempera good water colors to use?

A. No, they are opaque and will obliterate the engraving lines.

SEALING THE PRINT

Before cutting, you must seal the color into the paper. This is done with an application of sealer over all the colored areas. Gently flow the sealer onto the print and blot off the excess with a crumpled paper towel. This step is important for three reasons: 1. Sealing the color into the print prevents the varnish from discoloring the print. 2. The sealer also prevents the cutout paper from shredding apart when it is wet with paste and pushed around with the fingers. 3. The sealer makes the paper stiffer and delicate cutting is much easier. The colors appear to blend very subtly as soon as the sealing process is begun. Uncolored prints must be sealed to protect the ink, prevent varnish discoloration, and stiffen the paper for cutting.

CUTTING

Pick up the découpage scissors with the blade curve pointing away from you and in a very relaxed way slip your third finger and thumb into the scissors. Rest the scissor blades on your index finger. Open and close the scissors many times to get used to it. This is the way you will hold your scissors for almost all cutting. Take a practice piece of paper and feed it into the scissors, move the paper round and back with your other hand. The hand holding the scissors doesn't move back and forth, it only opens and closes the scissors in a very relaxed but exacting way. After some practice you are anxious and likely ready to cut out your print.

The first cutting will remove all excess paper from the outside of the print. Your straight scissors will do this more rapidly. You will cut next the inside details. After you have the inside areas cut out, begin to do the outside contours. Hold your scissors so the curve is pointed out—most people cut better this way. If this just doesn't suit you, try it with the curve pointing in.

Generally, you should cut the inside areas first. There are some prints in which the outside areas would be cut out first—doing some *incised* cutting when you are done. In this creative craft, you will learn by practice what is best for you to do in a given circumstance.

Avoid very long straight line cutting; instead, cut a *serrated* edge by wiggling the paper back and forth as you cut so as to produce a softer, blending edge. You will readily see the advantage of this preferable cutting technique when you compare the hard line with the *serrated* line. These details make for distinguished cutting.

Do not cut corner details so you destroy the crispness. For example, if you have stair steps to cut, each step should be squared and crisp on the leading edge, as well as a right angle where the riser joins the tread. This will appear to be a zigzag instead of rounded scallops.

All of your cutting should be done so that you further identify the material you are cutting. Clusters of leaves and satin fabrics should be rounded and soft. The character of trees and other hard materials should be cut to identify their texture.

Occasionally, it is necessary to turn the scissors—with scissors' curve cutting in the opposite direction. Whenever it is better to change scissors, by all means do. Some instructors feel it is best to hold the scissors at an angle so as to cut a bevel edge. This is not likely to produce a very different edge from straight cutting, as the scissors cut it the same from any angle. If you believe you cut better at an angle or a bevel, do it that way. I believe it is most important to be as relaxed and comfortable as possible to make cutting a pleasure. You will have a greater appreciation of your découpage when you appraise your cutting from the reverse side.

Découpage is the art of distinguished cutting. Accomplishing this superb cutting is possible for anyone who has good enough vision to thread a needle. Practice is of ultimate importance. Fine cutting doesn't happen when you try your first practice print. It is mastery of the scissors that makes the most beautiful découpage. The accomplishment of découpage can hold you a captive forever.

Hold the print with the left hand, cut from underneath so you can see your work. Uncut strips of paper "ladders" are left intact until ready to paste. Ladders are seen on scrolls at right.

Carefully study these cuttings to identify reverse cutting, incised cutting, foreground cutting, dry brush cutting, serrated cutting, straight cutting.

This fascinating jewelry box has a music box movement, which is wound from the front. Gold paper braid outlines the borders and drawer on a background of cobalt blue. Bright red velvet is used for lining the drawer and top interior, which features two mirrors. The prints are colored in the 18th century palette.

Study the types of cutting illustrated: feather cutting, drybrush cutting, foreground cutting, serrated edge, incised cutting, outline cutting and reverse cutting positive.

The character of the grass, leaves, feathers, branches is identified by the cutting. The bird at the right was cut apart to facilitate cutting. The ladders are still intact.

In this 6 x 9 inch découpage cutting, some intricate techniques can be identified. This 18th century cutting was done with a knife. The border illustrates banister cutting. The other styles are not used in découpage today. The tuft between the roosters shows feather cutting and reverse cutting, shadow. The necks of the roosters are done in outline cutting as are their body feathers and those of the owl. Stencil cutting is also seen in the leaves and small flowers in the foreground. Circa 1780.

From Belgium comes this old découpage cutting, circa 1740. Many of the flowers, the center pedestal and medallion are pinpricked. This cutting was done with a knife. All papers used for fine cutting are very light weight.

Children playing in this silhouette are lively and colorful, even though the entire work is black and white. A fine découpage cutting inked black would be a handsome ornament.

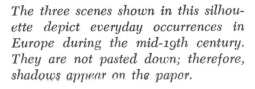

The three scenes shown in this silhouette depict everyday occurrences in Europe during the mid-19th century. They are not pasted down; therefore, shadows appear on the paper.

The more silhouettes we study the more conscious we are of the character of cutting. Although silhouette is a 19th century name, its origins were in the 18th century where and when découpage began.

This assembly of prints is shown from the back side, which is less distracting when studying cutting and the use of ladders. It is easy to detect the ladders from this illustration. Study carefully the design plan and try to identify which of the cut-outs came from the accompanying prints. See how important the scale is. Notice the textures identified by the cutting.

This engraved trophy by Berthault is translated for use in découpage by being printed on a special lightweight opaque paper and printed with a special ink. The following illustrations show how the cut-out parts are then assembled in a composition.

The open tulip in this print was bare, so two leaves were drawn in, colored and cut out—as seen in the assembled design. Study also placement of ladders.

The four English découpage pictures are cut from colored paper. The feather cutting is so delicate it appears almost lifelike. The light-colored birds are yellow; the dark ones are blue and wine, gray and lavender. Bright red flower blossoms and green foliage make a lively and colorful "painting." Circa 1800.

Styles of Cutting

Creative cutting is not done following the lines of the engraving. It is rarely shown in the print at all. For the most part you must decide where to use these cutting styles and how much detail to add. These styles of creative cutting make your work much more interesting to look at, and the art of cutting prints, distinguished as fine découpage.

1—Straight cutting—ladders
2—Reverse cutting—positive
3—Reverse cutting—negative
4—Reverse cutting—shadow
5—Feathering or feather cutting
6—Drybrush cutting.

7—Serrated cutting
8—Incised cutting
9—Foreground detail cutting

10—Outline detail cutting
11—Bannister cutting
12—Stencil cutting

1. *Straight cutting* is usually confined to border designs. This is accomplished by feeding the paper straight into the scissors with no movement of the hand holding the paper. Straight cutting is done on ladders as it is quicker.

2. *Serrated cutting:* This is the type cutting done on most figures, animals, flowers, trees and other designs which give a soft edge. It makes a much firmer bond when pasted down. The paper is moved back and forth as it is fed into the scissors to produce this type cutting.

3. *Feathering or feather cutting:* This is the same thing and the cutting is done in a manner to imitate feathers. Usually you determine where to place the feathering, which occurs most often at the lower right and left of a print motif.

4. *Drybrush cutting:* This type of cutting is an alternate to feather cutting. It is used at the lower right and left for the purpose of producing an imaginative lower edge detail. It is done to resemble a drybrush technique often used in watercolor and other artistic brush work. This cutting is done to appear to be an arc with a downward sweep.

5. *Foreground detail cutting:* This style of cutting is done to produce an attractive front edge. The grass tufts and other motifs you invent will make the print more exciting and produce an edge which will hold much better when pasted. Although this is usually done at the front edge of prints, it is also a suggested technique to finish a print motif which is cut off at one side or the other, such as buildings and trees. By doing this, it is possible to blend prints from one to another to make a continuous horizontal design, hiding the fact that many prints have been used in a line. This is convenient when designing a lamp shade or paper basket.

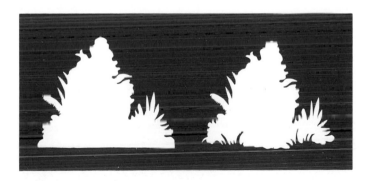

6. *Reverse cutting—negative:* This type of cutting creates an opening which appears to be a small plant or tuft of grass. This innovation in cutting is useful for many reasons. It offers an opportunity to accent a bland area of print. Gold tea chest paper can be used behind the opening,

creating a tuft of grass, or to enliven the same area with the background color paint. It is an opening which enables the varnish to hold to the paint—assuring you of continuous adhesion of the varnish film.

7. *Reverse cutting—positive:* Used for the same cutting advantage, and the same varnish adhesion advantage as reverse cutting negative. You see the positive motif or design cut in the paper with the paper tuft shown against the opening. It is possible to accent either type of reverse cutting by pasting metallic paper behind the reverse cutting. Both positive and negative can be used together. They add variety and interest.

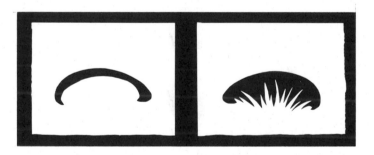

8. *Reverse cutting—shadow:* This technique offers further variety to the découpeur. A motif or tuft of grass is cut out of the print as if it were a shadow in which the cutout opening repeats the design in the print.

9. *Incised cutting* is usually done after a print is entirely cut out. The purpose of this cutting is to open up areas in a print which are entirely solid. The openings may be any size or shape—and are camouflaged in the print so as not to be noticed. The reason you should open up areas in a print is that this provides a hole to remove excess paste, and most important provides a spot where the varnish can touch paint and firmly tack the varnish film to the paint surface. This one trick can prevent many "blister under print" heartaches.

10. *Stencil cutting* is done with a knife or razor blade. It is difficult to handle this type of cutting with scissors. The openings produced are long crescents or S curves. When using a razor blade or a knife, cut against a hard surface for the best cutting (masonite or glass). Stencil cutting is done along lines in a scroll or parallel to accent lines.

11. *Bannister cutting:* This type is done with a knife or scissors. There are few opportunities to use this style but you should be aware of it when you need it. Many short vertical lines are cut between two lines. The bottom horizontal is cut from end to end, releasing all bannisters. They are then broken loose on alternate shafts to produce a series of bars—unattached at the bottom until they are glued.

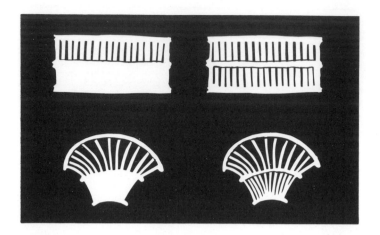

12. *Outline detail cutting:* Narrow crescents cut to accent the outline of flowers, fruit, figures, cloud formation, and other curves. A straight outline is accented with straight cutting. Either a knife or scissors is used for outline cutting.

Cutting Two Prints at Once

Sometimes there is a need for many of the same print. This is especially true of borders, ornaments and scrolls. It is not good for the beginner, who needs practice, to cut two prints at a time. As the experienced découpeur works on larger pieces, some monotonous cutting can be eliminated. Superimpose the printed images and pin right through the print with a very fine silk pin. The tiny hole is not noticeable when pasted down, and it is a good escape hole for air or trapped paste. Be sure to mark the ladders on the top print.

Drawing Ladders

As you look at your lovely colored print, you may feel you do not know where to start cutting. Do not cut until you determine where to draw the ladders. Take a colored pencil and draw in the *ladders* that you will need to keep the print intact while you are cutting, and to make it possible to handle them prior to pasting the prints into position.

Ladders are your third hand, which hold delicate tendrils of paper together until you are ready to paste. They are placed by the découpeur in strategic places to hold long stems or appendages intact while cutting. You draw in the connection with a pencil; then you cut around the ladder which you drew. The ladder remains in place until just before you paste. Then you snip them off as they have served their purpose. Sometimes ladders are left in place if they become part of the design. In this case, the ladder should be the color of the connecting motifs.

Study the print and join portions which will be weak or isolated on a long stem. In the cutting photograph, you can see a ladder between the scrolled curves at the right of the illustration. Make all these connecting ladders with a colored pencil before you begin cutting. Store the prints with the ladders intact as this facilitates handling.

PASTING THE PRINTS
IN PLACE

Before you open your paste—get a small bowl of water, sponge, and a small damp cloth. You will need them as you work. Dip your finger or two fingers into the paste and go over the entire area to be covered with cutout designs. Smooth this paste as evenly as you can, adding drops of water when necessary to have a good surface to receive the cuttings. Pick up your pieces from the temporary composition and place them on the pasted surface, working as rapidly as you can. Use a barely damp piece of cloth over the freshly painted work. Roll over the entire surface with a small roller. Rinse the paste out of the cloth and repeat, removing all traces of paste. If the cloth is too wet it will dissolve the paste under the prints, making it necessary to add paste later. The slight dampness of the cloth draws the paste up rapidly and leaves the surface clean.

Paste one side of a box at a time; however, relate each area to the next side or top. Sometimes a flower stem trails off the top to the sides —you may have a design start on the lid and follow down the sides to surround the subjects on each side. Occasionally, you may use the side as one design unit and a separate but related composition on the top.

Don't paste one layer upon another. This heavy build-up will make it necessary to add many extra coats of varnish. *Carefully* cut and fit edges next to each other. Remember the smoother your box, paint, and print, the easier it will be to apply the varnish evenly. One hazard in sanding is that thin spots in the varnish will be sanded through quickly with possible damage to the print. This will happen only if the print humps up here and there or overlapping prints make a high place. Another place to watch is the edges.

The paste referred to is the water-soluble découpage paste. It is removable, if the need arises. *Glue* is not water soluble and not removable. Paste is used exclusively on prints. Glue is used on fabric lining, gold tea chest paper and gold braid.

QUESTIONS AND ANSWERS

Paste

1. Q. I have heard of wonderful mixtures of something like Elmer's glue and some other paste where you have the advantage of both— what is this called?

A. Trouble. You may end up with the advantages of neither. Use the right adhesive and don't alter it. Don't mix your own and expect good results. It may work sometimes. The right paste, glue or adhesive is one made for découpage. Buy from a specialist. Use materials that are made to go together. A complete collection of materials for découpage that work together and fit the job right is like buying the right size clothes to fit an individual.

2. Q. I like to buy one brand of paste, another brand of sealer, and I just buy whatever varnish I can find. I have never had any problems. What about that?

A. Some people have all the luck!

3. Q. I had a magazine cover print lift after it was glued down flat. I used a heavy duty glue and I had sprayed the back of the magazine cover with aluminum paint to keep the printed type from showing through. What caused the trouble?

A. Aluminum paint or gold paint should not be used under prints. The glue holds to the metallic powder and the inadequate binder for the paint is absorbed in the paper. You may have trouble with metallic sprays of this type. It is best to put magazine prints on a darker background or not use them at all if you have type showing through. If you spray or paint a box with gold or other metallics, use Treasure Sealer* as a paint bonding adhesive.

4. Q. Why should I avoid vinegar water as a cleaner when I glue the prints on?

A. Vinegar is acid and can react on many things. It can give you problems with metal leaf or tea paper that cannot be corrected. If your glue or paste is not easily cleaned with plain water, change adhesives. You should *not* use a waterproof glue—it can't be cleaned off when dry.

5. Q. Why did my gold tea chest paper come loose after I was done with the box? I used glycerin to slow the drying so I could glue evenly.

A. Glycerin may slow the drying but it does damage the adhesion of the glue. The glycerin can prevent varnish from adhering, too. It acts as a separator. Do not alter your paste or glue with anything—unless directions on the label say so. Change paste, work faster, or work on smaller areas if the paste you use dries too fast.

* See page 170.

THE VARNISH FINISH

Almost everyone is astonished when you say, "It has thirty coats of varnish." This alone would set you apart from the crowd, but it is neither complicated nor difficult to apply a number of coats of varnish in order to achieve an incomparable finish. After your pasted découpage is thoroughly dry, assemble brush, varnish, soft cloth and paint thinner or turpentine for brush cleaning. Apply the varnish to your work in long flowing strokes. Do not brush too rapidly or in short choppy strokes. Be generous but not to the point that the varnish will sag or run. Pick the brush stroke up at the edges of a box or tray in order to avoid rollover (an accumulation of varnish on the edge of the box). Inspect your box each time you apply a coat of varnish, so you do not allow a sag or a drip to dry. Remove drips with the brush or a turpentine-dampened cloth.

Apply one coat of varnish every twenty-four hours or follow the instructions on the varnish can label. When you have applied ten coats, begin sanding with wet-or-dry sandpaper #400, available at most paint stores. You will be pleased with this sandpaper that you can use so effectively. Dip it in water; always keep the surface and the sandpaper wet. No dust is created to make you sneeze. After a thorough leveling with the sandpaper, begin the last series of six to ten varnish coats. If you are satisfied with a few more coats, this is your decision to make. If it takes sixteen or more coats to achieve the rich depth of varnish comparable to a fine deep porcelain glaze, continue until you are satisfied. You can apply too few coats, but it is unlikely you will apply too many. The last two coats of varnish should be a low lustre.

By adding a little detergent when you are wet sanding it is possible to obtain a smoother finish, as it tends to help eliminate small scratches.

Cleaning the brush: After each use of the brush, you should clean it with a solvent and shampoo the bristles thoroughly. Then squeeze the water out gently, setting the bristles in place to dry. Or, you can keep your varnish brush suspended in a glass baby bottle filled one-third deep with turpentine. Cut the rubber tip from the nipple so the brush will fit snugly and stay in place. A plastic bottle will not hold the solvent—use only glass.

Découpage, being the art of cutting out paper, has nothing actually to do with a specific finish. Varnish wasn't used on the original works. The 20th century examples are largely exhibited with many coats of varnish or other clear finishes which protect and enhance the lovely cuttings. Of the many examples which are currently done, the most effective are not antiqued or fly-specked. Those two finishes are connected with painted furniture and somehow have been added as an unnecessary conceit in découpage. It is best not to antique or color glaze in dark tones when finishing works of découpage. It is also best not to spatter with black paint to create artificial fly specks.

A subtle antique coloring is achieved with amber varnish. After a few years most varnishes will deepen in color and artificial antiquing also becomes much darker. For this reason, one should create a finish in as natural a coloring as is possible. If you use antiquing at all, it should be so subtle that an expert would find it difficult to detect. Any obvious anachronism is as bad as an artificial finish effect. The beautiful deep lustre of varnish is the most desirable and durable finish for découpage.

How to do the Varnish Finish

Assemble supplies for varnishing: Brush—varnish—small pan
Tack rag—paint cloth—turpentine
Brush saver bottle

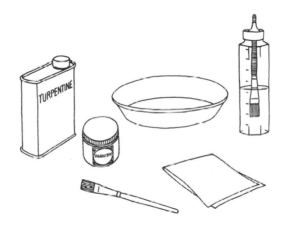

Assemble supplies for sanding: #400 wet or dry sandpaper sponge—
bowl of water
Steel wool—découpage wax

1. Pour a small amount of varnish into a pan. It is easier to hold and no evaporation or contaminating dust will damage the varnish remaining in the can. Pour in more as needed. Also, you can thin with turpentine as needed.

2. Dip your brush halfway up the bristle in the varnish. Lay the brushful of varnish on your work, draw it toward the edge, and lift it up from the edge. Do not draw down or apply pressure as you will deposit excess varnish. Work rapidly—do not rebrush when the varnish is beginning to set. Always remove bristles as they fall from a brush.

3. When the varnishing is done, set it aside to dry where no lint or dust will fall into the film as it dries.

4. Use your tack rag to pick up dust particles, as a regular ritual—before each coat of varnish is applied. Wait twenty-four hours between coats (unless otherwise specified on the label). Apply about ten coats before you begin to do any sanding.

5. *First Sanding:* Dip sandpaper in water and begin to level the varnish. Sand with the grain. As a paste is worked up from the water and sanding, remove with wet sponge. Be careful not to sand through a print edge or the paint at the outer corners of boxes. These are danger points for beginners. When the surface is reasonably level—use your tack rag to pick up any stray dust particles and apply six to ten more coats according to how thick or thin your layers of varnish are applied.

6. *Second Sanding:* This is done much the same as the first sanding except it must be very level this time. Use steel wool #0000 to get low places.

7. *Final Varnishing:* Apply two coats of low gloss varnish twenty-four hours apart, and use steel wool for a smooth surface.

8. *Waxing:* The final coating is a découpage wax or fine furniture wax. Apply very sparingly with a damp cloth. After ten minutes polish to an incomparable sheen.

QUESTIONS AND ANSWERS

Understanding Paint, Varnish and Lacquer

1. Q. Why does the enamel paint I'm using leave ridges? It seems too thick.

   A. It needs to be thinned. Use turpentine or mineral spirits.

2. Q. Are turpentine and mineral spirits the same? Where do they come from?

   A. Turpentine is made from the southern pine tree. Pure gum turpentine is made from the sap. Steam distilled is made by heating the stump of the tree to get the turpentine. Mineral spirits is also a solvent for paint but it is a petroleum product, distilled from crude oil. It is much weaker in its solvent strength than turpentine but is a comparable material for thinning. The products distilled from petroleum include mineral spirits, kerosene, naphtha, gasoline, acetone, xylene, and toluene. The last ones listed are the strongest solvents—used as lacquer thinner (in given proportions). Mineral spirits is much less expensive and lower in odor. It is also available as odorless mineral spirits—used in odorless paints.

3. Q. My paint seems to build up ridges when I apply the second coat. I have already thinned it. Does it need to be thinner?

A. Not likely. This happens when the undercoat is not fully dry. If you didn't wait twenty-four hours this will happen. You may also find you didn't mix the paint well and you are into a denser material near the bottom. If so, then it may need more thinner.

4. Q. How do I get a mellow old look? What varnish do I use?

A. The amber-colored varnish will build up to a mellow old look. You may also add a small amount—¼″—out of the small tube of oil colors, Van Dyke brown or burnt sienna. Mix this oil color with a teaspoonful of turpentine and add it to one-half cup varnish for one coat. If you want it deeper, do another coat. The darker the varnish and the more coats the deeper the antique coloring.

5. Q. How can I tell if I'm buying varnish that will go over flat enamel paints?

A. It will be labeled varnish—low luster, or gloss. If you learn to read labels carefully it will help you learn a lot about the materials you use. The harder the varnish, such as spar or deck varnish, the tougher it is to sand. This type must be sanded every coat or two. If you use a varnish made for découpage it will be much easier to sand. It has aluminum stearates and silicas which do not make a tough surface—these are built-in for easy sanding. So, many coats can be applied for a more rapid build-up, and you don't have to sand until ten to fourteen coats have been applied. Then, you can apply a spar or semi-gloss varnish for the last few coats. The varnish suitable to apply over flat enamel will usually have a typical varnish odor. If it smells like lacquer or nail polish—check the label—you will find a special solvent or lacquer thinner is used to clean the brush. This type of material will shrivel the enamel or oil paints.

6. Q. When do you use a sealer over the paint and why?

A. If you buy a paint you've never tried before—and it is not made for découpage—or if you use paints left over from other things— seal it. Sealer will prevent the varnish from causing the paint to bleed. Many paints will not bleed and you do not need to worry about this problem. You can always test this if you have a panel of the paint in question, by brushing on a varnish and stroking back and forth many times. Then apply the varnish left in the brush on white paper. If there is a pink coloring evident, the paint bleeds. This is assuming there is red pigment in the paint.

7. Q. How do I get a muted soft-colored varnish finish that is not amber or antique coloring?

A. There are many brands of varnish now available for découpage which are cloudy in appearance; some are a creamy gray color. These are usually alkyd resin varnishes that are pigmented slightly. They are easy to sand, give a rapid build-up and a lovely muted mellow color. For a final tough finish, it is best to use two coats of a low gloss varnish.

8. Q. Will lacquer give me an absolutely clear finish?

A. Yes. However, it *cannot* be used over flat enamel or oil paints. It can be used over poster paint, tempera, rubber base, and other water base paints. Ask for brushing lacquer.

9. Q. I have a piece two years old that has begun to get wide cracks in it. Why? I used lacquer.

A. Many coats of lacquer are apt to crack in this manner. It happened to me and I found out why. Most lacquer when sprayed on, such as a factory finish, is very thin and eight coats sprayed is the equivalent of three coats brushed on. From 18% to 34% solids are in brushing lacquer. Only 8% to 12% solids are in sprays because they must be thinned so much to prevent clogging the nozzle. Therefore, many coats of lacquer hand-applied cause a stress which eventually shows up as cracks in the finish. I am told this is true of clear lacquer in general. The pigmented lacquers used in import ware are very different from U.S. clear lacquer. I would not use lacquer for more than six coats to avoid cracks.

10. Q. Why sand between coats of paint?

A. A smoother finish is the result of careful sanding, especially between coats of paint. Be sure to use a tack rag to pick up dust from sanding.

11. Q. What is a tack rag? Why is it used?

A. It is a cloth (commercially ready to use) which is slightly sticky or tacky and it will pick up the dust from sanding paint or varnish. It is essential to a good finish. If you have dust on a varnished piece and do not remove it, your next coat of varnish merely embeds the dust and causes unnecessary little irregularities. Do not varnish while wearing a wool sweater, because it sheds lint and statically attracts dust.

12. Q. How can you tell what color a paint will be when it dries? Mine seems a shade darker.

A. Most paint dries a shade darker when it is dry and cured. You can tell after twenty-four hours. Make a test and dry it.

13. Q. How does the amber varnish affect colors of paint?

A. If you could look at colors through amber-colored glasses you would be able to gauge how your paint will be affected by varnish. The reds are intense and attractive as are orange, mustard and yellow orange. The pale pink becomes salmon. The pale yellow becomes deeper and white or off white seems yellowed. The blues all become slightly green and the greens seem richer and mellow. Brown is not affected. Lavender seems to become a neutral gray. Violet is also neutralized and seems brownish. The amber tone of varnish will change every color.

14. Q. In my varnish finish there are darker and lighter streaks. Why?

A. Uneven coats is the answer. If the base color of paint wasn't smooth, varnish will flow into the crevices and appear darker. If you apply heavy overlaps of varnish, the overlaps may be darker. If you use a brush which does not discharge the varnish well, you may have irregularities. Use a good brush—apply even coats. It is all a matter of experience and learning. Streaks and color variation can always be traced to inexperience or being in a hurry. An exception could be: using inferior materials.

15. Q. What causes sags in the varnish? How can I correct it?

A. If you understand the cause you should never have this happen. Too heavy an application of varnish will sag. If the varnish dries quickly on the surface, the under layer may slip to a sag. This can not happen if thin layers are applied—or if you let the varnish set to dry in a horizontal position. An ounce of prevention is worth a pound of cure.

16. Q. What causes edge build up, especially on boxes?

A. The brush continuously is discharging varnish at the edge because of the way you use your brush. Think of touching the brush down near the middle of a box lid and making an arc as you lift the brush near the edge. Finish each edge by attempting to pick up excess varnish at the edge.

17. Q. What is rollover and how is it caused?

A. Rollover of paint or varnish is caused by a brush stroke which discharges the varnish at the edge. It builds up on this outside edge or runs down and drips. You are brushing in the wrong direction or you have not checked the edge for possible drips or rollover. Be aware of this fault—it is easy to prevent—terrible to sand off!

18. Q. There are drips around the edge of a lid on which I am working. They are not dry enough to sand, too dry to remove with turpentine, how do I get them off? How do I prevent them?

A. Prevent this happening to start with by using a cloth dampened with turpentine all around this underside—before you leave it to dry. You remove these semi-dried drips with a knife or even your fingernail. Then wipe with a turpentine-dampened cloth. When dry, sand.

19. Q. Do you need as many coats of varnish on furniture as you use on boxes?

A. I would try to make a table top or desk top as smooth as you can, using more varnish on the horizontal surface as this will get the most wear. Boxes are easy to handle, easy to do and should be well finished. A large secretary may be difficult to have all designs buried in varnish. The originals and the reproductions available from Italy today have very little varnish.

20. Q. How do present-day varnishes differ from those used during the 18th century?

A. The earlier varnishes in the 18th century were often more like shellac or lacquer, called seed lac. These products dry by evaporation, which means a dried-out brush could be softened in its own thinner, a shellac brush in alcohol, a lacquer brush in lacquer thinner. The resins used in the 18th and 19th centuries dried by evaporation, such as the picture varnishes, damar varnish and spirit varnishes. Spirit varnish is one thinned with alcohol. Modern varnishes, if they dry in a brush, are not soluble in turpentine as they have polymerized—or changed their molecular structure—

and a stronger solvent must be used. Some paints and varnishes oxidize when they dry. Basically, paint is varnish with a pigment added. Latex paints are rather like the natural rubber latex for which they are named. They cure into a different material than they were in the liquid state. Varnish as we know it today is a 20th century product.

21. Q. Were the varnishes of the 18th century made to last?

A. Shellac was generally used as a finish, and we know now as they did then, that this resin will become very dark brown with time and dust embedded. Many of these pieces were cleaned off regularly and new shellac applied. Not everyone who inherited this furniture knew how to take care of this finish a generation or two later, so the finish became dark and often the piece was set aside as unattractive and not used. This happened also to paintings which were varnished with a turpentine soluble light varnish. Many people knew enough to have the varnish removed every thirty or forty years and fresh varnish applied to preserve the painting. Only recently some museums are restoring the varnish on paintings and other works of art which should have been treated years ago. So you see the varnishes used then were not identical to those we use now.

22. Q. I prefer to use a water base paint. Can I still use the antique varnish if I want the old amber color?

A. Yes. Varnish can be used over water base paint. The strongest objection to water base is the time necessary for it to cure out before the varnish or lacquer is used. The problems involved do not show up immediately. They start happening two to six years after you put in all that work, so I just feel it is best to use the oil base paint known to hold up under many coats of varnish.

23. Q. What is the main difference between spray can products and those you brush on?

A. The paint or varnish, lacquer, sealer, or acrylic, which is packaged in spray cans is very convenient and more people turn to these products daily. You can't beat them for many things you need to paint. They are much more expensive for the amount of paint, et al, you will use. You must use many more coats for the same coverage. Let's look at the label on the spray can. You will see 8% solids—92% vehicle and propellent, or some such ratio. Look at a paint can label—34% solids, resin, pigment, modifiers, etc. and 66% vehicle—thinner, driers, etc. This is one reason the aerosol paints dry so fast, a thin coat and fast drying vehicle. It may take four coats spray to equal one brush-applied. I believe you should enter into the spirit of découpage, an antique craft, with the idea that there is no big rush. Here is one refuge where there is no hustle-bustle. You do your best work and relax while doing it.

24. Q. What is varnish?

A. The natural and synthetic resins form the solids of a varnish. These are diluted with a solvent, turpentine or mineral spirits, and modified as to gloss, drying time, plasticity and resistance to abrasion and other external forces. The resin is generally amber in color. Many layers of varnish of this type add a soft antique glow to the work underneath.

   The synthetic varnishes are less amber. Some are nearly water clear. When the resin is modified, a milky or translucent liquid results. Either of these two basic types of varnish depends upon a solvent being evaporated and the layer of modified resins building a coating on the surface. The solids content is usually 34% to 45%. Turpentine or mineral spirits can be added to aid in leveling of the varnish. This information about varnish is much too simplified, but it does perhaps bring a little better understanding of this material. Basically, it is a natural product being used as a protective on wood. It bonds perfectly to the paint, being of similar material, and protects as well as enhances the surface.

25. Q. What is lacquer?

A. The lacquers, having nitro-cellulose solids, may be easier to understand. They dry by evaporation. They can be dissolved again in *their own* thinner. Varnish cannot; however, varnish can be dissolved by a stronger solvent system, such as the lacquer thinner.

   Alcohol does not dissolve lacquer nor, in many cases, varnish. It will dissolve shellac, which is its solvent. Mineral spirits is the weakest solvent and will not dissolve varnish, shellac, or lacquer. Turpentine is about twice as strong a solvent as mineral spirits and is by no means the same. Fumes from lacquer thinner should be avoided. They may seem mild but some people are easily overcome. Sprays in general are very handy and easy to use for many jobs.

26. Q. What is mineral spirits?

A. It is a petroleum distillate, like naphtha, gasoline, kerosene, xylol and toluol. It is used as a paint thinner and has a very weak solvent power. It is much weaker than turpentine as a solvent, but an equally good thinner. It dries from a surface without leaving a residue. It is often given other label names such as paint thinner, enamel reducer, varnish reducer. It costs half the price of turpentine.

27. Q. What is odorless mineral spirits?
    A. It has much the same properties of mineral spirits but it is a different petroleum distillate. It has no odor and is very pleasant to use; however, it does give off the same vapors that mineral spirits does and must be used in a ventilated area.

28. Q. What is acrylic?
    A. Acrylic is a water clear plastic—used as a synthetic resin. It can be used as a clear spray for many different surfaces. It is usually in a petroleum solvent vehicle.* Sometimes it is in a water base emulsion. The water base emulsion looks milky. When dry, it is perfectly clear. Sometimes this is used as a sealer—such as the bright drying floor "wax", self-polishing. Water base sealers must not be used on raw wood. They are suitable for plastic or use over painted surfaces. Avoid water base products for découpage—except, of course, the paste and glue.

29. Q. How do you make paint crackle?
    A. Add a slow drying oil such as raw linseed to the base coat and a drier or fast drying solvent to the top coat. The top dries rapidly and cracks away from the base coat. All crackling of paint is a flaw and is rarely controllable—so even if you have a successful crackle once, it may not be consistent.

30. Q. How do you make very fine gold lines with paint?
    A. Liquid Leaf paint can be used in a ruling pen and the fine lines ruled onto a box or other surface. It is then protected with Treasure Sealer and the varnish coats applied.

31. Q. I have a wooden box that warped. Why? How do I unwarp it?
    A. Uneven drying or lack of equal varnish on the outside and inside can cause a box to warp. The concave surface is the one which dried into the warp. On this surface, place two coats of one-half alcohol and one-half glycerine, mixed together. Forty-eight hours later, repeat. This action is slow but it works. Do not rush it.

* Krylon acrylic, Blair acrylic, Devoe acrylic, Sherwin Williams, Glidden, and many other clear plastic spray manufacturers.

113

32. Q. I have a dust free area to varnish, new varnish and I clean my brush carefully. I still have a lot of trouble.

A. You probably have varnish dried up in the ferrules of the brush, even if you have cleaned it as well as you can. Suspend it in clean turpentine between varnish coats. Experience will overcome all these problems.

33. Q. Explain what makes the best finish.

A. Use materials made for découpage. Use as thin a paper as is practical, a layer of paste worked into the surface before pasting the print, removal of excess paste from under the print and the edges, and thin layers of varnish, dried properly between coats. The final rubbed finish can be as smooth with 3M paper and steel wool as with rubbing compounds. It's your own experience that makes the difference. By all means, use découpage wax to protect your finish.

34. Q. What causes the print to have a blister under it after applying twenty-five to thirty coats of varnish on the box?

A. If you have a blister the paste or glue did not adhere. As the varnish dries and cures, it shrinks. This happens *after* six weeks, usually. The more coats of varnish, the greater the stress. This is like a slow drying skin on a drum head—it can pull up a print.

35. Q. What can I do to prevent blisters?

A. Use the right paste or glue for the right job, and press out all excess. Découpage paste is used for light-weight paper. A heavier glue is used for heavier paper. It is advisable not to overdo the varnish build-up. That is—most varnish available at the paint store is made to be built up to no more than four coats. The large number of coats, twenty-five or thirty, cause immense stress. The varnish may pull apart and crackle or lift the prints. Be sure to use thin coats. This makes it possible to dry thoroughly between coats—this causes less stress. Varnish made for découpage has been modified so it builds up rapidly but doesn't shrink after many coats. Spar or gloss varnish does give a good finish but was not made for the build up.

Varnish made for découpage is not as tough as other varnish, i.e., spar varnish, bowling alley varnish. The tough film you expect to last on a gym floor or traffic area should repel or resist abrasion. It is extremely difficult *to sand* these varnishes. They were not meant to be sanded. They would be usable for one top coat, but not for coat-on-coat application.

36. Q. What is the best way to keep varnish?

A. When you buy it in a large can, put it into several two ounce jars, which are absolutely clean and dust free, or buy the smaller sizes already packaged. This way a skin doesn't form over the whole can of varnish and waste so much and you can't contaminate the unused varnish with dust particles.

37. Q. Will antiquing or glazing with a darker tone make a découpage piece more authentic?

A. No. It is not a good idea to do any antiquing. This dark muddy effect will not improve the appearance in any way and it will continue in nearly all instances to get darker with age. Most varnish will deepen as it matures.

38. Q. Can you antique a finish a little?

A. Yes, if you need a tone to bring out contours in a particular piece of furniture or a box. Antiquing colors should be used in a very subtle manner—so you do not see streaks but a gentle accent on the old distresses. I would advise against it in general as the work will gain a used look naturally, if it is used.

39. Q. How do you do the spatter or fly specks?

A. Fly specks and faux texture of this type are a hangover from antiquing and they do not generally add to the finished work. In fact, most times when you see speckling or spattering it detracts from the design. I have seen some diluted color used so subtly that the antiquing spatter was attractive. Immediately after the spatter is applied, it was blotted so it was hardly evident. Then a spatter of plain naphtha or even lighter fluid was done, leaving tiny clean spatters. Do this only on old furniture and boxes.

40. Q. How do you make a piece look like a real antique?

A. If you are accustomed to seeing the real antiques (made before 1830) and the very fine objets décoratifs—you will not see any spatters or speckles. Indeed, the finest were well cared for and look old and authentic because of the exquisite workmanship and superb materials. If you want the appearance of a fine antique piece, do a real craftsman's job with designs of the period and do not antique or glaze at all! Rub wax into the finish.

41. Q. Why do you use steel wool in some instances and wet or dry sandpaper in others?

A. Wet or dry sandpaper is flat and will level out a varnish finish. If the varnish used was gloss, you will have some glossy depressions. Use steel wool to get into these areas. You must have an even surface to make an even gloss when you apply the wax. If you want a contoured surface, use the steel wool because it follows the embossing into high and low places.

42. Q. Do you like to see a smooth surface or one with the contour of the découpage?

A. In 18th century work one should try to have a smooth finish. On large pieces, it is possible to have a print contour showing on the sides, but the flat planes should be as level as you can make them. On Victorian découpage the embossed surfaces of the work are attractive if the finish is deep. Do not use sandpaper if you want a contour; use only steel wool, as it will not flatten any of the embossing. You can also do a final rubbing with pumice and oil.

THE WAXING

With a single coat of wax a magnificent transformation will take place. The slightly etched and dusty finish will assume the smooth texture of elegant porcelain and polishing will reveal depth and a richness only acquired in the classical method of a deep varnish finish. This hand-made, hand-finished piece may well be your proudest possession—a special piece you have made.

There is a wax made for découpage, different from all other waxes, and yet it can be used on any fine furniture. This is Royal Parquet découpage wax. Use a damp piece of knitted cloth or cheesecloth, wring all water from it, pick up a little wax and apply to the varnished surface. In about ten minutes polish with a dry cloth to a lustrous sheen.

BRIEF SUMMARY OF
THE VARNISH FINISH

1. Apply ten coats of gloss varnish before first sanding. All varnish coats must dry twenty-four hours between each.

2. The first sanding is done with #400 wet or dry sandpaper dipped in water for the sanding operation. Ever-soft sponge removes the sanding residue. The tack rag is used just before applying a coat of varnish.

3. Apply four to ten more coats according to the richness of finish and coloring you want. Sand smooth with #400 wet or dry sandpaper. This final sanding should leave a perfectly level finish.

4. Use a tack rag before final two coats of low luster varnish. Gently steel wool the surface with #0000 to remove the minute scratches as a result of sanding.

5. Application of wax: Use a découpage wax which is a varnish wax or a fine furniture wax. A SLIGHTLY DAMP CLOTH is used to pick up a small amount of wax. Rub firmly into the finish and polish shortly after application with a damp soft cloth first, a dry cloth last. Do a small area at first to get the feel of this procedure. It is a very important step.

QUESTIONS AND ANSWERS
Waxing

1. Q. Can any wax be used on the varnish finish?
   A. If your work is sanded or rubbed down it needs wax and any paste wax is better than none. The best wax to use is pure white and has a gentle fragrance of French spices. It will not distort the finish as yellow or brown wax does and the illusive fragrance remains.

2. Q. Why is it necessary to wax?
   A. After using sandpaper or abrasive rubbing powder and oil, the finish is minutely scratched all over. It has an etched surface. Scratches can more easily mar this finish and it can collect small amounts of dirt to make the appearance less attractive. After all your work so far, it is a shame to leave the surface open instead of finished with wax. A smooth finish is smoother after waxing. This is a time-honored procedure with all fine furniture or varnish technicians—the final waxing. It feels better and it looks richer. The real distinction between an ordinary finish and an extraordinary finish is how it looks and especially how it feels to the touch.

UNUSUAL TECHNIQUES

There are many exciting effects that are closely related to découpage. They cannot be placed in any of the three main areas of 18th century, Victorian, or Modern découpage as they are not any of these. We categorize this collection of methods as "unusual techniques." They are meant to expand your curiosity, to present a broad scope of imaginative ideas with which you can combine découpage cutouts, gold paper braid, marbleized paper, gold tea chest paper, and other materials. This is not a traditional collection of authentic types. Some of them can become traditional. After all, every tradition started somewhere. The traditions we have in découpage now will be the basis for ideas in new traditions of the future.

Finishes—Unusual Techniques on Glass

THE MOONSTONE FINISH—USING CLEAR DRYING WHITE GLUE

A mirror is used for the background. Paste prints on mirror with a coat of white glue. Brush a coat of white glue over the print and set aside to dry completely clear. Apply a total of six coats with no attempt to be perfectly smooth. Do not thin the glue at any time. The uneven surface is ripply over the mirror and it is softly diffused—giving the appearance of a mysterious inner light. Give three coats of gloss varnish; steel wool, and wax for finish.

SEEDED GLASS

Apply white glue on glass—not mirror. Set print or gold paper braid into glue and coat also with white glue. After being allowed to dry clear, apply six more coats capturing or creating bubbles by brushing fresh glue into a partly dried surface.

SMOKED GLASS MIRROR FOR DÉCOUPAGE

Hold a mirror above a candle allowing carbon to collect in a random pattern. Move the mirror slowly—raise and lower it to produce the effect you want. Frame this mirror as it is under a piece of thin picture glass. The picture glass should be ornamented with découpage before you frame.

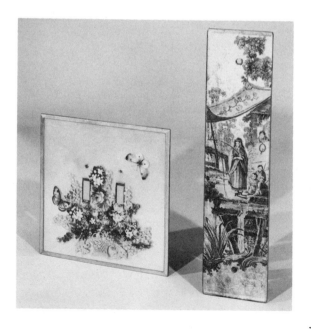

The double switchplate shows the moonstone finish bordered in gold and using Victorian découpage material. A mirrored switchplate is covered with six coats of white glue and dries to a nearly clear finish, which resembles moonstone. The pushplate is hand colored and backed with gold leaf.

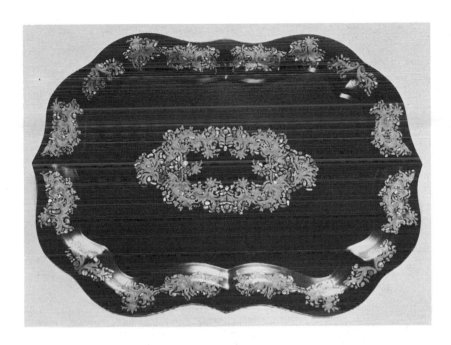

A large tray, using the Chippendale scrolls for the border and center designs, features lustrous accents of carefully cut-out mother-of-pearl. The use of mother-of-pearl adds great dimension to the elegant tray.

OPALINE

This iridescent coloring is relatively easy to do and is accomplished by the use of pearl paint or pearl spray. On a lamp base the sea shells and stylized scrolls make fine companion designs. After being colored in nacreous pastels and pasted to the inside of the glass, two coats of the pearl lacquer, or four coats of the spray are applied. Allow ample drying time between coats. The last step is to apply one coat of flat white or a pastel color to back up the pearl. An especially interesting illusion is created by using a metallic foil, silver leaf or Treasure Silver as a final step instead of the flat paint.

SMOKED GLASS DÉCOUPAGE

On a well-cleaned glass, spray an even coating of acrylic all over the backside. Dry thoroughly. Hold this glass over a lighted candle and move gently to accumulate the candle smoke where you want it to be. A beeswax candle will not smoke very much so use an ordinary one. When the coloring meets your approval, spray a fine mist of acrylic over the smoked surface to embed the carbon. Paste brightly colored découpage on a mirror and install behind the smoked glass, in a frame.

Bright reflections from mother-of-pearl add considerable interest to a switchplate. The very thin veneer sheets are easily cut after being soaked in hot water.

Mother-of-Pearl

The illusion created by using mother-of-pearl is incomparable. Glints of opalescent fire accent the print in strategic contours and add a dimension that cannot be achieved any other way. The best mother-of-pearl comes from the South Pacific. It is layered in a very thin veneer measuring about two inches by five inches.

To Prepare: Use a pencil to trace the pattern onto the translucent shell. While it is dry, the shell is brittle. Pour hot water over the shell, soak ten minutes, remove from water and begin cutting with the découpage scissors. Leave the shell in water during a long working period to avoid soaking from day to day. The left-over pieces can be used in many designs. Use the natural irregular bits on any contour without cutting a pattern.

To Apply: A thin coat of white glue is applied to the surface of the print and the mother-of-pearl. Dry to create a tacky instead of wet surface. A firm bond is made on contact. For small bits of mother-of-pearl, apply glue only to the print and press the shell into place. The white glue will dry transparent so there is no need to remove the excess. Apply a coat of clear sealer before you varnish.

Gold Leaf—Metal Leaf

First, we should distinguish between gold leaf and metal leaf, which is widely but erroneously called gold leaf. Real gold leaf is always packaged in squares 3" x 3". It comes in very few shades. The main two types of real gold leaf are standard and patent (or gild-in-the-wind) leaf. The latter is very lightly adhered to the paper so that a gilder working out of doors will be able to do gilding. This is easier for an amateur to work with. Tiny attached pieces can be easily handled and no waste occurs with this expensive material. Most leaf—real gold or otherwise—is twenty leaves to a book.

The metal leaf, though it is called "gold leaf," is easier to work with and much less expensive. In quantity purchases these 5½" x 5½" or larger sheets are inexpensive. Many paint stores carry the metal leaf and many also have "gold leaf" kits. The metal leaf is very susceptible to tarnish so sealer is used to prevent further tarnish. I have removed tarnish after a job was complete with a little diluted lemon juice, immediately neutralize with water, and dry. Then coat it with sealer.

This small chest can be used for practice when planning a full-sized piece. Here we see how the marbleizing is done, tapping across the surface to imitate marble. Last of all, the gold is applied to the edges.

The marbleizing on this Venetian shaped box was made by tapping gold accents on with a sponge. The turpentine-dampened sponge was dipped into Treasure Gold, and then applied to the box. The black center panel was painted on after the gold was dry. A print will be placed in the panel.

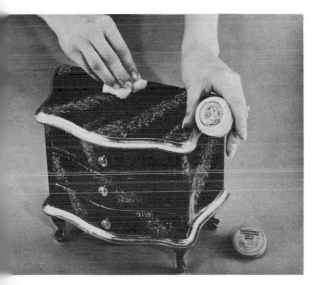

JAPAN GOLD SIZE

The mordant used varies. Mordant is the adhesive or varnish which is dried to the tacky stage and then receives the leaves of gold or other metal. Any gloss varnish could be used as a gold size. Any time you see the name "size"—this means adhesive. The name "Japan" on a gold size or drier means fast drying, and it really is. You may not be able to work fast enough to keep up with it. Apply a test patch, about 8" x 8", and time the drying. After twenty minutes it may be tacky enough to work well. Touch the surface ever so lightly; if there is a tacky click it is ready for applying the leaf. Continue to dry the test area. If it seems to have lost its tack after ten to fifteen minutes, that is all the time you have to work. If you have a fast drying gold size and it dries too rapidly, it can be removed with a rag dampened in turpentine. Then start again with another application of size. If you permit the gold size to dry twenty-four hours you can apply another coat and start again.

EIGHT HOUR MORDANT

Slow drying gold size may take four to eight hours to become tacky but you have one to two hours working time. If you use a fast size, cover a little at a time. Do as much as you can in twenty minutes, apply more size and wait until tacky and then place more leaf.

GOLD LEAF KITS

Gold leafing kits are abundant on the market now and generally work very well. One I have used seems very satisfactory. I don't like the disposable paste brushes that are included as you can't apply the adhesive evenly. The adhesive is rather like a thin latex and stays tacky a long time (twenty-four hours).

PREPARING THE GOLD LEAF

First, cut across the fold of the book of gold leaf so you have all single sheets. I handle the metal leaf sandwiched between two of the papers used in packaging. The leaf should be positioned so it extends one-half inch out of the papers; then lay this one-half inch of exposed leaf into the tacky surface and slip the leaf out of the papers easily onto the surface. After laying many leaves, I use a cotton ball and gently smooth down the leaf so it attaches evenly to the mordant. Go only in the direction of the grain as the gold leaf is so delicate it shows scratches if you smooth in circles. After the cotton polishing, collect the left-over scraps of gold leaf and save in a little jar. After much work you'll find these scraps handy fill-ins. Last, cover all metal leaf with découpage sealer, which is crystal clear.

Dissolve four empty gelatin capsules in a half cup of boiling water. Use this diluted gelatin mixture for a mordant on glass. (Most drug stores can supply you with the empty gelatin capsules.) The gelatin must dry only until tacky, then lay the leaf on the glass. Again, cotton is used to smooth the gold onto the surface. Silver or aluminum leaf will have the appearance of an old mirror, especially if your application is not perfect.

The Creil Technique

The original pieces were done during the 18th century. An invention of John Sadler, an English designer and engraver, is the basis of this exquisite ware. He discovered a method by which an engraved copper plate image could be transferred directly to white porcelain. He sought to guard his secret; however, he was imitated and the making of printed ware was soon widespread in England. There was a great demand for this beautiful ware, not only in his home land but throughout the entire European continent. Nowhere was there a livelier nor more enthusiastic demand than in France, where it became very serious competition for the domestic faience.

Therefore, the French potters began also to imitate the English work

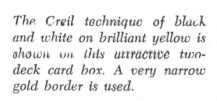

The Creil technique of black and white on brilliant yellow is shown on this attractive two-deck card box. A very narrow gold border is used.

The chinoiserie cut-outs are used in the Creil technique on a yellow ground. Creil often features a border such as this.

in order to meet the competitor, and recapture their lost market. The first such factory was at Douai, which had arranged to have the Leech brothers from England oversee the manufacture of printed wares in France. They brought with them, also, experienced workers to train local potters in the craft.

In 1796 the Creil factory was established and soon was well known for the production of this type of transfer printed pottery. Their production was so well established that all French pottery of this type was known as Creil whether it was from this factory or not. The reason for their success was that they had been able to engage the service of Bagnall, an English engineer, and thirty workmen from the factory at Chantilly, who had been carefully trained by Bagnall.

The more important early factories making printed wares in France were Johnston, Montereau, Choisy, Sèvres, and Val-sous-Mendon. The Montereau factory was purchased by Creil in 1819. The Creil factory continued its production until 1895. The Choisy factory continued until 1914. By the time of Napoleon's Consulate, 1799–1804, there were twenty-nine factories and forty-six merchants in Paris alone. Napoleon himself ordered several services for different châteaux and the officers' mess.

Most of the Creil was painted in black on all white, some was done with black on white using yellow borders. A lesser amount was done by transferring black to all yellow. The rarest combination was a sepia on olive green. By the end of the 19th century many of these designs were done in multicolored decorations on a white ground. Many collectors of this beautiful ware consider the black on yellow to be the most flattering for "terre imprime." Varying from lemon yellow to earthy ochre, this coloring is most eagerly sought for today.

Many of the pottery shapes are typical of the English silver of the period of the Napoleonic Empire. There were certain French shapes developed from other forms and especially adapted for their own dinner services.

During the Empire period gelatin transfers were developed and for all practical purposes were a good replacement for the original method of direct transfer. This method soon replaced all others.

It is fairly accurate to assume the costume depicted is a key to the date of the piece. During the Directoire period pre-romantic designs were in vogue. Battles, processions and other great events were depicted. Madame Blanchard's balloon ascension was a frequent subject. Other favorite subjects were street vendors, marionette theatres, fables of La-Fontaine, the monuments of Paris, views of Venice and other Italian scenes, and provincial scenes. There were also drawing room settings, coach and horses, and favorite farm animals. There was little Chinese influence in the Creil designs.

The central designs were always accompanied by classic border material. Some of this was acanthus leaves, laurel wreaths, flower garlands, and other casual and formal accent motifs. Trophées were always popular in France. This subject called for a simple border selection.

The best Creil is characterized by delicately printed designs made with perfect transfers. Some pieces show hand retouching where a transfer had been mended. These pieces are not as collectible.

Toleware With Creil Designs

From the time the handsome idea of Creil was invented, a variety of imitations came into being. Many provincial pieces of tinware or tole were given a ground color of yellow (from pale yellow to mustard) and hand painted in delicate scrolls or garlands of laurel with the central motif of the trophy. This work was done largely on trays, lavabos, boxes, cache-pots, and planters. This tinware was largely for the provincial people. Since tin was more durable and could more readily be crafted by the tinsmith, the country people had their imitation of Creil. This particular interpretation of the original is a highly collectible commodity today. Much of the tole was handpainted to resemble closely the character of the pottery.

The original French provincial "tole" or tinware came into being as a suitable and available substitute for the very expensive porcelains and pottery. The free-hand painted tole motifs of field flowers, garlands, and borders are used on many of today's casual accessories.

I have mentioned these two techniques of decorating tin—or tole-ware—because it relates directly to the use of our Creil design cutouts for trays, tole lampshades, lamp bases and other metal ware. The soft yellow ground is a very good color to use in the home today. Like gold, it seems to enhance the setting in which it is used.

The prints for the Creil technique are to be used generally without coloring (sepia being an exception). The black and white is very smart on a yellow ground. Any simple ornament, trophy or figure surrounded by a border in the right scale mounted on yellow, white or olive green ground could be an interpretation of Creil. If you plan to use the olive green, color the print with #64 terra cotta and #54 Van Dyke brown pencils gently. It must be in the character of the Empire or Directoire period. The Creil designs should be on utility ware or accessories. Your selection of prints with which to do this could be based on costume or the aforementioned subject of soldiers, triumphal procession, transportation, ladies and gentlemen in Napoleonic costume or animals, particularly goats.

In most of our cities, large and small, it is possible to find ceramic hobbyists who have many shapes of boxes and trays available in bisque. This ware has been fired but not glazed. It is very suitable to use for découpage. You must seal the surface first, just as you do a wooden box, and apply two coats of flat or semi-gloss enamel for the ground on which to paste the découpage. Paste your cutouts in position, apply the borders, remove excess paste and allow to dry. Use many coats of varnish just as if you were working on wood. When a sufficient number of varnish layers are applied, sand the surface with wet or dry sandpaper. Next, use #0000 steel wool, polish over all to remove scratches. Last of all, wax the entire piece and polish to a gentle sheen.

Boulle

A French invention for the surface decoration of fine furniture was named after M. Boulle. He used tortoise shell and fine gauge brass laid together and cut out. When the assembly was finished and affixed to a surface, the brass scrolls were seen on a ground of tortoise shell. The beautiful warm reds of the shell were reversed for the companion piece, so no material was wasted.

Process: In order to make an effective scroll and not waste the inside pieces, this cutting will require a knife. The scrolls and motifs must fit the area to be done, if it is a small motif. They must fit in segments if it is larger. This handsome work should be done with gold tea chest paper and tortoise shell paper. Borders are used on all of this work.

Seal the tea chest paper on the back with sealer. Use a coat of gloss varnish on the front as sealer may remove gold color. Seal the front and back of the tortoise shell paper to make it stiffer and crisper to cut. Use very sharp blade. You can also cut out the tea chest paper only and lay it on the tortoise shell ground. In this instance, cut two gold layers at a time. Your work will be speeded along.

Marquetry

A popular French technique involving the use of light colored wood veneers inlaid on a ground of darker wood. The fruit and nut woods, as well as satinwood and boxwood, were used for the motifs. Mahogany,

Marquetry at its finest is seen in an 18th century example from the Civic Museum in Milan, Italy. It will provide design inspiration for use in découpage.

burl woods and crotch veneers were used as dark background. Flowers, birds and foliage in beautiful profusion were used to decorate furniture fronts, table tops, and drawer facings.

Process: Cut together wood veneer paper and the scroll print pattern. Paste on natural wood grain or simulated wood grain. Varnish.

Silhouette

Another Frenchman has his family name connected with a shadow detail technique of doing portraiture—and later applied to all flat black and white cutout work. This work was looked down on when it was introduced as it was done to obtain an inexpensive portrait likeness—avoiding the high cost of miniature paintings or porcelain portraits.

Process: Cut scrolls, flowers, people. Stain either side with india ink. Apply to white background. If reverse work is your plan, use the white prints on black background.

Intarsia (Inlaid marble)

This technique involves the use of marbleized papers to effect an inlaid appearance on furniture. Usually a wide flourish is established for a border and various colored marble tones are laid out in an effective front and top pattern.

Process: Cut designs from a main pattern. Paste onto the painted surface and sink under many layers of varnish.

Trompe l'oeil

Trompe l'oeil and découpage go together. The French word *tromper* means to fool or to deceive and *oeil* means eye. We now see a growing interest in this marvelous technique and there will be more and more in the future. The fruit or other objects which are used as cutout material depend upon the hand-painted shadows to complete the illusion.

In the color illustration opposite, the cutouts, all life-size, were applied to make-believe pigeonholes and drawers that had been blocked out in paint on the surface of the cabinet and shaded to trick the eye into seeing a third dimension. Actually the cabinet, 12 inches square by 18 inches high, has one door, no drawers. Book, wineglass, key, clock face and rose motifs were snipped from pages of magazines. Butterfly and apple were cut out of inexpensive prints. Playing cards and letters are real, but ribbon is a strip of paper that was pressed flat and pasted on. Each pigeonhole was charted first on paper.

The use of Boucher's cherubs and the Abbé de St. Non garlands have made an exquisite transformation from a piano into a very grand piano indeed.

Découpage in the trompe l'oeil manner embellishes an eye-defying cabinet. The cutouts, all life-size, were applied to make-believe pigeonholes and drawers that had been blocked out in paint on the surface of the cabinet and shaded to trick the eye into seeing a third dimension.

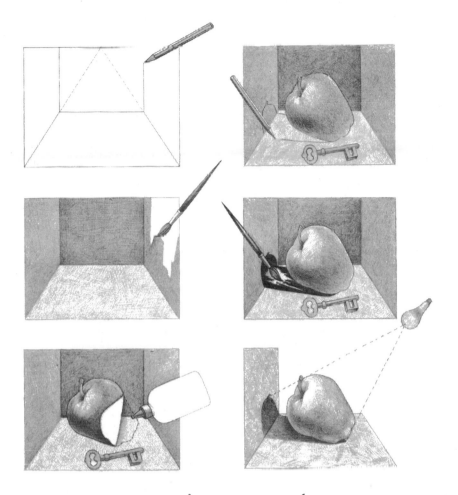

HOW TO PLOT AND PAINT TROMPE L'OEIL PIGEONHOLES[1]

1. Starting in center of top boundary for pigeonhole, draw diagonal lines to bottom corners. Join diagonals at mid points with line parallel to bottom. From same points, draw vertical lines to top. Erase lines indicated by dots.

2. Shade with paint each section of pigeonhole to give the effect of depth, varying darkness of shading to suggest direction of light source.

3. Glue cutouts on "floor" of pigeonhole.

4. To determine the realistic pattern of shadows cast by the cutouts, select a real apple, key, etc., place nearby and direct a light on them.

5. With soft pencil, copy the outlines of the real shadows around the objects in the pigeonhole.

6. Fill in shadows with shades of gray.

[1] Reprinted from House and Garden Magazine, Copyright © 1963 by the Condé Nast Publications, Inc.

The violin is done in découpage, rubbed to an ivory lustre, and mounted with old sheets of music to create a handsome framed picture.

A flat panel gains depth and an illusion of three dimensions in the trompe l' oeil work shown here. Pre-colored prints are used and shadows are painted in afterwards.

Reproduction (with a few liberties) of a primitive painting in the Garbish art collection. Background table and base are freehand painted and dishes are drawn and painted on heavy paper, then cut out. Prints used are antique and reproductions of old prints in full color. Old curly maple frame is used.

Repoussé

This very attractive technique involves filling the cavity of an embossed print with papier mâché or other hardening material. It is necessary to use a print on heavy paper. If the print was done in watercolor, be sure to apply two coats of sealer. Dry thoroughly. Soak the print in warm water twenty minutes to soften it so it will contour easily. The contour is created by pressing the print from the back side to stretch the paper into a convex shape.

Against a turkey-red grained background are placed three yellow-green finches on a pine bough. The side lighting helps set off the sculptured bodies in this handsome repoussé.

Yellow wild roses in repoussé shown on a cut-out panel of antique white. A green wooden wastebasket repeats the foliage color.

HOW TO DO A BIRD IN REPOUSSÉ

1. Hold the print to a window or other light, and trace the outline of the bird on the reverse side of the paper. This is done so you will know where to press the paper to create the bird's body shape.

2. Place the wet print on a piece of plastic foam, such as Oasis or styrofoam. With the burnishing tool or other rounded metal object begin to press on the area that you want the deepest. Continue pressing in gentle circles until you have come to the edge of the penciled outline. You are scooping out or hollowing a negative contour from the reverse side that will appear as a raised or embossed surface on the printed side.

3. When the shaping is complete, apply two coats of white glue and dry. Fill the cavity up to within one-eighth of an inch of the outline so the cutting will be easy, and the edge will flatten out when you glue. Use a ready mixed papier mâché or make a filling of wadded tissues and white glue. It is possible to use plastic wood or self-hardening clay, plaster, or spackling compound. On a cylindrical or other contoured surface, use a papier mâché filler as it will bend.

4. After the work is completely dried, cut out the bird, and glue to the surface with white glue. Begin the varnish finish. After ten coats you

are ready to sand. Use steel wool on the contoured bird and sandpaper (#400 wet or dry) on the flat areas.

The print can be cut out before stuffing, but for most people it is a little more difficult to handle this way.

QUESTIONS AND ANSWERS

Repoussé

1. Q. My print is on thin paper. What can I do to use it?
   A. Seal the print first, then glue or paste it to a heavier grade of paper, such as water color paper. Then proceed with the repoussé work.

2. Q. Where can you use repoussé birds when they are finished?
   A. They are beautiful on screens or boxes. An attractive wood stain can be a natural setting for birds. They are used on the top of basket purses and on wastebaskets.

3. Q. Can I combine repoussé flowers with Victorian découpage, and contour a gold paper braid basket for a container?
   A. Yes. That would be very attractive. It would be interesting to use a gold tea chest paper background for the flowers and gold basket.

4. Q. Should I stuff or contour a butterfly for use in a shadowbox picture?
   A. No. A butterfly's natural shape is flat except for the body.

5. Q. How many coats of varnish should I use if I plan to do flowers in repoussé in a shadow box?
   A. Two or three coats may be sufficient for a shadow box. If you need more, use more.

6. Q. Would it be permissible to glue gold cord or colored string when doing work in repoussé?
   A. Related materials such as gold cord, string, woven matting, grass cloth, and perhaps natural plant material such as twigs could be used. Fabrics can be used in repoussé.

7. Q. Are animals sometimes used as designs?
   A. Yes. There are no limits to the number of subjects that can be used.

8. Q. Can I use mother-of-pearl in the contours?
   A. Mother-of-pearl accent is beautiful and will contour on many surfaces.

Projects to Try

The following projects are easy to do if care is observed at each step. Read the instructions through completely and if you do not understand the procedure with the aid of the illustrations, go to the next project, and come back to this project later. (You will understand it.) Do not feel baffled if there are parts that seem to confuse you or that you do not understand. After all, you will find even in a class with the best instructor this situation arises. Relax, learn what you can, and upon returning to the project with a clear fresh mind, all will be clear and easy to understand.

Beginner Project: How to do a Metal Tray with Modern Prints

Prepare the tray. Wipe with alcohol if previously painted. If it is very glossy, use fine sandpaper to create a good surface for adhesion.

1. Choosing the background color is easy. You want the prints you choose to be against a color that will accent their beauty. This is a good place for an accent color you enjoy. Remember the varnish will mellow considerably, so use blue, green, red or soft yellow.

2. Apply two or three thin coats of paint. If your first coat has ridges, thin the paint with solvent and continue to apply a smooth coat. Sand very gently between coats.

3. Apply sealer to the front of the print. If the paper is heavy, you will need many extra coats of varnish to cover the edges. It is possible to taper these prints with sandpaper or wet it and roll off a layer of paper —this is hazardous for the beginner.

4. Cut out prints carefully, serrating the edges of the leaves by wiggling the paper back and forth to create a softer edge as you guide the paper into the scissors.

5. Apply paste to the tray and gently press the print into place. Roll out any excess paste, using a brayer (looks like a small rolling pin) or a wallpaper tool. A slightly damp cloth placed over the design prevents smearing paste as you roll.

6. Use gold paper braid as a narrow border—adhere with white glue. Apply sealer evenly over the entire surface before varnishing.

7. Now, begin the beautiful process which will make your tray permanently attractive and useful. Apply the varnish to the entire surface. Do not drag the brush across the edge of the container as this creates bubbles. Always pour the amount of varnish you will be using into a separate container, so you will not contaminate the entire can with dust and foreign matter. Keep the brush in turpentine from day to day.

The Basket Purse

The basket purse is a fashion accessory which is becoming increasingly popular all over the United States. Exquisite samples are seen in the smartest resort boutiques and specialty shops in many of our larger towns. The woman who appreciates these handmade, beautifully finished basket purses will part with a considerable sum of money in order to possess one. They are carried with casual clothes and street wear. They always attract attention! Some smaller basket models are made for dress-up and done with delicate prints and metallic coloring. Other small models are made for smaller women or little girls in this fashion-conscious world.

A white ground is used for the forget-me-not blue garland. A matching blue velvet ribbon is placed over wide pale green ribbon to trim the edge and handle. Sapphire and green amber are rubbed on the wood for a stunning effect. Blue and green berries are woven on the lining fabric.

Louise Hoyt of Grosse Pointe designed and taught how to make the basket purse in découpage. Her work has been featured on television stations and in national publications. These instructions are basically the ones used in Mrs. Hoyt's classes.

1. Sand the box and lid carefully with fine garnet sandpaper.

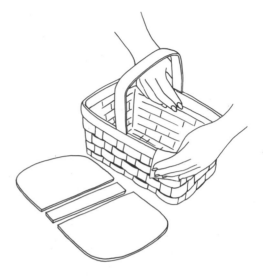

2. Stain the lid and basket with oil stain or Treasure Jewels thinned with turpentine.

3. Rub the stain color in wet with wet or dry emery paper. Do handle, lid and outside of the basket—not inside. This makes an incomparably smooth finish.

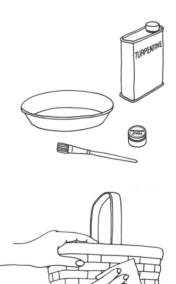

4. Seal prints, lid and basket. Cut out print for lid and under lid designs. Sealer makes the print easier to cut—prevents tearing when wet with paste.

5. Paste on motifs. Remove excess paste. Dry. Seal the surface of print and lid, top and underside. Also, seal the stain on the basket.

6. Begin the varnish finish. Apply ten coats. Then sand with wet or dry paper dipped in water. Apply six to ten more coats of varnish. Sand. Apply two coats wax.

Fabric lining the basket purse:

7. Cut two sides and one bottom strip. Apply two coats acrylic spray to stiffen and protect lining.

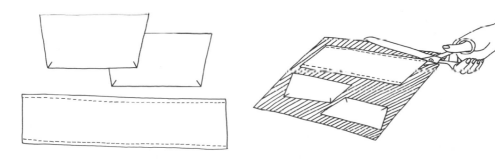

8. Glue lining. Glue in both sides first and center panel last. Glue on nylon ribbon or gimp braid available at upholstery shops. Make bow trim.

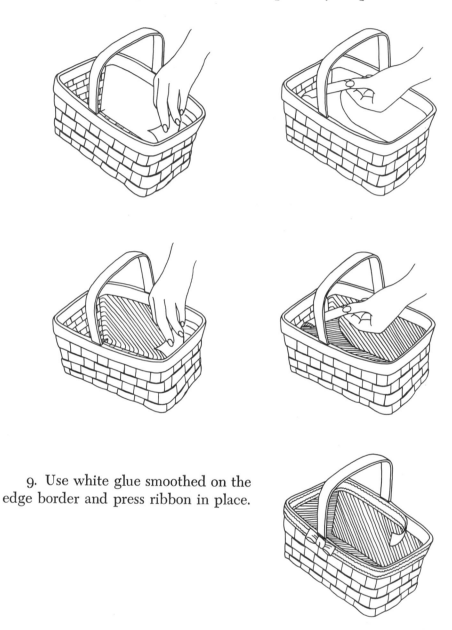

9. Use white glue smoothed on the edge border and press ribbon in place.

10. Place hinges ½" from edge of lid. Slip under handle into place and install handle screw to secure center lid panel.

Finished basket

How to do a Shadowbox Picture

Assemble your materials:

    Frame
    Colored cutout prints: tiny ship or gondola
    Cement glue
    Paste
    Sponge
    Water
    Tiny matchbox
    Glass
    Gold Paper braid border

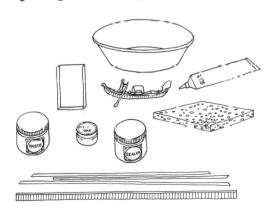

1. Wash glass with ½ and ½ vinegar water. Dry. Paste foreground prints onto the glass. Apply découpage paste over the area the print will cover. Press out excess paste. Remove with sponge. Set aside to dry. Clean all excess paste. Must be very clean.

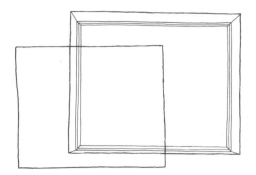

2. Place tiny print panels and people in the matchbox which will be the scene in the left foreground. Tiny people can be cut from découpage print catalogs showing prints in miniature.

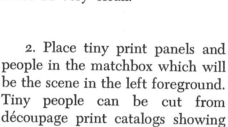

3. Glue the matchbox to the back of the building so this setting can be seen through the open windows. Also, paste into place the canal panel.

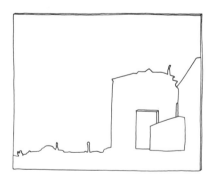

Seen from rear

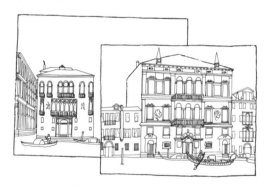

Canal panel

4. Paste gold tea chest paper to the back board (corrugated). Seal tea paper on both sides before using it. Allow pasted paper to dry thoroughly. Paste background print on gold tea paper. Use small gold paper braid

motifs inside open doors and windows to resemble grill work. Install small gondola or ship with glue or Plasti-Tak.

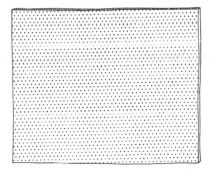

5. Paste in a strip of black cardboard allowing ¼″ for the back board (corrugated) to fit against. (Use shirtboard painted black with ink or paint.)

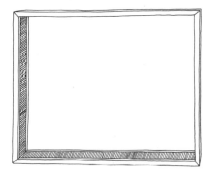

6. Use cement glue (Duco or other) to hold glass onto outside of the frame. Place glass immediately before glue sets. Cover edge with gold paper braid.

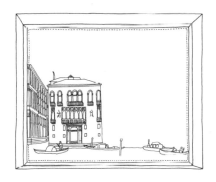

7. Nail backboard in place. Cover the back with dust paper and install a center pictured ring.

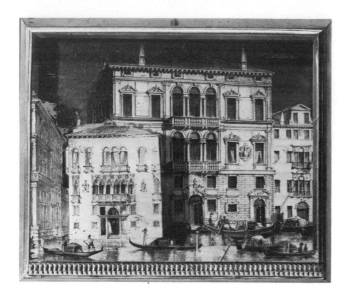

Venetian shadowbox showing placement of palazzos along the canal to give depth and create a vue d' optique. The building in the foreground has doors and windows opened into a matchbox scene.

The inside story is told when we see the matchbox attached to the print on the glass and the tiny silver filigree gondola in the canal on the back print. Hand-colored prints in pastel are framed in gold leaf shadowbox.

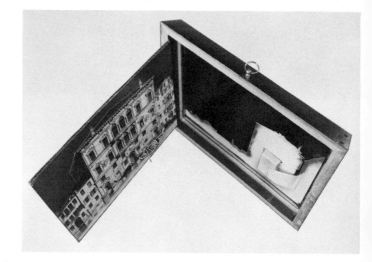

Chinoiserie shadowbox with a vue d' optique is colored in the 18th century palette and placed on a gold tea chest paper background. Three prints were used for this piece.

This large panel is one of a pair to be used on either side of a door. The prints are uncolored. The various shades of the ink used on the antique engravings make an interesting though very subtle color under the many coats of varnish.

This drawing for a bronze ormolu clock was cut out and laid against gold tea paper, accented with embossed gold braid and fitted with a battery-operated movement. The deep shadowbox molding conceals the works.

Ribbon Découpage—antique cut-out showing the various ribbon patterns through the cut-out designs.

Ribbon découpage showing a pair of Englebrecht prints cut out to reveal brocade in a kelly green and gold behind the uncolored print. The white paper was antiqued with tea before cutting.

How to do Ribbon Découpage

This lovely antique technique was not called by this name traditionally, but ribbon découpage is a good name to use when you place ribbon or brocade behind the cutout print. Many of the varieties of cutout work did not have a standard name. Probably this is due to the fact each artist designing this work felt he had created something nobody else ever did. In so doing, he may or may not have given it a name. Many exquisite shadowbox cutouts were done as portraits of a favorite saint, usually performing a miracle.

1. Antique the print first. Moisten both sides of the print—lay on a flat table surface—drip tea or coffee to stain. Instant tea or coffee can be blown from the open hand to the print to create random age spots. Blot these if they are too intense and add more water or tea. Dry flat.

2. The print is not colored; however, if you wish to add subtle accents in pencil now is the time to do it. Seal the print back and front.

3. Cut out portions of the pattern that you wish to ornament with gold paper accents. Paste the gold paper in place on the back of the print—very carefully.

4. Cut the areas of the print where you wish to have the brocade showing through. It is not necessary to do anything to prepare the fabric if it lies flat. If you want to use a few spray coatings of acrylic plastic the fabric will be stiffer for smooth mounting; however, you might lose some of the color or alter the sheen. Spray-test first.

5. The print is somewhat wrinkly like an antique print. I do not think this is objectionable. You can dry mount the print flat with rubber cement or a photography shop can dry mount it to a board to be perfectly flat —this is your preference. I like the natural easy state of the print—wrinkly.

6. Cut a mat for the print or have the mat cut at the shop where you get your frame. Mount gold border strips and tortoise shell paper strips to make an inner border on the mat to make a French mat. Install in frame. Mount print on back board—set in place. Nail in the whole assembly. Paste dust paper and attach wire in screw eyes.

How to do a Lamp

Coordinating the size of the lamp base and the shade could be the most difficult part of this project. Be sure to have your lamp shade before you begin the découpage. Many electric repair companies have lamp parts and also the glass hurricane cylinder or chimney. If you buy all of your parts from a company they can also assemble your finished work. *Buy the shade before you begin.* Plan to use a related print border on the shade.

1. Assemble your materials.

2. Plan the design on the hurricane lamp base. Clean the inside and out with vinegar water to remove any oil or fingerprints. All work will be done inside the glass.

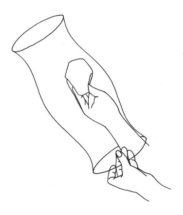

3. For work under glass do not seal the print. This is the secret of the perfectly clear paste job. If the print is very intricate you should seal very lightly on the back.

4. A china marking pencil or crayon can be used to indicate on the outside of the lamp the placement of motifs. Also, use a rubber band around the piece to make border indications. This can be moved up and down to the border edge. If you want an antiqued finish, this goes on before you paste, wipe or streak, or brush paint an antique glaze on.

5. Lightly apply paste on the *front* of the print which is to be used in the center area. Place the center motif first and the outer border last. Carefully press out excess paste and tap up with a damp sponge.

6. Follow the border rubber band and press your pasted border material into place. Do not overlap at the final piece; make it appear continuous.

7. If you want any gold accents, now is the time while the paste is still intact. Apply little pieces of bright gold foil behind openings, particularly areas which are reverse cut. *Lay lamp base on the side* in an airy place so the inside has an opportunity to get dry.

8. Dry overnight. Remove any excess paste when the individual motifs are dry underneath and will not move when touched with a slightly damp eversoft sponge. Set aside to dry again. You could use an electric fan now to dry quickly.

9. Use clear sealer over the entire design —this will prevent any paint from sneaking under the print. This is an important step so cautiously cover every little edge and especially where there might be an overlap. Dry thoroughly—use an electric fan.

10. Paint the inside of the lamp and the backside of the prints. I use a cloth pad—not a brush—inside, so I can easily pounce on a perfect layer of paint. Starting in the middle, pat the paint in an even layer in a wide spiral toward the outside edge. Turn over and do the same from the center to the outer edge. If you plan a contrasting band of Treasure Gold behind the border, now is the time to apply the gold with your finger. Tap it on at first, dry a little, and give a second coat to make the gold richer. You need a second coat of paint after twenty-four hours.

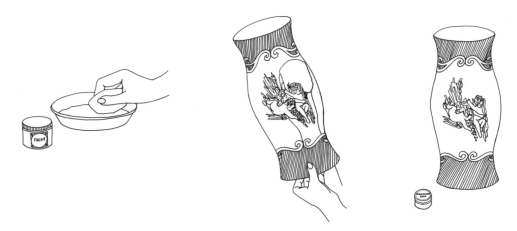

How to do a Lamp Shade

When doing the lamp base, you worked in reverse under glass. The traditional name for work under glass is reverse painting. Now, when you do the shade, the work will be the standard procedure. A plain ivory silk shade can be used or you can make the lamp more attractive by making a shade designed with the same prints as the base.

1. Assemble materials:
   Parchment shade
   Gold or silver spray paint
   Découpage paint and brush
   Clear spray
   Border cutouts
   Paste
   Sponge
   Water

2. Cut out the border material, either more of the lamp base prints or something related.

3. Paint the parchment paper shade with a silver or gold metallic spray to make it opaque. Do not get spray on the inside. This must be sealed with Treasure Sealer.

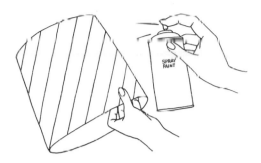

4. Paint the background with a pad dipped into the paint to imitate the texture of the base. You could use a small trim roller if you have one. Dry twenty-four hours. A second coat may be needed if the first coat wasn't even. Sand very lightly and wipe the dust away. Make measured *marks* on the edge for the border.

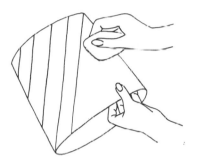

5. Apply paste to the area on which you intend to apply the border. Position prints and press on with a damp sponge. Do an area of about ten inches at a time, or whatever is near your border size. Repeat until you are finished. Allow paste to dry. Remove excess paste with a damp sponge.

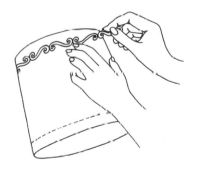 

6. Paste any motifs on the lamp shade. Glue on narrow contrasting ribbon.

7. Dull plastic acrylic spray is used to fix the paint and protect the prints.

8. Have lamp assembled.

9. Which finial to use? Be sure to finish your shade (when it is assembled to the base) with an attractive finial. It could be painted the base color, but this is the finishing touch of a well-designed lamp.

Covering a Box With Paper

1. Apply paste evenly to sides and bottom of box. Place box in center of paper.

2. Smooth the paper across the bottom and up the sides of the box. press firmly to top edges and corners.

3. Cut off "loops" at corners, carefully so that edges of paper meet.

4. Fold paper over top edges of box, paste down firmly.

5. Miter top edge (shown in circle) by cutting through overlap at 45 degree angle.

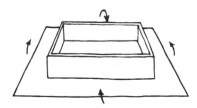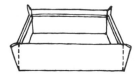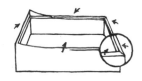

Lining Boxes

One of the special marks of a well done piece is choosing a related lining inside the box and finishing the underside of the box with great care.

Either use small brass feet on the bottom or a border design protected with varnish. On boxes which are heavy, you might prefer to use a felt or cork pad for the protection of furniture. It should not be glued on.

Each of us will devise a variation of his own on lining the box. I do believe a good lining is essential. There are at least three variations suitable for a box. An 18th century jewel box replica would surely have to be lined with a fine brocade, silk or velvet—either padded when using silk or flat when using the brocade or velvet.

The fabric lining is a bit tricky; with patience it will be a very successful lining, perhaps the easiest and most rapid of the three to do.

The découpage lining: a box to be used in the living room would be most intriguing if designs were carried out on the inside in the same manner as the outside.

The paper lining: the third type of lining is a solid lining of gold or silver tea paper, silver leaf, gold leaf or metal leaf—or a select marbleized book-binding paper for the tailored taste.

HOW TO DO LININGS

The fabric lining: cardboard from a dress box or shirt box or even a tablet will be quite suitable for the backing. Cut a piece to fit the bottom, minus ⅛″ all around the border. This seems terribly small, but wait till the fabric is glued on! Cut pieces now for the two ends and two sides, minus the ⅛″ border. It is easiest to do one side and an end together, so lay the cardboard on the back side of the fabric and cut it out allowing ½″ extra border. Cut V's at the crease and cut diagonally across ends. (Practice this on paper first if you are unsure. Fold the paper down all around and you will see how nicely the lining will fit.) Cut into your fabric and paste it down on the back side. Cut and paste both ends and sides. To make a final check on the fit, place the linings in the box, where they are to remain and slip the bottom piece (to which the fabric is pasted and ready) into place.

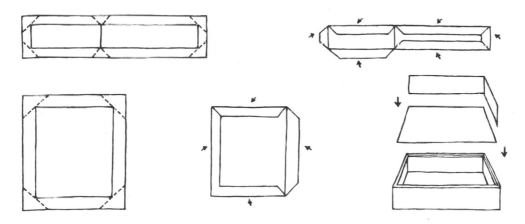

151

If you have no further alterations, paste the sides and bottom into position. The inside of the box was sealed and painted when the box was being prepared. This helps prevent warping of the box.

Go through the same procedure to line the top of the box. If the lid is too narrow for side pieces cover the cardboard for the inside top of the lid and glue in place a decorative cord around the edge to finish it. You may select a woven braid which would be in keeping and glue it in for the sides.

The découpage lining: this decorative lining is done using additional designs cut out for the inside. Two coats of paint are needed inside. This should be done when you are preparing the outside of the box. You may choose to make a contrasting color inside. At any rate, your basic preparation is just the same as the outside of the box. Plan the design, smooth paste over the section you are to apply the cutouts and arrange them, pressing as much paste from under the cutouts as is possible. A rolling pressure with thumb or index finger should accomplish this. After all the designs are in place, remove *excess* paste—picking it up with a *damp, but not wet,* sponge. Continue to tap up all the excess paste, then permit the work to dry—do not accelerate with heat at any time.

After twenty-four hours' drying, check to see that all the segments are tightly glued. A toothpick and a touch of white glue is used for any stragglers. Next, brush a thin coating of sealer and dry an hour. Now, apply the first coat of varnish, evenly but not generously. Follow the varnish label for drying interval—every twenty-four hours is safest. About four coats should do for the inside. Sand after the final coat of varnish—not between coats.

The paper lining: since the paste you use is a water base paste it would stretch and warp any lining paper, so be sure to use *sealer* on the front and back of your lining paper, dry thoroughly and cut the paper to fit the sides and the bottom. Paste in the section for the bottom first. Smooth paste evenly on the bottom of the box and press the paper into place. Using a wet finger and paste for lubrication press the paper down firmly and try to get any excess paste out at the edges. Apply paste to the sides and having the lining paper creased at the corners, lay it into place. Next, use the thumb or finger with a rolling movement to remove excess paste.

Use a damp sponge again to clean the excess paste from the inside surface of the box. Dry twenty-four hours and apply a coat of sealer. You do not need any further varnish as your paper now has two coats of sealer. There should be no bubbles or areas which did not stick. If a bubble or a blister should occur, slit through it with a razor blade and fill it with white glue applied with a toothpick or artist's tiny spatula and smooth into place.

A sumptuous serving tray by Hiram Manning is ornamented in the Sèvres porcelain fashion with embossed gold filigree paper to produce the effect of chasing. Small cutout floral garlands are used in the center. Background enameled in apricot and antique white. Under the varnish a glazed porcelain appearance results from the many coats of varnish.

Octagonal box—Mrs. Kimball Powning. Mrs. Powning chose a scenic design and mounted it on a soft Pompadour blue background, which turned to mellow absinthe green under the antique finish.

Ideas for Accessories

All of these designs can be cut out by the amateur wordworker. The illustrations include: pencil and stationery box, book ends, key board, desk paper holder, either note size or business size, wooden shields, wooden clothes hanger, and special letter box with a drawer on each side and crest design.

Your First Découpage

Somewhere among your magazine clippings you have probably saved an idea you would love to try in découpage. You may have seen a lovely basket purse, a fabulous tray or stunning little box which you'd like to duplicate. You may have seen what you thought was a priceless antique accessory with mother-of-pearl inlay, only to be told that it was made just recently by a person who has no more training nor ability than you have. Right then and there you decide you can learn découpage, too!

You must start by deciding what project will be your first. Then get prints which will be suitable in scale and character. Assemble all your materials and begin. It is really about as uncomplicated as that! It is also important that you plan to work where and when you can find a time free from needless interruption. Only then, with materials set neatly for work in a light, airy and comfortable place, can you find freedom for creative expression and become absorbed in découpage—in such a setting fine work can be done.

In preparing to do découpage the following materials are necessary: print, pencils, paste, sealer, paint, brushes, sandpaper, steel wool, scissors, varnish and wax. There are other handy things to have but these are essential.

Prepare the piece to be done in découpage by painting and sanding very evenly and smoothly. Color a black and white print to coordinate with the background paint or use the print without coloring. In either case the print must be sealed. The cutout prints are placed in a pleasing arrangement and pasted down firmly. The final step is applying ten or more coats of varnish and sanding level. The varnish finish is complete when wax has been applied and polished to a sheen. Each step is relatively simple and when done with care the results are very pleasing.

Project Suggestions for a Beginner

Plan a group of three projects to learn working with wood, metal and glass. Relate the projects to bathroom, desk, vanity—such as

    Game accessories—cardbox, ashtray, bonbon dish
    Desk accessories—letter holder, ashtray, stamp box
    Entry hall—switchplate, serving tray, wastebasket
    Dressing room—vanity tray, switchplate, jewel box

Further Projects

For men—young and older:
    The crest box for jewelry or pocket items
    Organizer box—chest-top box
    Hobby box—boat box, model car box
    Stationery box—lap desk
    Good grooming kit—shoe polish, etc.
For young women:
    Curler box, sewing stand
    Vanity box, mirror
    Box purse

Basket purse
Stationery box
For the home:
Candle table
Small desk
Mirror
Tole planter
Large tray
China cabinet
Lamp base and lamp shade
For special gifts—all ages:
Bachelor's chest
Doll bed, dresser
Lap desk
Picnic basket
Courtin' basket
Trinket box
Poodle bed
Shadowbox
Découpage pictures

Panels, Screens, Pictures and Plaques

When working with only two dimensions, width and height, you have a different design problem than with three dimensions, width, height, and depth. When planning a composition for a picture, many prints will be used—either in a landscape, figure presentation, or flowers and fruit. The reason for a découpage picture is purely ornamental. "Beauty is its own excuse for being," Emerson says.

In planning a decorative panel or a useful screen your purpose may be to provide a subtle, but ornamental background. In this instance use less contrasting colors, a pale ground color and pastel colored or uncolored prints. This screen or panel will take its place quietly in a room setting. If your plan is to have the screen or panel a dominant design factor in the setting, it can be very ornamental and amount to a considerable factor in furnishing a room. This screen should show a sharp contrast in ground color as well as greater strength of design and color in the prints.

Plaques are used as beginner projects and test panels. They are quickly done and very good to do to learn découpage techniques. Usually a single print is cut out, applied and varnished.

The background of the box and plaque are opalescent blue. The Boucher palette of colors is used on the cherubs and also the box.

Broken gold leaf is used for the background. Marbleized paper is cut out for the basket and stand. Reproductions of Redouté's roses, fruits and flowers are used in gay profusion.

The little shepherdess and shepherd are shown in a typical French setting. The overhead arch is a cartouche of scrolls and cherubs selected from various prints. The uncolored prints are laid on a muted yellow ground.

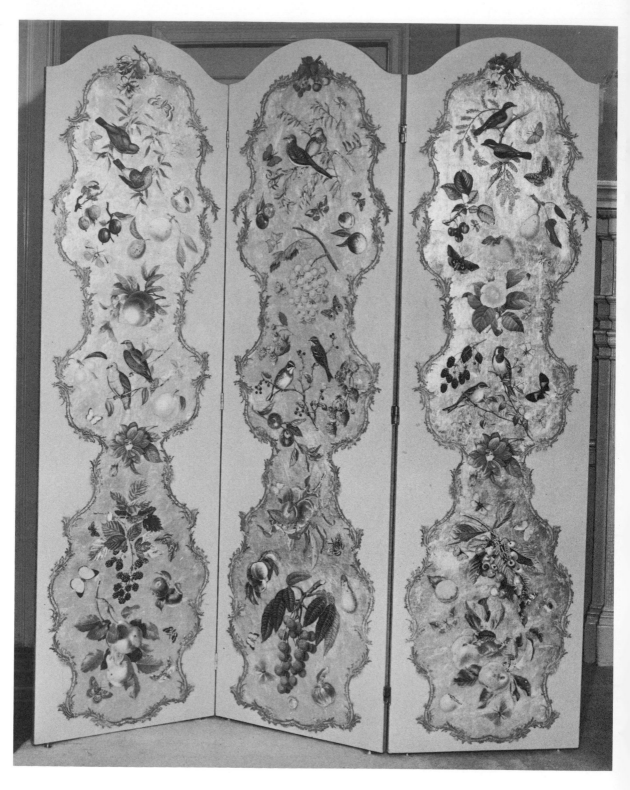

An outstanding example of a three panel screen. It is painted pale green outside with gold leaf background, enclosed in the cartouche border. Some prints are antique, some are Gould's tropical birds, Redouté's camellias and fruit reproductions. Only the cartouche is hand colored green and gold. This screen is one of the most arresting works in contemporary découpage.

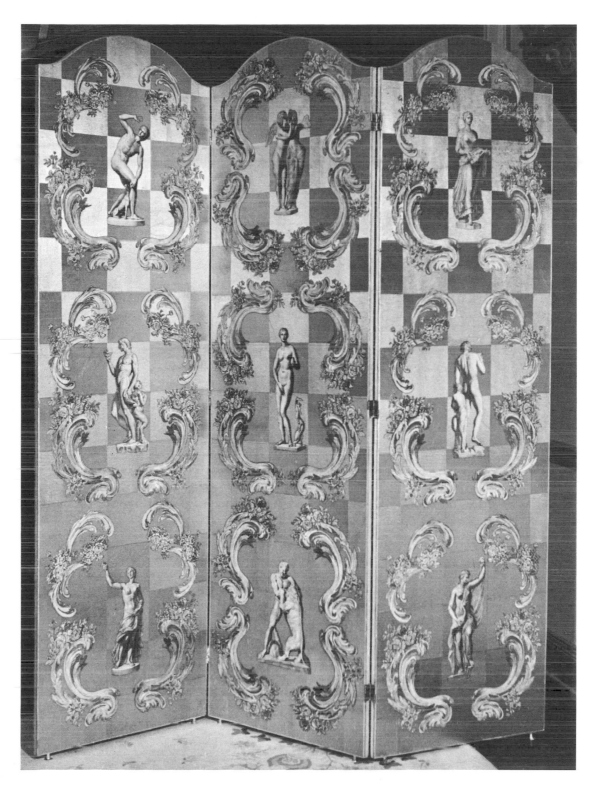

Screen is 6 feet tall with a background of silver tea paper cut in squares. The 18th century engravings are reproductions of Tessier, painted in black and sepia water color, matching the Greek gods and goddesses. This original piece is a classic example of découpage at its best.

SOURCES OF SUPPLY

The best place to buy supplies is at a shop specializing in découpage materials. Usually, they have instructors available for classes or for a program to local clubs. These people are very glad to help you get started with or without lessons. Art supply shops carry a wide array of material and often have a special découpage department, which would include Derwent pencils, other pencils, erasers, artists' paint brushes, sealer, varnish, paste, glue, découpage scissors and special découpage materials. Artists' materials distributors, listed in the yellow pages, can tell you who would have découpage supplies in your community.

Boxes are available at art and craft supply shops. If you don't have some choice raw material stored somewhere, second hand shops and antique shops as well as gift shops have a variety from which to select. You may not always be able to find what you're looking for. Ask the sales person for a jewelry, glove, trinket or stamp box, a large silverware or a photograph box.

Small pieces of accessory furniture are to be found in these same little shops. Look for a candle stand, small pick-up table, smoking stand, sewing box (footed or not), lap desk, Bible box, or magazine rack. Any of these will require very little cutout ornament, and the style of the piece will determine what type découpage you will choose.

The following firms have boxes, scissors, 18th century reproduction black and white prints, full color prints, sealer, paste, glue, paints and varnish. Many have also mother-of-pearl, brass feet, hinges, ornamental pressed brass, wastebaskets, glass switchplates, and other accessories to decorate.

Antique Prints and Scrapbook Pictures: Brandon Memorabilia, Inc., 13 E. 53rd Street, New York, N. Y. 10022

* Artists Materials: Arthur Brown & Bro. Inc. 2 West 46th Street, New York, N. Y. 10036.

Baskets: Wicker World, 20651 Mack Avenue, Grosse Pointe Woods, Michigan 48236

*Découpage Supplies: Patricia Nimocks, Inc., 12200 Shelbyville Road, Middletown, Kentucky 40043

Hurricane Globes: Davis Lynch Glass Co., P. O. Box 4286, Star City, West Virginia 26501

Lamp Bases: West Virginia Glass Specialty Co., Weston, West Virginia 26452

* Lamp Parts: Angelo Bros. Co., 2333 N. Mascher St., Philadelphia, Pennsylvania 19133

*Tin Ware—tole unpainted: Carson and Ellis, 1153 Warwick Avenue, Warwick, Rhode Island 02888

Trays: Colonial Handcraft Trays, New Market, Virginia 22844

* *Catalog available*

DECOUPAGE SHOPS AND STUDIOS

Anderson Découpage Studio
7736 Dublin Street, Woodlawn East, Wichita, Kansas 67206

Aristocrafts
22070 Michigan Avenue, Dearborn, Michigan 48124

Billy Arthur, Inc.
Eastgate Shopping Center, Chapel Hill, North Carolina 27514

The Blue Mussel
478 Fifth Avenue S., Naples, Florida 33940

Bob's Florette, Inc.
4276 Tennyson Street, Denver, Colorado 80212

Boca Bazaar
20 S. Dixie, Boca Raton, Florida 33432

Bulwinkle Découpage Studio
4250 Jordan Lane, Mobile, Alabama 36608

Bunny's Crafts
2532 Monroe Boulevard, Dearborn, Michigan 48124

Cambridge House
7630 State Line, Prairie Village, Kansas 66208

Jane Christensen Découpage Studio
1655 Kingsmere Circle, Rochester, Michigan 48063

Christman's Découpage Art Studio, Village Green, Worthington, Ohio 43085

Creative Cove, Inc.
2218 Peachtree Road, N.W., Atlanta, Georgia 30309

Creative Hands Company
P. O. Box 11602, Pittsburgh, Pennsylvania 15228

Creative Hands Studio
7604 Madison Street, Forest Park, Illinois 60130

Cricket Cage
Box N, Route 10, Denville, New Jersey 07834

Cross Hobby House
600 Rawson Avenue, Fremont, Ohio 43420

Davis Paint Associate Store
207 East Main Street, Shawnee, Oklahoma 74801

163

Découpage Studio
421½ Northwood Drive, West Palm Beach, Florida 33407

The Découpage Studio
4337 Lovers Lane, Dallas, Texas 75225

Découpage Unlimited
P. O. Box 73, Northfield, Illinois 60093

Design Associates
3552 Maryland Parkway, Las Vegas, Nevada 89109

Emmons's House of Handicraft
1930 Fourth Street, Jackson, Michigan 49203

Flair Flowers & Gifts
5119 South Lewis, Tulsa, Oklahoma 74107

A. H. Herman and Son
1514 Vincennes Avenue, Chicago, Heights, Illinois 60411

Hobby and Art House
Village Center, Little Rock, Arkansas 72204

Hummel House
1638-40 Orrington, Evanston, Illinois 60201

The Idea House
3846 Government Street, Baton Rouge, Louisiana 70806

Kraft Korner
5842 Mayfield Road, Mayland Annex, Cleveland, Ohio 44124

La Petite Boutique
50 South Washington Street, Hinsdale, Illinois 60521

Lewis Sales Company
623 Towson Avenue, Fort Smith, Arkansas 72901

Marie Mitchell's Découpage Center
16111 Mack Avenue, Detroit, Michigan 48224

Patricia Nimocks, Inc.
12200 Shelbyville Road, Middletown, Kentucky 40043

Protective Paint Co., Inc.
3019 N. State, Jackson, Mississippi 39216

Will Rogers Gift Shop
2112 So. Harvard, Tulsa, Oklahoma, 74114

Suzanne's Art Center
239 Portage Street, Kalamazoo, Michigan 49001

The Talent Tree
618 West Bough, Houston, Texas 77024

The Talent-ry, Inc.
1169 Floyd, Birmingham, Michigan 48009

Van's Hobbies & Raceways
1544 University Avenue, Midway Shopping Center, St. Paul, Minnesota 55104

Valley Paint & Wallcovering
P. O. Box 1097, Columbus, Georgia 31901

Village Bazaar
713 South Mendenhall Road, Memphis, Tennesse 38117

Vilage Hobby Mart
2414 Bolsover, Houston, Texas 77005

Vonda's Trunks & Treasures, Ltd.
1341 N.W. 24th Street, Oklahoma City, Oklahoma 73106

Windwhistle Studios
1269 Furnas Road, Vandalia, Ohio

Frances Wing Studio
P. O. Box 311, Sarasota, Florida 33578

June Zimonick's Découpage Studio
300 South Quincy Street, Green Bay, Wisconsin, 54301

GLOSSARY

ADDÉ DE ST. NON   18th century artist designer of ornamental French trophées, who was a collector and a friend of Fragonard.

ALKYD-RESIN   Basic ingredient for varnish, made from soya bean.

APPLIQUÉ   Ornamental design motifs applied to a surface.

ARTE POVERO   The poor man's art. Italian name for imitations of oriental lacquer furniture.

BANNISTER CUTTING   Parallel line cutting done to resemble bannister rails, used in border cutouts and other decorative areas such as a basket.

BIEDERMEIER (Bee-der-myer)   Early 19th century German furniture style with solid geometric mass designs frequently incorporating pillars and claws, decorated with ormulu mounts.

BLEEDING PRINT   A print in which the ink is alcohol or soluble, causing a blurred appearance when sealer is applied.

BOMBÉ (Bom bay)   Furniture which is contoured with a vertical swell on the sides or front or both. This style prevailed in Europe during the 18th and 19th centuries.

BOUCHER, FRANÇOIS (Boo-shay)   1703–1776. An outstanding artist and engraver, famed for his unusually charming cherubs and well drawn ladies of history and mythology.

BOULLE (bool)   A style of ornamental inlay for furniture. It was made of fine gauge brass which was tooled and laid in natural tortoise shell for a background.

BOULLE, ANDRÉ CHARLES (Bool)	1642–1732. Made fine furniture during reigns of Louis XIV, Louis XV and Louis XVI with various fine woods, tortoise shell and gilt bronze ornaments and mountings.
BURNISHER	A metal or agate tool used to compress paper and bevel the edge of a pasted print so the surface is smoother for applications of varnish.
CARTOUCHE (car-toosh)	A stylized scroll border used as a frame around 18th century subjects, to make a border of cutout material resembling the cartouche.
CERAMIC BISQUE	A piece of clay which has had a single firing to harden it, but no glaze applied to make a surface finish.
CHINOISERIE (Shin-wah-zer-ie)	A term used by the French to describe the Chinese influence or to express work done in the Chinese manner.
CREIL (Cray)	Ornamental designs transferred in black ink directly to the ware, originally copper plate engravings, later different designs applied to yellow or ochre colored ware.
DÉCOUPAGE (Day-coo-pahge)	The art of decorating surfaces with applied paper cutouts.
DRYBRUSH CUTTING	Découpage style of cutting showing an edge cut in the manner of a stroke from a nearly dry brush.
EMPIRE PALETTE	A selection of colors used together to express the taste in color used during the reign of the Emperor Napoleon Bonaparte.
ENGLEBRECHT, MARTIN	1684–1756. Made many copper plate engravings of prints for decorative purposes, designs to cut out for scrap books, peep shows and découpage.
FEATHER CUTTING, FEATHERING	Découpage technique of cutting to resemble feathers, especially outer motifs in intricate and graceful tufts. Feathering usually refers to the tufts of feather cutting in a print. It is also used in some regions to describe the serrated edge. It is referred to as feathered cutting or feathered edge.
FOREGROUND DETAIL CUTTING	Transforming a straight line at the bottom of the print into an interesting irregular line defining material or motifs on this edge or on either right or left side of the print.

FRAGONARD, JEAN HONORÉ (Frag-o-nar)	1732–1806. Artist, engraver, whose work was sought by collectors and royalty. His exquisite engraving is a graphic record of the opulent court life of the French Royalty.
FERRULE	A ring of metal put around a slender shaft to strengthen it or prevent splitting; the metal band which holds bristles of a brush in place.
GALBÉ (gal bay)	An elongated ogee curve used as a furniture contour similar to bombé.
GESSO (jes-oh) like the g in gesture	(Italian for gypsum)—A plastic prepared with glue for use in painting a smooth surface or making bas reliefs; a paste prepared from Spanish whiting and rabbit skin glue spread on a surface as a gilding base. Gesso-instant: Liquitex gesso, ready mixed.
GILDING	To overlay with or as if with a thin covering of gold—to give an attractive appearance to a surface.
GOLD LEAF	A sheet of gold ordinarily varying from four to five millionths of an inch in thickness that is used especially for gilding.
GOLD PAPER BRAID	Ornamental foil paper which is embossed with intricate designs and die-cut into delicate filigree. The designs are borders, scrolls, frames, corners, alphabets, and numerous other stylish motifs used in Victorian découpage.
GRISAILLE (gree-sail)	A decorative painting in gray monochrome; gray coloring used to resemble shadow and form of marble sculpture.
INCISED CUTTING	Découpage cutting in which the print is opened in contoured areas—not noticeable as a special pattern. The purpose is to prevent large areas without openings.
INTARSIA (in-tar-sha)	A mosaic usually of wood fitted and glued into a wooden support popular in 15th century Italy for decoration, later in the 18th century interpreted in marble and semiprecious stones used as rectangular inlays in furniture.
LADDER	Paper strips left uncut to hold delicate parts of the print together for further cutting and handling.
LADIES AMUSEMENT	"Ladies Amusement, or The Whole Art of Japan-

ning Made Easy": a book printed in London in 1760 for Robert Sayer containing some 1500 fascinating original drawings and designs, incorporating chinoiseries, birds, butterflies, flowers, landscapes and Oriental figures and a variety of borders and patterns. This book had an important effect on the designs of later Georgian craftsmen.

LATEX
A general group of water base enamel paints, originally made of rubber base resins, currently not made with rubber.

MARBLEIZED
The technique of creating a marbleized finish on furniture or other surfaces.

MARBLEIZED PAPER
Decorative papers of many designs and colors usually swirled in random patterns to resemble the effect of marble.

MARQUETRY
(mar-ket-ree)
A decorative process in which elaborate patterns are formed by the insertion of pieces of wood, shell or ivory into a wood veneer that is then applied to a piece of furniture.

MORDANT
An adhesive used to hold gold leaf or metal leaf onto a surface—it is usually a slow drying varnish.

OUTLINE DETAIL CUTTING
Narrow lines are cut into the print following the lines of the engraving. This may be done to accentuate birds' feathers, clouds, or straight lines of windows, building details or folds in fabrics.

OXYDIZE
To combine with oxygen; to dehydrogenate, especially by the action of oxygen.

PASTE
A preparation usually of flour or starch and water used as an adhesive or a vehicle for mordant or color.

PILLEMENT, JEAN
(Peel-mont)
1719–1808. French artist and designer during the reign of Louis XV and XVI. Much of his work was based on Oriental fantasies.

PLASTI-TAK
A plastic adhesive used for temporarily mounting prints or designs on surfaces.

POLYMERIZE
(plem-er-ize)
A chemical reaction in which two or more molecules change structure. A given material completely changes its identity.

POMPADOUR
Jeanne Antoinette Poisson, Marquise de Pompadour, 1721–1764; mistress of Louis XV of France.

PROVINCIAL GARDEN PALETTE	A group of colors consisting of lavenders and fragile blues, pinks and greens; used with a soft pastel background color on furniture or boxes.
REDOUTÉ, PIERRE-JOSEPH (Reh-doo-tay)	Botanical artist, who enjoyed the patronage of Marie Antoinette and Josephine Bonaparte. His fame rests in part upon the love dedicated to his favorite subject, the rose.
REPOUSSÉ (reh-pou-say)	A raised or embossed motif which has been shaped from the underside to give a sculptured appearance.
REVERSE CUTTING positive negative shadow	A découpage technique of cutting an area from a print to show a tuft of grass or other ornamental motif in either positive or negative according to whether you see a negative tuft of grass or a positive against the background. Shadow cutting repeats a reflection of the motif directly above.
SAYER, ROBERT	1725–1794. A print and map seller in London. Published "Ladies Amusement or Whole Art of Japanning Made Easy" in 1760.
SCISSORS, DÉCOUPAGE	Small sharp precision steel scissors with curved blades used for intricate cutting.
SCRIVAN	Italian name for secretary-desk. It is also spelled scriban in old French references.
SEALER	A coat (as of size) applied to prevent subsequent coats of paint or varnish from sinking in; used as a coating to prevent bleeding of inks or oil pencils.
SERRATED EDGE CUTTING	Notched or toothed on the edge. Cutting a serrated edge makes adhesion of print smoother, optically blends to background when pasted on.
SHADOWBOX	A shallow enclosing case usually with a glass front in which something is set for protection and display.
SHADOW CUTTING	See reverse cutting.
STENCIL CUTTING	A découpage technique of cutting crescent or S curves into the print as accent lines in the engraving. Usually done with a knife.
STRAIGHT CUTTING	Generally confined to border cutting and ladders.
SHELLAC	Purified lac resin usually prepared in thin orange or yellow flakes by heating of filtering and often

	bleached white; a preparation of lac dissolved usually in alcohol and used chiefly as a wood filler.
SILHOUETTE	From Etienne de Silhouette—controller of finances; a representation of the outlines of an object filled in with black or some other uniform color.
SIZE	A water-base gelatinous adhesive or paste.
TOILE DE JOUY (twal-duh-zwee)	An 18th century French scenic pattern usually printed on cotton, linen, or silk in one color on a light ground.
TREASURE GOLD	A wax metallic used in gilding.
TREASURE JEWELS	Wax metallics in color.
TREASURE SEALER	A water clear, alcohol soluble sealer, used on prints, and other porous surfaces. Also, used as a paint bonding adhesive on glass or metal.
TROMPE L'OEIL (tromp-loy-yah)	To fool the eye—a technique used in painting and découpage in which objects create an illusion of three dimensions.
TROPHÉES (tro faze)	An architectural ornament representing a group of military weapons; also, a drawing or etching of a group of articles related to a profession or trade.
VARNISH	A liquid preparation that when spread upon a surface dries forming a hard lustrous typically transparent coating.
VIGNETTE (Vin-yet)	To describe or sketch briefly; a running ornament (as of vine, leaves, tendrils, and grapes) put on or just before a page or at the beginning or end of a chapter; a picture that shades off gradually into the surrounding ground or the unprinted paper.
VUE D'OPTIQUE (view-dop-teek)	A three dimensional setting enclosed in a box or frame depicting a scene, or stage with figures in an elevated perspective.
WHITE GLUE	A polyvinyl resin adhesive—water soluble in liquid state but generally dries waterproof.
WATTEAU, JEAN ANTOINE	1684–1721. A French painter.
WAX, DÉCOUPAGE	A special white scented wax made for fine furniture and boxes. It does not distort color.
WAX GILT	A metallic wax used for gilding.

BIBLIOGRAPHY

ADHÉMAR, JEAN, *Graphic Art of the 18th Century*. McGraw-Hill Book Company, New York, 1964

The Art of Wood Finishing, H. Behlen & Bros., Inc., in collaboration with Qualatone Products, Inc. Laboratory, Kearny, N. J., 1957

BRAZER, ESTHER STEVENS, *Early American Decoration*. The Pond-Ekberg Company, Springfield, Massachusetts, 1940

BRITISH MUSEUM, "Some Wonderful Paperwork", The Queen, November 18, 1911

CANONERO, LELIO, *Barocchetto Genovese*, Aldo Martello, Editore, Milano

GARDNER, HELEN, *ART Through the Ages*. Harcourt, Brace and Company, New York, 1926

HALSEY, ELIZABETH T., *Book of Interior Decoration*, Ladies Home Journal, The Curtis Publishing Company, Philadelphia, and Doubleday and Company, Garden City, 1954

HARROWER, DOROTHY, *Découpage—A Limitless World in Decoration*. M. Barrows and Company, Inc. New York, 1958

HOARE, ALFRED, *A Short Italian Dictionary*, Cambridge University Press, The Macmillan Company, 1945

House and Garden Craft Guide, Condé Nast Publications, Inc., New York, 1963

Ladies Amusement or The Whole Art of Japanning Made Easy. Facsimile of the original published for Robert Sayer at the Golden Buck, 53 Fleet Street, London 1760, by the Ceramic Book Company, Newport, Monmouthshire, Wales, 1959

MANNING, MAYDELLE, "Découpage—Hobby or Vice?", American Home, January 1949, p. 26

MAZZARIOL, GUISEPPE, *Mobili Italiani*, Antonio Vallardi, Editore, Milano

Mobili e Ambiente Italiani Dal Gotico Al Floreale, Volume Primo, Bramante Editrice, Milano

MOTTAHEDEH, Catalog of Creil Decorative Accessories, Privately published, New York, 1966

O'NEIL, ISABEL, *Bench Book,* Printed privately and used exclusively for her classes; distributed from the Isabel O'Neil Studios, New York, N. Y.

SODERBERG, GEORGE A., *Finishing Materials and Methods,* McKnight and McKnight Publishing Company, Bloomington, Illinois, 1952

STALKER, JOHN and PARKER, GEORGE, *A Treatise of Japanning and Varnishing 1688,* Quadrangle Books, Chicago, Illinois, 1960

Webster's Third International Dictionary, Unabridged, 1961, G. & C. Merriam Company, Springfield, Massachusetts

WING, FRANCES S., *The Complete Book of Découpage,* Coward-McCann, Inc., New York, 1965

PICTURE CREDITS

173

30 Courtesy Mrs. H. Paul Gant

31 *Top and bottom:* the author. Photographs by Lin Caufield
Center: courtesy Mrs. Maurice F. Dufour. Photograph by Noel Blakeley Studio

32 *Top and center:* courtesy Ferdinand Fromholz. Photographs by Lin Caufield
Bottom: courtesy Mrs. Vonda Jessup. Photograph by Pipkin Photo Service, Oklahoma School Pictures, Inc.

33 The author. Photographs by Lin Caufield.

34 Courtesy Mrs. H. Paul Gant.

35 The author. Photographs by Lin Caufield

36 *Top:* courtesy Christine Payne (tray) and Beth Person (boxes). Photographs by Photographic Associates
Bottom: courtesy Mrs. Martha West. Photograph by Carl & Esther Tammen Photo

37 *Top:* courtesy Mrs. Vonda Jessup. Photograph by Pipkin Photo Service, Oklahoma School Pictures, Inc.
Bottom: courtesy Mrs. Maurice F. Dufour

38 Collection of the author. Photograph by Lin Caufield.

39 Courtesy Mrs. W. James Moore, Jr.

41 Courtesy Mrs. Frank Boos. Photographs by Gene Butler

44 Courtesy Jesse Nimrocks. Photograph by Lin Caufield

45 Courtesy Mrs. Vonda Jessup. Photograph by Pipkin Photo Service, Oklahoma School Pictures, Inc.

46 *Top:* courtesy Shirley Hodges
Center: courtesy Louise Hoyt. Photograph by Eddie McGrath, Jr.
Bottom: courtesy Mrs. Marie Mitchell. Photograph by Eddie McGrath, Jr.

47 *Top:* courtesy Mrs. Dola Bice
Bottom: courtesy Mrs. Frank Boos. Photograph by Gene Butler

54 Photograph by Lin Caufield

55 *Left:* photograph by Photographic Associates
Right: photograph by Lin Caufield

61 Courtesy Miss Mary Carman. Photograph by Lin Caufield

63 Courtesy Mrs. Walter Rebmann. Photography by Les Wallace

64 Courtesy Margaret Bennett. Photography by Lin Caufield

68 The author. Photographs (left) by Lin Caufield, (right) by Photographic Associates

69, 70, 71 The author. Photographs by Lin Caufield

73 The author. Photograph by Photographic Associates

175

IN COLOR

This Book
Belongs
To

Dragonfly
Beetle
Butterfly
Bee

Maryjo Koch

SWANS ISLAND BOOKS

THIS EDITION PUBLISHED IN 1998 BY SMITHMARK PUBLISHERS, A DIVISION OF U.S. MEDIA HOLDINGS, INC.,
115 WEST 18TH STREET, NEW YORK, NY 10011.

SMITHMARK BOOKS ARE AVAILABLE FOR BULK PURCHASE FOR SALES PROMOTION AND PREMIUM USE. FOR
DETAILS WRITE OR CALL THE MANAGER OF SPECIAL SALES, SMITHMARK PUBLISHERS, 115 WEST 18TH STREET,
NEW YORK, NY 10011; (212) 519-1300.

PUBLISHED IN 1996 BY COLLINS PUBLISHERS SAN FRANCISCO, 1160 BATTERY STREET, SAN FRANCISCO, CA 94111

A SWANS ISLAND BOOK

LIBRARY OF CONGRESS CATALOG CARD NUMBER: 98-60010

ISBN 0-7651-0761-9

PRINTED IN HONG KONG
10 9 8 7 6 5 4 3 2 1

For my dear sister Diane

Beetle god Kheperu
symbol of life
from ancient wall in Egypt

Evolution: Web of the World

Living intimately with nature, the ancients believed consciousness pervaded the whole of creation, weaving all vital things into a vast web. Powerful symbols of nature, conveyed in myths, described human culture and condition. The mysterious behavior, metamorphosis, and life cycle of insects baffled and intrigued our ancestors, who bestowed potent associations upon them.

One classical Greek metaphor refers to the human spirit itself as an insect: since ancient times the word psyche has come to mean both "soul" and "butterfly." Finnish folk wisdom held that even vegetables had butterfly souls. In the Noh plays of Japan, the butterfly is a propitious symbol of the transformed human soul, and in Calabria, Italy, when a white butterfly flits around a baby's cradle, the people say it is the child's spirit.

Insect totems can supposedly protect the clan or the individual they represent. The Arunta, a tribe of central Australia, call upon numerous insects, including the cicada, longhorn beetle, grub, and honey ant. Only the headman of the tribe is exempt from the taboo on eating the totem creature, which is tantamount to eating one's relative.

A legend from Orissa, India, tells of a deadly battle that obliterated the gods, leaving only their eyes - in the form of fireflies - as a luminous reminder of divine valor and eternal vigilance.

How Fire Came to Earth (or the Bowl on the Water Spider's Back).

Cherokee tradition honors an insect as the creature who brought fire to their ancestors. Pitying the animals and birds who struggled to keep warm on the cold, dismal earth, the thunder gods shot a lightning bolt down to a small island, setting fire to a hollow sycamore tree. The animals held a council to determine how to bring the fire to the mainland. After much debate, the humble water spider spoke up. She offered to weave a little bowl from her silk and attach it to her back so that she could scamper across the water's surface and carry back a live coal. The animals agreed, and the water spider brought warmth to the world.

EVOLUTION: PREHISTORIC SCIENCE

In the primeval world, small primitive plants established themselves between the realms of wet and dry, begetting a blush of green that slowly spread out from the margins of ponds, lakes, rivers, and seas. In its wake came life's conquest of the continents. The collaborative effort of flora and fauna spawned the early arthropods — animals with jointed legs — about 400 million years ago.

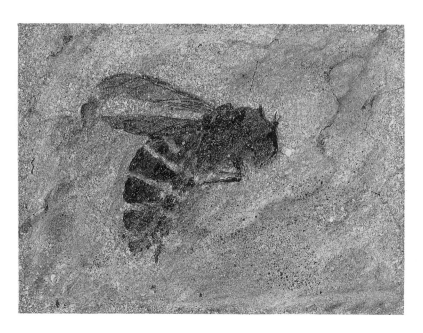

Fossil bee from Oligocene epoch, 35 million years ago.
Colorado Florissant fossil bed.

The phylum arthropoda includes crustaceans, millipedes, centipedes, insects, and arachnids and is by far the largest phylum in the animal kingdom. The insects alone outnumber all other animals by about four to one.

OVER THE EONS, THE EVOLUTIONARY CAREER OF INSECTS HAS SPANNED FOUR PRINCIPAL STAGES. IN THE FIRST, INSECTS WERE WINGLESS. THE NEXT WITNESSED THE ORIGIN OF PRIMITIVE WINGS, LAUNCHING INSECTS INTO THE AIR AS THE FIRST CREATURES TO TAKE FLIGHT. THEY WOULD REMAIN THE SOVEREIGNS OF THE SKIES FOR 100 MILLION YEARS, ACQUIRING FOLDABLE WINGS DURING THE THIRD STAGE OF EVOLUTION. THEIR STREAMLINED SILHOUETTES NO DOUBT MADE THEM LESS CONSPICUOUS, PROTECTING THEM FROM PREDATORS WHILE AT REST. THE FINAL INSECT INNOVATION WAS THE PROCESS OF METAMORPHOSIS, WHICH COMPLETELY TRANSFORMS THE MATURING INSECT FROM ITS ORIGINAL STATE TO AN ENTIRELY DIFFERENT ADULT SHAPE.

A termite in amber—
30 million years old

MANY LIFE-FORMS THAT HAVE EVOLVED WITHOUT BONES OR TEETH HAVE LEFT BEHIND AT BEST A SKETCHY FOSSIL RECORD. SOME ANCIENT INSECTS SLEEP IN TINY TRANSPARENT TOMBS OF AMBER, THE SOLIDIFIED OOZE OF RESIN FROM CERTAIN TREES. AMBER HAS PRESERVED THEIR EXTERNAL ANATOMY IN EXQUISITE DETAIL, YET THEY REMAIN PHANTOMS. ANY ATTEMPT TO UNLOCK THE GOLDEN VESSELS WILL REDUCE THEIR PREHISTORIC TENANTS TO DUST.

THOUGH THE PARTICULARS OF THEIR EVOLUTIONARY SUCCESS MAY REMAIN A MYSTERY, INSECTS HAVE COME TO FILL COUNTLESS ECOLOGICAL NICHES IN NEARLY EVERY BIOME.

PROTURONS (Protura)

SILVERFISH AND ALLIES (Thysanura)

IAPYGIDS AND ALLIES (Entotrophi)

SPRINGTAILS (Collembola)

ROACHES, GRASSHOPPERS, CRICKETS AND ALLIES (Orthoptera)

EARWIGS (Dermaptera)

ELEANOR DOORLY
The Insect Man

A PUFFIN STORY BOOK · ONE SHILLING AND SIXPENCE

L'Harmas Jean Henri Fabre
-ENTOMOLOGISTE-
1823-1915
SERIGNAN DU COMTAT. 84830.

COME COME COME
COME IN YOUR BILLIONS
TINY SMALL FEET
AND HUMMING LITTLE WINGS
CRAWLERS AND CREEPERS
WIGGLERS AND STINGERS
SCRATCHERS BORERS AND SLITHERERS

ARCHY AND MEHITABEL
DON MARQUIS 1916

ORIGINAL KARLSBADER INSEKTENNADELN · No 3

COMPASS DUDLEY 10X

THRIPS (Thysanoptera)

BUGS LEAF-HOPPERS SCALES AND ALLIES (Hemiptera)

MAYFLIES (Ephemeroptera)

DAMSELFLIES AND DRAGONFLIES (Odonata)

NERVE-WINGED INSECTS (Neuroptera)

SCORPION-FLIES (Mecoptera)

STONEFLIES (Plecoptera)   TERMITES (Isoptera)   EMBIIDS (Embioptera)   PSOCIDS, BOOKLICE AND ALLIES (Corrodentia)   ZORAPTERONS (Zoraptera)   BITING LICE (Mallophaga)   SUCKING LICE (Anoplura)

Buzzwords

No wonder Adam ultimately succumbed to the temptation to eat the forbidden fruit of the tree of knowledge, for one of his first tasks was to name all the creatures in the garden of Eden. In the animal kingdom, the phylum Arthropoda is by far the largest grouping. The current tally of arthropods is estimated at thirty-five million species, with quadrillions (thousands of trillions) of individual insects currently inhabiting the earth.

Why it isn't called arthropodology

In the fourth century B.C., Aristotle, the Greek philosopher and naturalist, referred to the class of animals with segmented bodies as entoma, from which the word entomology, the study of insects, derives its name.

A purist would define entomology as the scientific study of insects, but entomologists often study many other classes of land-dwelling arthropods as well as insects because of their similar features. These include terrestrial crustaceans like sow bugs and wood lice, Diplopoda (such as millipedes), the centipedes and other Chilopoda, and the Arachnida, which encompasses spiders, scorpions, ticks, and mites. All insects and honorary insects share two main characteristics: jointed legs and a rigid, waterproof, waxy-coated exterior, or exoskeleton.

Modern entomology still involves a great deal of descriptive taxonomy, the systematic classification and naming of species. The class Insecta alone boasts close to one million identified species, and some experts claim that those waiting in the wings number in the millions. Entomologists describe twenty-six different orders of insects with distinct anatomical characteristics.

CADDISFLIES (Trichoptera)   MOTHS AND BUTTERFLIES (Lepidoptera)   BEETLES (Coleoptera)   REPSIPTERONS (Strepsiptera)   WASPS, ANTS, BEES, AND ALLIES (Hymenoptera)   FLIES (Diptera)   FLEAS (Siphonaptera)

WHAT'S A BUG?

To an entomologist, only the Hemiptera (hemi=half, ptera=wing) are true-blue bugs. Most of these creatures sport piercing, sucking mouthparts and wings that are leathery at the base and membranous at the tip. Many have names that describe what they do and where they do it. Bed bugs, shore bugs, seed bugs, leaf bugs, stink bugs, assassin bugs, ambush bugs, and pirate bugs are all aptly labeled.

After J.J. Grandville

BUG TALK: AN ETYMOLOGICAL VIEW OF ENTOMOLOGY

BUG: AN IMPERFECTION

BUG WALK: A LOW BED

BUG: AN IDEA OR A SUGGESTION

BUG RAKE: HAIR COMB

BUG WASH: HAIR OIL

BUG: A FANATIC

TO BUG: TO ACCEPT A BRIBE INSTEAD OF MAKING AN ARREST

BUG EYES: PROTRUDING EYES

BUGSY: THE NOTORIOUS GANGSTER

BUG JUICE: CAMPERS DRINK IT

BUG OFF!:

GO AWAY!

BUG AND FLEA: COCKNEY RHYMING SLANG FOR TEA

TO BUG OUT: TO LOSE CONTROL

BUGS: THE FAMOUS CARTOON BUNNY

TO BUG: TO PLANT A HIDDEN MICROPHONE

TO BUG: TO GET ON SOMEONE'S NERVES

BUG OVER!: HAND IT OVER!

nsect

HAPPY INSECT! WHAT CAN BE
IN HAPPINESS COMPARED TO THEE?
FED WITH NOURISHMENT DIVINE,
THE DEWY MORNING'S GENTLE WINE,
NATURE WAITS UPON THEE STILL,
AND THY VERDANT CUP DOES FILL...
UNKNOWN

Camouflage

When frightened, these Flatid sap-suckers fall away like rose petals from branches.

It seems humans are the only predators indifferent to the savory appeal of insects. Frogs, lizards, shrews, foxes, monkeys, and bats all enjoy various arthropods du jour. Probably half the species of birds would perish of starvation were it not for nature's vast menu of insects.

Found in Madagascar, their actual size is 3/8".

*I*NSECTS ARE ZEN MASTERS IN THE ART OF
BECOMING ONE WITH THEIR SURROUNDINGS. OVER TIME,
MANY HAVE DEVELOPED DECEPTIVE APPEARANCES THAT
BLEND PERFECTLY WITH THEIR HABITAT. MOTTLED, BARKLIKE
COLORATION IS ONLY THE BEGINNING. TEXTURE, BODY FORM, AND
SILHOUETTE ALL HELP TO CONVINCE WOULD-BE PREDATORS THAT BEFORE
THEIR VERY EYES THEY SEE LEAVES, PETALS, TWIGS, LICHEN, ROCKS, OR
SAND RATHER THAN INSECTS.

Senses and Traits

A GOOD MANY INSECTS HEAR WITH THEIR KNEES AND TASTE WITH THEIR FEET. IF THAT WERE THE CASE WITH HUMANS, WE'D ALL HAVE TO WEAR SHORTS AND BE MORE CAREFUL OF WHERE WE STEP.

GWYNN POPOVAC 1993

*T*HE LOVE SONG OF THE CRICKET MAY IN FACT MAKE HIS INTENDED WEAK IN THE KNEES, FOR IT IS THERE THAT THE DRUMLIKE MEMBRANE CALLED THE TYMPANUM, THE INSECT VERSION OF AN EAR, IS LOCATED. CERTAIN HAIRS ALSO ACT AS MECHANICAL RECEIVERS, BROADENING THE RANGE OF SOUNDS HEARD BY INSECTS TO INCLUDE FREQUENCIES BOTH HIGHER AND LOWER THAN THOSE HUMANS CAN PICK UP.

J.J. Grandville

A Concert at The Wedding Party

THE SETAE, BRISTLE-LIKE HAIRS OFTEN LOCATED ON INSECTS' LEGS CONTAIN NERVE ENDINGS THAT ARE STIMULATED WHEN AIR CURRENTS, WATER MOVEMENTS, OR ANY OTHER VIBRATIONS STIR THEM.

NERVE-PACKED TACTILE ORGANS CALLED PROPRIOCEPTORS ARE EMBEDDED IN PITS IN INSECT EXOSKELETONS. EXTREMELY SENSITIVE, THEY CAN DISTINGUISH GRAVITATIONAL FORCES AT PLAY, A NECESSITY FOR CREATURES WHO LIVE MUCH OF THEIR LIVES OFF OF THE GROUND.

INSECT ANTENNAE ARE COVERED WITH MICROSCOPIC HAIRS OR CONELIKE STRUCTURES, CALLED PEGS, THROUGH WHICH INSECTS PERCEIVE CHEMICAL SIGNALS OR ODORS AND CHANGES IN HUMIDITY, TEMPERATURE, AND OTHER STIMULI.

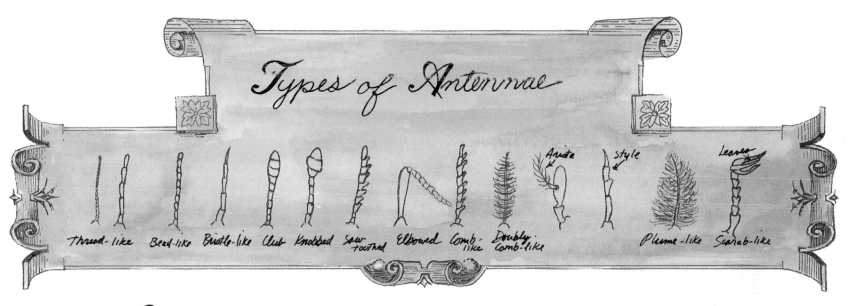

Types of Antennae

Thread-like Bead-like Bristle-like Club Knobbed Saw-toothed Elbowed Comb-like Doubly Comb-like Arista style Plume-like Scarab-like Leaves

OLFACTORY RECEPTORS ANALOGOUS TO TASTE BUDS ARE FOUND IN ABUNDANCE NOT ONLY NEAR INSECTS' MOUTHS BUT ALSO ELSEWHERE. THE PETITE HAIRY FEET OF THE RED ADMIRAL BUTTERFLY ARE ABOUT TWO HUNDRED TIMES MORE SENSITIVE TO THE PRESENCE OF SUGAR THAN THE HUMAN TONGUE.

THE ABILITY TO SENSE CHEMICAL SIGNALS OFFERS A NUMBER OF ADVANTAGES. SUCH INFORMATION CAN BE PERCEIVED IN THE DARK, AS FAR AWAY AS SEVERAL MILES, AND FOR LONGER PERIODS OF TIME THAN EITHER SIGHT OR SOUND. MORE IMPORTANT THAN ANY OTHER STIMULI, CHEMICAL SIGNALS GOVERN VIRTUALLY EVERY ASPECT OF INSECT LIFE, FROM COMMUNICATION TO MATING TO BURIAL OF THE DEAD.

"The passions are expressed by sounds"

From "Episodes of Insect Life", 1867

Song

Allegretto
3/4

JUST AS THE PASSION FOR OPERA DIVAS HAS LED NOTABLE CITIZENS ASTRAY, SO, TOO, HAS THE PASSION FOR CRICKETS. MALE FIGHTING CRICKETS FACE OFF WITH SONGS OF TERRITORIAL RIVALRY AS MAJESTIC AS ANY ARIA. THE DECLINE OF THE SOUTHERN SUNG DYNASTY IN CHINA HAS BEEN ATTRIBUTED IN PART TO THE OBSESSION OF PREMIER JIA SIDAO WITH CRICKET FIGHTING, WHICH CAUSED HIM TO NEGLECT STATE AFFAIRS. TODAY, CHAMPION FIGHTING CRICKETS, KNOWN AS SHOU LIP, BECOME NATIONAL HEROES IN CHINA, AND THEIR MATCHES ARE TELEVISED IN SHANGHAI.

California Tree Cricket ⅝"

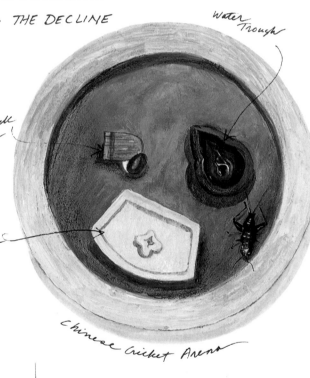

Water Trough

Food rack with Bean

Cricket House

Chinese Cricket Arena

CRICKETS AND THEIR RELATIVES MAKE MUSIC BY A PROCESS CALLED STRIDULATION, THE RUBBING TOGETHER OF VARIOUS BODY PARTS. MOLE CRICKETS USE THE LENGTH OF THEIR SUBTERRANEAN BURROWS TO AMPLIFY THE SIGNALS THEY MAKE.

Secret Cave Cricket 1"

Northern Mole Cricket 1⅜"

Small Talk

Like all animals, insects need to communicate. Besides courtship and mating songs, they compose warning songs, triumphal songs, kin-to-kin songs, calling songs for long-distance communication, and more. Each species' unique songs are characterized by distinct frequencies and pitches. Some species vary their sounds regionally, producing the insect equivalent of an accent.

The amazing variety of insect sounds is produced following one of two strategies. When stridulating, modified body parts are slammed, stroked, or vibrated together, or body parts are struck against the ground or another hard surface. Every part of the body can be used as a resonating chamber. Except for the mouth, which is always busy feeding. No insect can ever be accused of speaking with his or her mouth full.

Bleuet Et Coquelicot

Grandville del.   Ch. Geoffroy sc.

Cicada is the loudest insect in the world

Cicada

Cricket Whistle

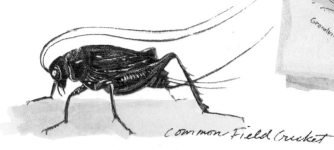

Common Field Cricket ———— 1"

Courtship

The selected reflections of Amorous Insects

ACT I

HE: IT WAS AN IRRESISTIBLE CHEMICAL ATTRACTION - I WAS DOWN WIND A COUPLE OF MILES AND I KNEW SHE WAS THERE.

SHE: I IMAGINED HIM, THE STRANGER, WHO WOULD BECOME MY BELOVED. WHEN HE ARRIVED, HIS SCENT FILLED ME WITH LONGING.

HE: I HEARD HER BUZZING ARIA INSISTENTLY BECKON ME. I SANG MY REPLY.

SHE: WHAT DOES HE THINK THIS IS, SEX FOR A SONG?

SHE AND HE: YOUR APPEAL OUTSHINES THE MOON.

HE AND SHE: SHE WILL BE MINE!

SHE AND SHE: HE HAS REMARKABLY GOOD TASTE!

"The First Kiss" WILLIAM BOUGUEREAU

TRANSLATION: FEMALE INSECTS PRODUCE LONG-RANGE PHEROMONES TO ATTRACT MATES, AND MALES OF AT LEAST SIXTY SPECIES (INCLUDING FLIES, MOTHS, COCKROACHES, BEES, AND BUTTERFLIES) ARE KNOWN TO PRODUCE APHRODISIACS. INSECTS ALSO SING LOVE SONGS TO THEIR INTENDED, FEMALE MOSQUITOES WITH THEIR WINGS AND MALE CICADAS WITH DRUMHEAD-LIKE MEMBRANES ON THEIR ABDOMENS TO DAZZLE PROSPECTIVE MATES. EACH SPECIES OF FLASHY FIREFLIES EMPLOYS A UNIQUE, ILLUMINATED MORSE CODE OF VISUAL DOTS AND DASHES. MALE INSECTS IN PARTICULAR OFTEN COMPETE FOR MATES: HEAVILY ARMORED STAG BEETLES WRESTLE FOR POWER AND TERRITORY, WHILE MALES OF MANY SPECIES OFFER NUPTIAL GIFTS OF FOOD.

Episodes of Insect Life 1867

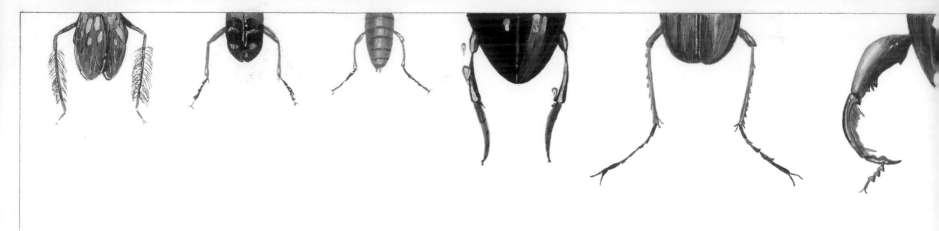

LEGS

𝒜 CENTIPEDE WAS HAPPY QUITE
  UNTIL A TOAD IN FUN
SAID, "PRAY WHICH LEG MOVES AFTER WHICH?"
  THIS RAISED HER DOUBTS TO SUCH A PITCH,
SHE FELL EXHAUSTED IN THE DITCH,
  NOT KNOWING HOW TO RUN.

RAY LANKESTER 1889

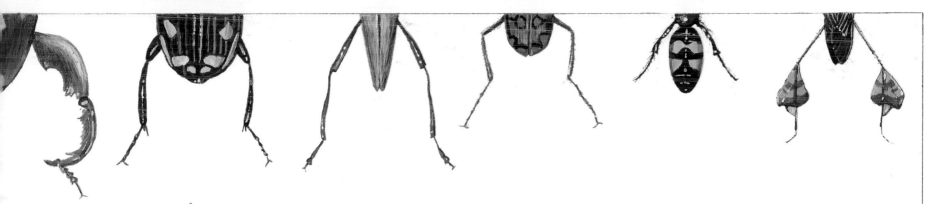

IN A BIRD-EAT-BUG WORLD, THE ABILITY TO MAKE A FAST ESCAPE IS CRITICAL TO INSECT SURVIVAL. HENCE THE EVOLUTIONARY ADAPTATION: JOINTED LEGS INCREASE SPEED. WHERE VELVET WORMS CAN WRIGGLE ALONG AT A MAXIMUM SPEED OF THREE-EIGHTHS OF AN INCH PER SECOND, WOLF SPIDERS CAN HOTFOOT IT AT ABOUT TEN INCHES PER SECOND, ABOUT FIFTY TIMES FASTER.

THE ARCHETYPAL INSECT HAS JOINTED LEGS, EACH MADE UP OF FOUR SEGMENTS. OTHER ORDERS OF ARTHROPODS, LIKE SPIDERS, HAVE EIGHT LEGS, WHILE CENTIPEDES HAVE AN AVERAGE OF ABOUT THIRTY (NOT ONE HUNDRED) AND THE HYPERBOLIC MILLIPEDES HAVE A MAXIMUM OF ONLY FOUR HUNDRED.

DEPENDING ON THE HABITAT, INSECTS' LEGS SERVE A VARIETY OF MIRACULOUS FUNCTIONS. LONG, FLATTENED LEGS KEEP THE WEIGHT OF WATER STRIDERS DISTRIBUTED EVENLY SO THAT THEY CAN WALK ON WATER WITHOUT BREAKING THE SURFACE TENSION.

SOME CRICKETS' POWERFUL HIND LEGS HAVE A SMALL FILELIKE SURFACE THAT THE INSECT RUBS AGAINST ITS WINGS TO CREATE ITS MATING SONG.

MANTIDS' GRASPING, OR RAPTORIAL, LEGS GRAB AND HOLD BOTH PREY AND MATES.

BEES' KNEES – WELL, THEIR LEGS, AT LEAST – INCORPORATE LITTLE BRUSHES AND BASKETS FOR COLLECTING POLLEN.

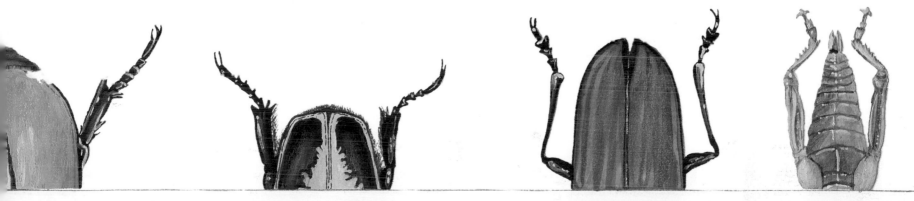

SIGHT: BEGINNING TO SEE THE LIGHT

INSECTS HAVE HIT UPON WAYS TO SEE, TASTE, FEEL, HEAR, AND SMELL THAT HUMANS CAN ONLY IMAGINE. SO UNLIKE OURS, THESE TECHNIQUES ARE EXCEEDINGLY SUCCESSFUL FOR MASSIVE NUMBERS OF LIVING INSECTS.

DO INSECTS SEE A KALEIDOSCOPE OF REPEATED IMAGES OR A MOSAIC OF LIGHT AND DARK SPOTS? THE DEBATE AMONG ENTOMOLOGISTS CONTINUES ---

SOME INSECTS HAVE SIMPLE EYES, CALLED OCELLI. THESE VARY IN STRUCTURE BUT GENERALLY CONSIST OF A DOME-SHAPED CORNEAL LENS AND A LIGHT-SENSITIVE LAYER OF NERVES, THE RHABOMERES. DEPENDING ON THE INSECT, SIMPLE EYES ARE FOUND IN DIFFERENT NUMBERS AND LOCATIONS.

COMPOUND EYES FEATURE INDIVIDUAL LIGHT-PROCESSING UNITS CALLED OMMATIDIA, EACH CONSISTING OF A CRYSTALLINE CONE TOPPED BY A HEXAGONAL CORNEAL LENS DIRECTING LIGHT TO THE RHABDOME BELOW. DIFFERENT SPECIES MAY HAVE AS FEW AS A DOZEN OR MORE THAN TWENTY THOUSAND LENSES PER EYE.

AN OLD MOTH' Leonardville

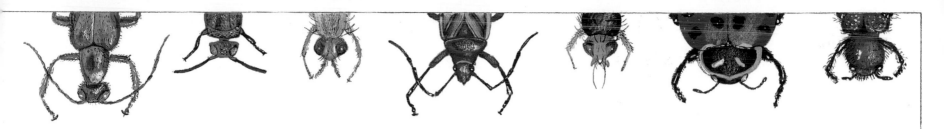

Not only can many insects see color, they can detect polarized light — the angle of light waves — so that they know the position of the sun even when it is hidden by cloud cover.

Like a moth to a flame

Much like devoted sunbathers, dragonflies keep their bodies in a fixed transversal position in relation to the sun. Some nocturnal insects do the same in relation to the moon and stars. Artificial light sources, such as candles and light bulbs, have no natural equivalent in their capacity to confuse insects. Night-flying moths that attempt to maintain a fixed position relative to such nearby illumination must make constant directional shifts that seem to disorient them. They tend to spiral in toward the light in a bizarre and apparently self-destructive behavior that has long fascinated humans.

Grasshoppers

THE INSECT ORDER ORTHOPTERA, WHOSE NAME MEANS "STRAIGHT-WINGED," INCLUDES THE GRASSHOPPER AND ITS RELATIVES THE CRICKETS, CICADAS, AND KATYDIDS. KNOWN FOR THEIR POWERFUL BACK LEGS, THEY CAN VAULT SKYWARD WITH A SLING-SHOT LEAP AND KEEP CONTINUOUSLY ALOFT FOR THOUSANDS OF MILES ON LEATHERY WINGS.

Locust

IN AESOP'S FABLE OF THE ANT AND THE GRASSHOPPER, ANTS ARE INDUSTRIOUS WORKERS AND GRASSHOPPERS ARE LAZY CREATURES CONCERNED ONLY WITH THE PLEASURES OF THE MOMENT. DESPITE THE BAD RAP, GRASSHOPPERS KEEP QUITE BUSY. A SCOURGE TO HUMANKIND FOR CENTURIES, THEY HAVE WREAKED HAVOC ON ENTIRE NATIONS WITH THEIR DESTRUCTIVE APPETITES. THE DESERT LOCUST, MENTIONED IN THE BIBLE THIRTY-FOUR TIMES FOR ITS VORACITY, ONCE CONSUMED ENOUGH ETHIOPIAN GRAIN IN A SIX-WEEK RAMPAGE TO FEED A MILLION PEOPLE FOR A YEAR.

African Grasshopper

RUSTLING UP SOME GRUBS.

Flutacea Bird Grasshopper on a diet

Food carriers with grasshoppers. From an ancient Assyrian sculpture in the Palace of Sennacherib in Nineveh.

THE ARABS AND THE HOTTENTOTS CONSIDER COOKED GRASSHOPPER A GOURMET DISH, SAVORING BOTH THE FLAVOR AND THE NUTRITIONAL VALUE. DURING WORLD WAR I THE SURVIVAL MANUAL ISSUED TO THE AMERICAN ARMED FORCES LISTED GRASSHOPPERS AS AN EMERGENCY FOOD. FOR THE FARMER, WHOSE CROPS ARE TARGETED BY THESE HEARTY EATERS, A QUICK SAUTÉ OF A LOCUST OR TWO MIGHT MAKE A SATISFYING DINNER INDEED.

IN THE BEARTOOTH MOUNTAINS OF MONTANA, APPROXIMATELY ELEVEN THOUSAND FEET ABOVE SEA LEVEL, A GLACIER WITH DARK BANDS ACROSS ITS FACE IS SLOWLY MELTING. WITHIN THESE BANDS ARE LAYER UPON LAYER OF THE NOW-EXTINCT ROCKY MOUNTAIN GRASSHOPPER. THE FROZEN INSECTS HAVE BEEN SO WELL PRESERVED IN THEIR ICY GRAVES THAT AS THE "GRASSHOPPER GLACIER" MELTS, FISH AND BIRDS HAVE BEEN SEEN FEEDING ON THEM.

CRICKET THERMOMETER

WHAT? YES, IF YOU ARE LISTENING TO A SNOWY TREE CRICKET, COUNT THE NUMBER OF CHIRPS IT MAKES IN FOURTEEN SECONDS AND ADD FORTY: YOU WILL HAVE THE TEMPERATURE IN DEGREES FAHRENHEIT.

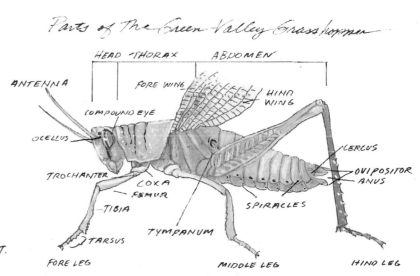

Parts of The Green Valley Grasshopper

HEAD · THORAX · ABDOMEN
ANTENNA
FORE WING
HIND WING
COMPOUND EYE
OCELLUS
CERCUS
TROCHANTER
OVIPOSITOR
ANUS
COXA
FEMUR
SPIRACLES
TIBIA
TYMPANUM
TARSUS
FORE LEG
MIDDLE LEG
HIND LEG

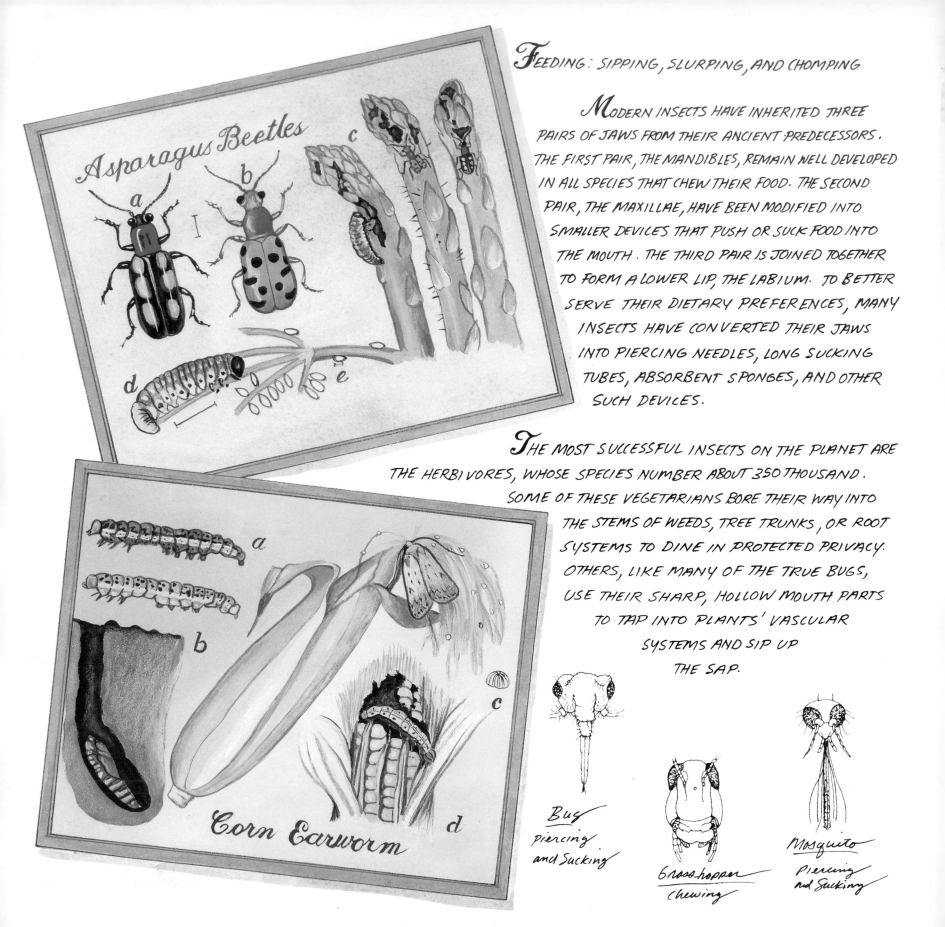

Asparagus Beetles

a b c
I
d e

Corn Earworm

a
b
c
d

FEEDING: SIPPING, SLURPING, AND CHOMPING

MODERN INSECTS HAVE INHERITED THREE PAIRS OF JAWS FROM THEIR ANCIENT PREDECESSORS. THE FIRST PAIR, THE MANDIBLES, REMAIN WELL DEVELOPED IN ALL SPECIES THAT CHEW THEIR FOOD. THE SECOND PAIR, THE MAXILLAE, HAVE BEEN MODIFIED INTO SMALLER DEVICES THAT PUSH OR SUCK FOOD INTO THE MOUTH. THE THIRD PAIR IS JOINED TOGETHER TO FORM A LOWER LIP, THE LABIUM. TO BETTER SERVE THEIR DIETARY PREFERENCES, MANY INSECTS HAVE CONVERTED THEIR JAWS INTO PIERCING NEEDLES, LONG SUCKING TUBES, ABSORBENT SPONGES, AND OTHER SUCH DEVICES.

THE MOST SUCCESSFUL INSECTS ON THE PLANET ARE THE HERBIVORES, WHOSE SPECIES NUMBER ABOUT 350 THOUSAND. SOME OF THESE VEGETARIANS BORE THEIR WAY INTO THE STEMS OF WEEDS, TREE TRUNKS, OR ROOT SYSTEMS TO DINE IN PROTECTED PRIVACY. OTHERS, LIKE MANY OF THE TRUE BUGS, USE THEIR SHARP, HOLLOW MOUTH PARTS TO TAP INTO PLANTS' VASCULAR SYSTEMS AND SIP UP THE SAP.

Bug
piercing and sucking

Grasshopper
chewing

Mosquito
piercing and sucking

CERTAIN INSECTS COMMANDEER THE HORMONAL SYSTEMS OF PLANTS TO INDUCE THE FORMATION OF SPECIALIZED GROWTHS CALLED GALLS, WHICH PROVIDE BOTH FOOD AND LODGINGS. THE FRUIT OF THE GALL WASP'S LABOR, FOR INSTANCE, INCLUDES SO-CALLED OAK CURRANT, OAK CHERRY, OR OAK APPLE GALLS LOCATED ON OR NEAR THE LEAF VEINS OF OAK TREES.

WINSOME BUTTERFLIES MAY DAINTILY SIP FLOWER NECTAR THROUGH ELONGATED PROBOSCISES, BUT TOUGHER INSECTS EARN THEIR LIVING BY STEALTH AND HUNTING SKILL. EVEN IN THE SUBURBS, IT'S A JUNGLE OUT THERE FOR THESE GANGSTER GOURMANDS. TRAPPING, AMBUSHING, ASSASSINATING, POISONING, STALKING, AND ALL FORMS OF FOUL PLAY COMPRISE THE TRICKS OF THEIR PREDATORIAL TRADE.

GIANT WATER BUGS FEED ON RELATIVELY LARGE PREY SUCH AS SNAKES, FISH, AND FROGS BY FIRST INJECTING A PARALYZING VENOM AND THEN SIPHONING OUT BODY FLUIDS WITH THEIR BEAKS.

European Corn Borer

E. MELADY

Potato Beetle

Fly
Sponging

Bee
Lapping

Butterfly
Siphoning

Net-winged Midge

Moth Fly

Saw Fly

Green Lacewing

Wings

BEFORE PIONEERING INSECTS TOOK THEIR FIRST TENTATIVE FLIGHTS UP FROM SWAMPS AND LAGOONS, THE SKY WAS A LIFELESS, SILENT VOID. NOW, INSECTS HAVE BEEN ON THE WING FOR SO LONG THAT THEIR ABILITY TO FLY IS INNATE AND NEED NOT BE LEARNED. EVEN THE COMMON HOUSEFLY CAN TAKE OFF LIKE A ROCKET.

Common Skimmer

Spongillafly

Broad-Winged

Honey Bee

Small Carpenter Bee

Bumble Bee

Epiplemid Moth

Insect flight requires the right body temperature, readily available fuel, and glorious wings.

Unlike those of birds and bats, insect wings are not modified forearms, and they contain no muscles or tendons. Instead they are aerodynamic surfaces controlled and powered from the thorax. Muscles at the base of each wing adjust the angle and thus determine the direction of flight. The veins sandwiched between the two chitinous layers of an insect's wings do contain some blood, but their main function is to provide strength.

Parnassian Butterfly

Most modern insects, such as wasps and butterflies, have two pairs of wings that flap in unison. Older species, like dragonflies, have two pairs that function independently.

Centuries of observation have allowed earthbound humans only brief flashes of insight into insects' effortless exploration of the heavens. Recent studies of insect flight have revealed that some of the established principles of aerodynamics are violated by the insect world's bizarre wing shapes and impossible angles of flight.

Swallowtail Butterfly

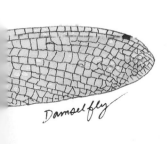

Damselfly

Paper Wasp

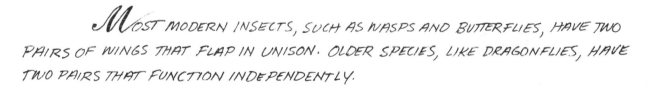

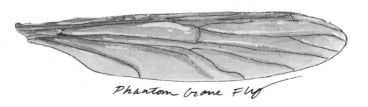

Phantom Crane Fly

Like many birds, some insects migrate. What causes their mass movements with seasonal regularity? Do they have feeding or breeding motivations? Many insects, such as grasshoppers, butterflies, ladybugs, and dragonflies, periodically engage in a frenzy of migration, traveling up to two thousand miles. Though scientists have observed the migratory movement of flying insects for a long time, what causes it and how insects navigate remain largely unsolved mysteries.

Best way to hold a butterfly—at the base of the wings. Do not squeeze the thorax.

Migration

SOME MONARCH BUTTERFLIES, BORN SEXUALLY MATURE, LIVE FOR ONLY FOUR OR FIVE WEEKS DURING SPRING OR EARLY SUMMER, MATING, REPRODUCING, AND DYING. OTHERS HATCH AT THE END OF SUMMER, NOT READY TO MATE. ONLY THESE MONARCHS MAKE THE MYSTERIOUS, ARDUOUS TRIP FROM CALIFORNIA TO MEXICO, GLIDING AS MUCH AS EIGHTY MILES A DAY ON EASTERN WINDS. PULSES, OR WAVES, OF THOUSANDS OF THE BLACK AND ORANGE FORMS CREATE DARK CLOUDS IN THE SKY AND COMPLETELY COVER THE BRANCHES AND LEAVES OF TREES WHEN THEY LAND.

TOWARD THE END OF FEBRUARY, MIGRANT MONARCH BUTTERFLIES WAKE FROM HIBERNATION TO MATE. THE MALES DIE IMMEDIATELY AFTERWARD, BUT THE FEMALES FLY INSTINCTIVELY NORTHWARD TOWARD THE MILKWEED FIELDS IN WHICH THEY WILL LAY THEIR EGGS AND DIE. THEIR OFFSPRING COMPLETE THE JOURNEY NORTH.

LEFT, RIGHT, LEFT, RIGHT.

LEFT, IN THE DESERT OF AUSTRALIA'S NORTHERN TERRITORY, PROCESSIONARY CATERPILLARS MIGRATE AFTER DEVOURING ALL THE LEAVES ON AN ACACIA TREE. MORE THAN A HUNDRED LINE UP HEAD TO TAIL IN A CHAIN UP TO EIGHTEEN FEET LONG. THEY MARCH RELENTLESSLY OVER THE SAND, TRAVELING MOSTLY AT NIGHT AND SPINNING CONTINUOUS SILK THREADS THAT HELP KEEP THE CHAIN TOGETHER UNTIL THEY FIND ANOTHER TREE.

BEST WAY TO HOLD A CATERPILLAR — ON AN ARTIST BRUSH.

monarch

ragonfly

TODAY I SAW THE DRAGON-FLY
COME FROM THE WELLS WHERE HE DID LIE.
AN INNER IMPULSE RENT THE VEIL
OF HIS OLD HUSK: FROM HEAD TO TAIL
CAME OUT CLEAR PLATES OF SAPPHIRE MAIL.
HE DRIED HIS WINGS: LIKE GAUZE THEY GREW;
THRO' CROFTS AND PASTURES WET WITH DEW
A LIVING FLASH OF LIGHT HE FLEW.

ALFRED LORD TENNYSON 1809 1892

Doubleday's
Bluet
Damselfly

Vestalia
Damselfly

Red Bluet
Damselfly

Four-spot Skimmer
Dragonfly

Southwestern
Short Damselfly

Neurobasis
Damselfly

Civil
Bluet
Damselfly

Stocky
Leaten
Damselfly

Biddie
Dragonfly

12-Spot
Skimmer
Dragonfly

Black-faced Skimmer

Black-wing Damselfly

Short-stalked Damselfly

Violet Tail Damselfly

White Tail Skimmer Dragonfly

Largest Damselfly - Megaloprepus

Ruby Spot Damselfly

Dark Lestes Damselfly

Circumpolar Bluet Damselfly

Common Forktail Damselfly

Water Prince Skimmer Dragonfly

Green Darner Dragonfly

Dragonflies and Damselflies

*The burnished dragonfly is thine attendant.
And tilts against the field,
And down the listed sunbeam rides resplendent
In steel blue mail and shield.*

Henry Wadsworth Longfellow 1807–1882

The appellation "dragonfly" conjures images of fire-breathing, castle-wrecking beasts rather than of the delicate insects known for their bright, metallic bodies and gauzy wings. Perhaps if these creatures were enlarged to a few thousand times their current size, they might look as ominous as their name sounds. Certainly, to the dragonfly's prey, the name is appropriate. A voracious feeder, the dragonfly consumes thousands of flies, mosquitoes, and other insects during its lifetime. The little dragons buzz around people quite harmlessly; the Anax junius—Lord of June—is a summer favorite.

Neither a young maiden nor a female dragonfly, the damselfly is a smaller relative of the dragonfly and has a similar appearance and lifestyle.

Faster than a speeding dragonfly

One of the most ancient insects in the world, the dragonfly has been flitting around for more than three hundred million years. The primeval dragonflies were impressively large: some of them had wingspans of two feet or more. Today, the dragonfly's four wings generally span three to four inches, each pair moving independently to allow for skillful maneuvering. The insect can also achieve great speed and has been clocked flying sixty miles per hour.

The magical shimmer of a dragonfly's wings can only be seen while the insect is alive. The iridescence appears when sunlight strikes a thin film of liquid suspended between the layers of the wings. When the dragonfly dies, the liquid dries up and the rainbow brilliance disappears.

Circumvision

With eyes that extend almost completely over the top of its head, the dragonfly has a virtual three-hundred-sixty-degree perspective. Its compound eyes have as many as twenty-five thousand facets, so it makes sense that eighty percent of the dragonfly's brain is given over to analyzing what it sees.

"Fascination of Nature" painting on silk
XIE CHUFANG · YUAN DYNASTY 1321

South African Bagworm

Bagworm's Silken Case incorporating The Thorns of an Acacia Tree

Mating

BIRDS DO IT, BEES DO IT. ALL ANIMALS CREATE MORE OF THEIR OWN KIND, BUT THE REPRODUCTIVE PROWESS OF SOME INSECT SPECIES IS LEGENDARY. THE QUEEN TERMITE IS CAPABLE OF STORING MILLIONS OF SPERM TO FERTILIZE THE MILLIONS OF EGGS SHE CAN PRODUCE OVER A LIFETIME THAT MAY LAST FOR YEARS. IN SOME CULTURES QUEEN TERMITES HAVE BECOME FERTILITY SYMBOLS.

THE VAST MAJORITY OF INSECTS REPRODUCE SEXUALLY, DIRECTLY DEPOSITING MALE GAMETES (SPERM) INTO THE FEMALE REPRODUCTIVE TRACT, WHERE THEY MAKE THEIR WAY TO THE FEMALE GAMETES (EGGS). THE TIME-PROVEN PRACTICE OF INTERNAL FERTILIZATION INSURES THAT THE MAXIMUM NUMBER OF EGGS WILL BE FERTILIZED. INSECTS OUTSHINE ALL OTHER ANIMALS IN THE DIVERSITY OF REPRODUCTIVE TECHNIQUES. THEIR GENITALIA ARE SO VARIED THAT SCIENTISTS OFTEN USE THEM TO IDENTIFY SPECIES.

Bagworm larvae emerging from their mother's case

The south african bagworm (eumeta hardenbergi) feeds off of the thorns of the acacia tree and then weaves a silk case in which to pupate.

The female bagworm is primarily an egg-laying machine. After spinning a cocoon around herself, she awaits the male bagworm, who approaches her through the open end of the silk sack. Tragically, once the eggs within her are fertilized, she dies. Soon the larvae will emerge from the cocoon as they mature, spinning silk threads on which they will be blown away by the wind.

Insect mothers-to-be are very discriminating about where they deposit their eggs. They usually place eggs directly upon the food source of choice, or as close to it as possible. Herbivorous insects therefore deposit their eggs on plants, while parasitic species deposit their eggs in areas frequented by the host--or within the host itself.

Certain predatory insects such as digger wasps must stock their larder before laying their eggs. Each step of the process must be done in ritual order with no interruptions, or they go back to square one. The wasp first digs a burrow, then carefully seals it before leaving to hunt for caterpillars. It stings each and every body segment of the prey it catches and drags the immobilized creature back to the burrow. Only after opening and inspecting the burrow and carrying the prey inside does the wasp finally lay a single, solitary egg on the caterpillar's corpse.

PARTNERSHIPS: WORKING TOGETHER

ON A HOT MIDSUMMER DAY, CLOUDS OF MAYFLIES DANCE OVER STREAMS OR RIVERBEDS IN MASS NUPTIAL FLIGHTS. SWARMS OF INSECTS ALSO GATHER TO FIND NEW FEEDING AREAS, TO MIGRATE AWAY FROM OVERCROWDED TERRITORIES, TO DEFEND AGAINST INTRUDERS, OR IN RESPONSE TO ENVIRONMENTAL CONDITIONS. WHATEVER THE CATALYST, INSECT GROUPS GENERALLY BAND TOGETHER FOR COLLECTIVE PHYSICAL STRENGTH AND PROTECTION.

SOME INSECT SOCIETIES USE THEIR UNIFIED STRENGTH TO CONTROL BANDS OF OTHER INSECTS. MUCH LIKE DAIRY FARMERS WITH HERDS OF COWS, HONEYDEW ANTS KEEP, CARE FOR, AND MILK TINY HERDS OF APHIDS. KIND MASTERS, THE ANTS PROTECT THE PLANT LICE FROM PREDATORY BEETLES, BUILD THEM SHELTERS, AND SOMETIMES EVEN PIGGYBACK THEM TO JUICY FOOD SOURCES. THEIR APHID APPRECIATION PAYS OFF HANDSOMELY: APHIDS CAN PROVIDE AS MUCH AS SIXTY PERCENT OF AN ANT COLONY'S NOURISHMENT. UNDER THE ANTS' ATTENTIVE SUPERVISION, APHIDS OVERFEED ON PLANT SAP, SECRETING THE EXCESS IN THE FORM OF HONEYDEW— A SUGARY SYRUP FERVENTLY ENJOYED BY ANTS. AN ANT WILL GENTLY STROKE AN APHID WITH ITS ANTENNAE AND FEET UNTIL THE APHID RESPONDS WITH A DROP OF DEW. THE MILKING SPEEDS UP APHID METABOLISM SO THAT THEY GROW AND REPRODUCE FASTER, ENLARGING THE ANTS' SUPPLY OF HONEYDEW.

Ant getting a droplet of honeydew from an aphid (enlarged).

Insect Architecture: Below

*E*XPERTS IN SURVIVAL, MANY ANTS HAVE DEVELOPED PERFECT TUNNEL HOMES BELOW THE SURFACE OF THE EARTH. THE UNDERGROUND NESTS CONCEAL THE ANTS AND THEIR YOUNG FROM PREDATORS, STORE AMPLE SUPPLIES OF FOOD, AND PROTECT THE INHABITANTS FROM THE ELEMENTS.

*A*NTS' LABYRINTHINE HOMES REACH DOWN AS MUCH AS FIFTEEN FEET BELOW GROUND. ABOVE, MOUNDS MADE OF EARTH, TWIGS, AND GRASS COVER AND DISGUISE THE MANY ENTRANCES. ANTS CONTINUALLY REARRANGE AND RECONSTRUCT THESE MOUNDS, CARRYING NESTING MATTER UP FROM BELOW THE SURFACE AND RETURNING BELOW WITH MATERIAL FROM ABOVE. THE CONSTANT TURNOVER ALLOWS MATERIAL FROM THE HUMID INTERIOR OF THE NEST TO DRY OUT REGULARLY, HELPING TO PREVENT MOLD FORMATION.

*S*EVERAL HUNDRED SEPARATE ENTRANCES MAY LEAD INTO A SINGLE ANT NEST VIA LONG TUNNELS. WITHIN THEIR NESTS, AMBITIOUS ANT ENGINEERS BUILD UNDERGROUND CITIES. THE LARGEST CUT-ANT NEST YET DISCOVERED CONTAINED 1,920 SEPARATE CHAMBERS. IN THESE ROOMS THE ANTS BUILD FUNGUS GARDENS, GUARD THEIR OFFSPRING AND QUEEN, AND EVEN STORE THEIR REFUSE.

*T*HE ANT WORKPLACE IS AS ORGANIZED AS THE ANT HOME. SOLDIER ANTS GUARD THE NEST, WORKER ANTS FARM THE GARDENS, NANNY ANTS PROTECT AND CARE FOR THE YOUNG, AND A QUEEN ANT REPRODUCES.

Uncle Milton's Fascinating Ant Farm

Specialization

Like humans, who secure survival via an infinite array of professions and activities, insects compete for a living in countless unique ways. Most insects are farming or foraging plant eaters, but  from herbivorous origins have also evolved honest hunters and crafty trappers.

Winged Ant Lion

The industrious nature of the harvester ant earned it one of the first mentions given insects in Western literature. The ant reaps but does not sow: instead of farming, it collects and saves plant seeds for future consumption. In storage caves located in their nests, the harvesters carefully monitor their provisions, making sure they do not become damp and germinate. If the seeds do get wet, they are quickly dragged outside to dry.

Ant lion larvae are devious predators. They dig pits in sandy ground and wait for prey at the bottom. When an ant walks by or tumbles in, the ant lion furiously throws sand up, creating a miniature avalanche. The landslide invariably drives the prey deep into the pit and into the predator's clutches. Placed in a clear glass bowl of sugar or salt, the ant lion can be observed happily digging pits.

cut-away view 8.
An Ant Lion larva catching prey
— enlarged

Insect Architecture: Above

Guided by pure instinct, insects create architectural wonders to rival the work of human engineers and designers. Consummate examples of originality and precision, specialized insect homes are constructed of clay, wood, wax, grass, and feathers.

Like Clockwork

In the deserts of Africa and Australia, strange pointed mounds dot the landscape. Reminiscent of Egyptian pyramids, these structures can soar to lofty heights of more than twenty feet. Inside each live as many as five million teeming termites, more than the entire human population of New Zealand.

The hardy, weather-resistant termite mound tops a primary cave nine feet deep, with additional caves extending to depths of more than thirty feet. Within, a complex maze of trails, air ducts, storage facilities, fungus gardens, and the queen termite's breeding chamber comprise a huge termitary. The external mound's hard casing, formed of soil and termite saliva, regulates the interior climate and protects the colony against predators. Naturally air-conditioned by its shape, the porous termite mound allows hot, moist air to pass out of the cave to venting chimneys. The temperature within the nest never varies more than one degree.

Height is 20 inches

Umbrella Nest of the African Cubitermes

Inside a Termitarium in Tropical Africa

— outer hard layer
— subterranean entry passages

Store of woody material

Air passages
fungus gardens

Royal cell

height is 9 feet

Paper Houses

Was it by observing and emulating the nest-building techniques of the wasp that humans were inspired to create paper? The paper wasp scrapes wood shavings from weathered beams, posts, and boards, mixes in saliva, and shapes the resulting pulp into horizontal layers of hexagonal cells, each designed to hold a single larva. Building from top to bottom, the wasps add tier after tier, constructing a giant, feather-light globe that hangs from a rafter, branch, or gutter like a gray boulder. Inside, larvae incubate at precisely 86° Fahrenheit. The paper makes an efficient insulater, keeping the workers' heat in and the cold drafts out.

Queen

Worker

Drone

Bald-faced Hornet
Paper Wasp

BEE

TO MAKE A PRAIRIE IT TAKES A CLOVER AND ONE BEE.

EMILY DICKINSON 1830-1886

WORKER HORNET 5/8"

BRACONID WASP 3/16"

WHEAT JOINTWORM WASP 3/16"

POTTER WASP 3/4"

RED-TAILED ICHNEUMON WASP 3/4"

'JEWEL' CUCKOO WASP 1/2"

CALIFORNIA OAK GALL WASP 1/4"

SCELIONID WASP 3/16"

YELLOW-AND-BLACK MUD DAUBER WASP 1"

PAPER WASP 1"

GOLDEN-YELLOW CHALCID 3/8"

DRONE HORNET 3/4"

EASTERN SAND WASP 5/8"

TRICHOGRAMMATID WASP 1/32"

QUEEN BALD-FACED HORNET 3/4"

GIANT ICHNEUMON WASP 5"

BLUE-BLACK SPIDER WASP 3/4"

WORKER HONEY BEE 3/8"

WORKER BUMBLE BEE 3/4"

MINING BEE 5/8"

AMERICAN PELECINID WASP 2"

DRONE BUMBLE BEE 5/8"

DRONE HONEY BEE 5/8"

QUEEN GOLDEN NORTHERN BUMBLE BEE 7/8"

VIRESCENT GREEN METALLIC BEE 3/8"

QUEEN HONEY BEE 3/4"

APPLE SEED WASP 1/4"

SWEET BEE 7/16"

COLLETID BEE 7/16"

FAITHFUL LEAFCUTTING BEE 1/2"

GREAT CARPENTER BEE 3/4"

HAIRY FLOWER BEE 1/2"

Numbering 108

THOUSAND SPECIES IN ALL, THE ORDER HYMENOPTERA INCLUDES INSECTS WITH MEMBRANOUS WINGS, SUCH AS BEES, WASPS, SAWFLIES, AND SOME ANTS. ONLY THE SAWFLIES LACK THE VICTORIAN WASP-WAISTED APPEARANCE PRODUCED BY THE FUSION OF THE FIRST SEGMENT OF THE ABDOMEN TO THE THORAX.

THIS THIRD LARGEST INSECT ORDER IS PERHAPS THE MOST DIVERSIFIED, BOTH IN FEEDING HABITS AND HABITATS. ARCTIC BUMBLEBEES BUZZ AROUND THE NORTHERNMOST EDGES OF GREENLAND, WHILE LION ANTS SWARM IN DESERTS FAR TO THE SOUTH. EMPLOYMENT OPPORTUNITIES ABOUND FOR THESE INDUSTRIOUS CREATURES. ANTS ALONE WORK AS ARCHITECTS, FARMERS, HUNTERS, HERDERS, AND HARVESTERS AND MAKE UP, EXPERTS ESTIMATE, HALF THE PLANET'S ENTIRE BIOMASS.

UNEXPECTEDLY, MANY OF THE INSECTS OF THIS ORDER ARE SOLITARY, NOT SOCIAL.

HOW THE BEE MOVES ITS WINGS IN FLIGHT

THE WINGS PUSH THE AIR DOWNWARD AND BACKWARD DURING THE DOWN STROKE.

MONEY-SWEETENED · THOMAS KEMPER SODA CO.

Hymenoptera: Bee Basics, Wasps and Kin

Though the females of many social or parasitic species of bees and wasps are equipped with venomous stingers, they are for the most part nonaggressive. The wasp most likely to sting is the startled one, caught snoozing in the shady comfort of a boot on the veranda, rather than the wasp out and about on its daily errands.

For bees, outright self-defense comes at a suicidally high price. Their stinger ends in a barbed hook that becomes embedded in the flesh of their target. The bee leaves behind not only its stinger but also part of its abdomen, thus sustaining a mortal injury.

Admire the dexterity of the leaf-cutter Bee.
Episodes of Insect Life 1867

FIRST AID
Stings of Insects

ARMY

For centuries, the people of the Brazilian Amazon have sutured wounds with the aid of Atta soldier ants. These minisurgeons have massive jaws with which they tenaciously grip the sides of an open laceration. Once the ants lock their jaws, the human healers quickly break off the thoracic and abdominal sections of the ant. The jaws remain in place and dissolve at the same pace at which the wound heals.

MEDICS

EPISODES OF INSECT LIFE 1867

ollination

INSECTS AND THE SEX LIFE OF FLOWERS

FIRMLY ROOTED IN THE GROUND, PLANTS CANNOT WANDER IN SEARCH OF A MATE. INSTEAD, THEY SEDUCE INSECT SURROGATES WITH NECTAR AND COLORFUL, SCENTED FLOWERS. VISITING INSECTS GET A DUSTING OF POLLEN AND CARRY THE MALE PLANT GAMETES TO THE FEMALE GAMETES OF A DIFFERENT FLOWER. WITHOUT INSECTS' ASSISTANCE, SOME OF THE WONDERS OF THE PLANT WORLD WOULD NOT EXIST.

THE MAGNIFICENT MIDGE AND THE MARVELOUS MELIPONE: CHOCOLATE AND VANILLA

THE AZTECS USED CACAO BEANS AS CURRENCY — A HUNDRED WOULD BUY A SLAVE — AND DAILY DRANK 2,000 PITCHERS OF CHOCOLATE IN MONTEZUMA'S COURT. THE ITZÁS FED CHOCOLATE TO HUMAN SACRIFICES, SANCTIFYING THEIR VICTIMS' JOURNEYS TO THE NEXT WORLD. LINNAEUS, THE FATHER OF MODERN BOTANY, NAMED IT THEOBROMA, "THE FOOD OF THE GODS." CHOCOLATE IS TRULY ONE OF NATURE'S MOST PRECIOUS INVENTIONS, AND THE MINUTE MIDGE FLY BEARS SOLE RESPONSIBILITY FOR ITS PROPAGATION. NO MORE THAN A SIXTH OF AN INCH LONG, THE MIDGE FLY IS THE ONLY INSECT THAT POLLINATES THE FLOWER OF THE CACAO TREE, WHICH GROWS ONLY BETWEEN THE LATITUDES OF TWENTY DEGREES NORTH AND TWENTY DEGREES DEGREES SOUTH OF THE EQUATOR. THE FLY'S TINY DIMENSIONS ALLOW IT TO SHIMMY INTO THE VIVID YELLOW MAZE OF THE PLANT'S BLOOM TO GATHER NECTAR AND CARRY POLLEN AWAY. EVEN WITH THIS SPECIAL ATTENTION, ONLY 30 OUT OF EVERY 10,000 CACAO FLOWERS MAKE IT TO SEED.

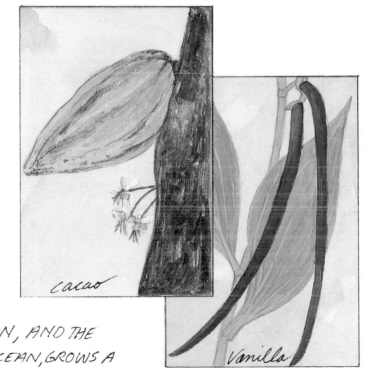

Cacao

Vanilla

ON MADAGASCAR, RÉUNION, AND THE COMOROS ISLANDS IN THE INDIAN OCEAN, GROWS A CLIMBING ORCHID SPECIES THAT PRODUCES MOST OF THE WORLD'S AROMATIC VANILLA PODS. A DEVOTEE OF THE EPHEMERAL BLOSSOM THAT LASTS ONLY ONE DAY, THE TINY MELIPONE BEE POLLINATES THE SCENTLESS ORCHID. HUMANS SOMETIMES TAKE ON THE BEE'S DUTIES, HAND FERTILIZING THE FLOWERS TO INSURE A GOOD HARVEST.

ANCIENT EGYPTIAN TOMB DECORATIONS SHOW THAT HUMANS HAVE KEPT HONEYBEES FOR CENTURIES, NOT ONLY FOR THE SWEET TREAT THEY MAKE, BUT FOR THE ARTFULLY CONSTRUCTED WAX COMB THAT HOLDS IT. APIS MELLIFERA CREATES ITS HONEYCOMB IN HIVES THAT MAINTAIN A STATIC INTERNAL TEMPERATURE OF 95° FAHRENHEIT, ALLOWING THE WAX SECRETED

BUG BY-PRODUCTS
BEESWAX

FROM THE BEE'S ABDOMINAL POCKETS TO REMAIN PLIABLE.

EACH PRECISELY SHAPED HEXAGONAL CELL HAS WALLS OF UNIFORM THICKNESS, CAREFULLY SHAPED WITH GREAT ECONOMY OF MOVEMENT. THE THRIFTY HONEYBEE EVEN RECYCLES OLD WAX, IF IT HAS NOT FIRST BEEN HARVESTED BY HUMANS FOR USE IN ADHESIVES, PAINTS, CANDLES, OINTMENTS, CANDIES, LUBRICANTS, OR SHOE POLISH.

From "Memorable Journeyings of Old Man Toad"
A bee-housemaid in the hive giving her duties bread
and honey — J.J. Grandville 1803-1847

BURT'S BEESWAX LIP BALM

QUEEN BEE

WORKER BEE

BEESWAX CANDLES

SMOKER AND HIVE TOOL

NEVIS $6
Queen Bee and workers

NEVIS

BEESWAX CANDLES

DRONE BEE

Honey

Bees gather nectar from flowers to make honey, sucking it into a special honey sac in their abdomen, where enzymes digest the natural sugars. Depositing the product in wax honeycomb cells, the bees fan it to evaporate excess moisture. The reduced liquid, eaten by both larvae and mature bees, is honey.

To produce two pounds of honey, bees must make approximately ten million nectar-collecting trips. If the flowers they visit are within a mile of the hive, the total distance traveled roughly equals ten laps around the globe.

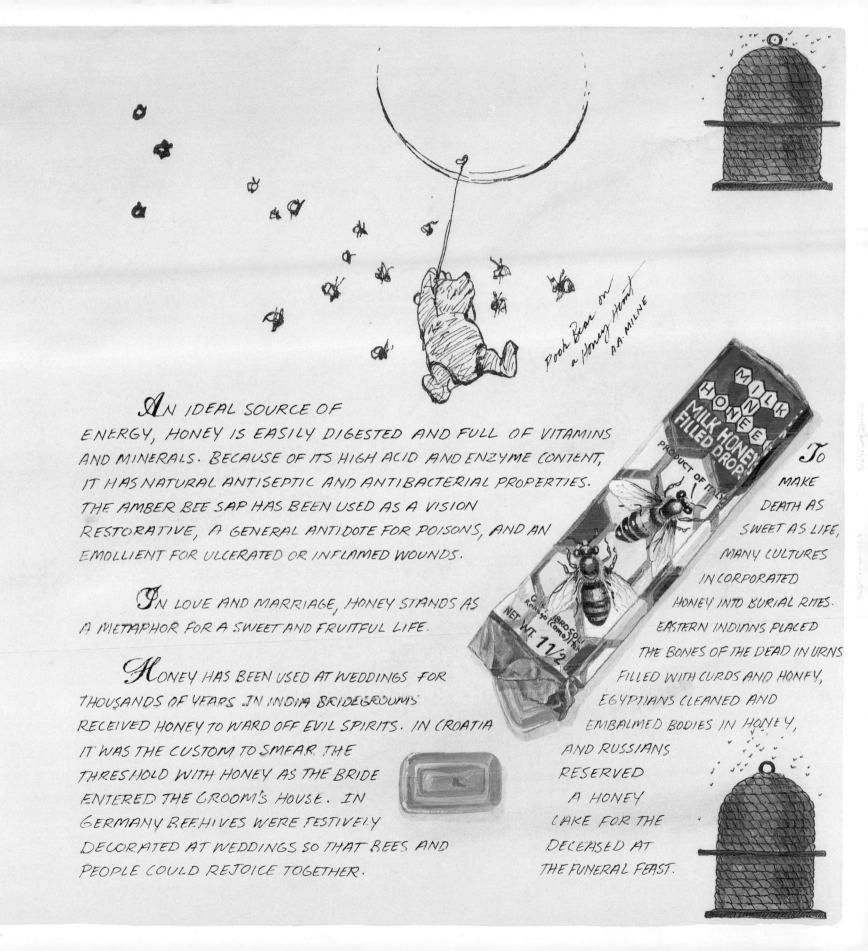

Pooh Bear on a Honey Hunt
A.A. MILNE

An ideal source of energy, honey is easily digested and full of vitamins and minerals. Because of its high acid and enzyme content, it has natural antiseptic and antibacterial properties. The amber bee sap has been used as a vision restorative, a general antidote for poisons, and an emollient for ulcerated or inflamed wounds.

In love and marriage, honey stands as a metaphor for a sweet and fruitful life.

Honey has been used at weddings for thousands of years. In India bridegrooms received honey to ward off evil spirits. In Croatia it was the custom to smear the threshold with honey as the bride entered the groom's house. In Germany beehives were festively decorated at weddings so that bees and people could rejoice together.

To make death as sweet as life, many cultures incorporated honey into burial rites. Eastern Indians placed the bones of the dead in urns filled with curds and honey, Egyptians cleaned and embalmed bodies in honey, and Russians reserved a honey cake for the deceased at the funeral feast.

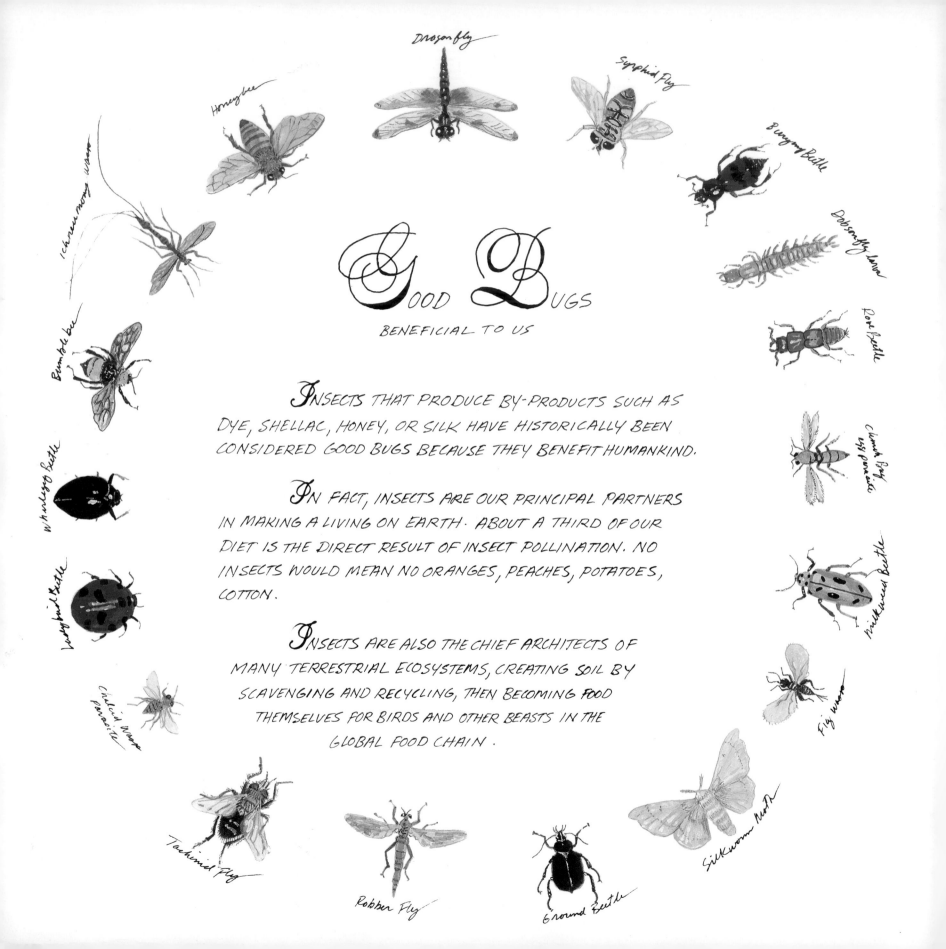

Dragonfly

Honeybee

Syrphid Fly

Burying Beetle

Ichneumon Wasp

Dobsonfly larva

Rove Beetle

Bumble bee

Good Bugs
BENEFICIAL TO US

Chalcid Frog egg parasite

Whirligig Beetle

Insects that produce by-products such as dye, shellac, honey, or silk have historically been considered good bugs because they benefit humankind.

In fact, insects are our principal partners in making a living on earth. About a third of our diet is the direct result of insect pollination. No insects would mean no oranges, peaches, potatoes, cotton.

Insects are also the chief architects of many terrestrial ecosystems, creating soil by scavenging and recycling, then becoming food themselves for birds and other beasts in the global food chain.

Milkweed Beetle

Ladybird Beetle

Fig wasp

Chalcid Wasp Parasite

Silkworm Moth

Tachinid Fly

Robber Fly

Ground Beetle

Bad Bugs

HARMFUL TO US

June Beetle

Cotton-boll Weevil

Cucumber Beetle

Larder Beetle

Apple Twig borer

Squash Bug

Termite

Granary Beetle

Chinch Bug

Clothes Moth

Cockroach

Corn Billbug

Mosquito

Cicada

House Fly

Carpenter Ant

Potato Beetle

Grain Weevil

INSECTS ARE PART OF WHERE WE HAVE COME FROM, WHAT WE ARE NOW AND WHAT WE WILL BE. THAT'S A PRETTY GOOD REASON FOR GETTING BETTER ACQUAINTED WITH THEM.

MAY R. BERENBAUM 1995

IT'S A TRICKY BUSINESS, DUBBING INSECTS GOOD BUGS OR BAD BUGS.

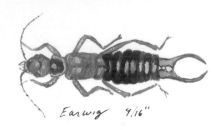

Earwig 9/16"

Moth Fly 1/16"

Vinegar Fly 1/16"

King Termite 3/8"

1/4"

Bed Bug

1/2"

Clothes Moth

*G*OD IN HIS WISDOM MADE THE FLY
AND THEN FORGOT TO TELL US WHY.

OGDEN NASH 1943

Bee Fly
1/2"

Biting
Stable Fly 3/8"

Buffalo
Gnat 1/8"

Velvet Ant 3/8"

Blow Fly 5/16"

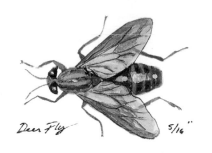
Flea 1/16"

Deer Fly 5/16"

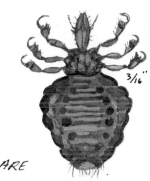
3/16" Sucking Louse

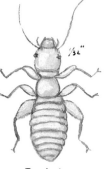
1/32" Book Louse

1/16" Biting Midge

Curiously, the most persistent and pervasive of humanity's adversaries are one-millionth of our size. Ask any flea or mosquito: humans are merely something good to eat.

The philistines were so plagued by nits and nibblers that they believed there was a god exclusively devoted to the affairs of insects. They worshiped Beelzebub, Lord of Flies, as a malevolent but divine master.

Carpet beetles, centipedes, clothes moths, cobweb spiders, earwigs, house dust mites, and termites all make unwanted houseguests and make for hellish housekeeping. Cockroaches, fruit flies, flour beetles, houseflies, and silverfish are kitchen companions who can make almost anyone lose their appetite.

Skin-piercing, blood-feeding insects have altered human history. Chiggers, body lice, crab lice, scabies, and above all, fleas and mosquitoes, are responsible for the transmission of a laundry list of noxious diseases. Malaria, yellow fever, typhus, encephalitis, the bubonic plague, and dengue fever are all deadly arboviruses, arthropod-borne maladies.

Bad bugs?

875 thousand known species of insects, but only one species of human, roam the planet at this moment. Given their numbers and the eons through which we have successfully coexisted, how bad can any bug really be?

Mosquito 1/4"

Hornet 3/4"

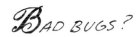
Biting Louse 3/32"

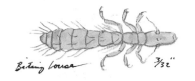
Silverfish 3/8"

eetle

EXTRAVAGANT COUTURIERE
BRIGHTEST BEETLES' READY-TO-WEAR,
INSPIRATIONAL, DEBONAIR.
MASTER METALLICS PAINT THE AIR
BEJEWELED IN NATURE'S BEST BUGWEAR.

SHELLEI ADDISON 1995

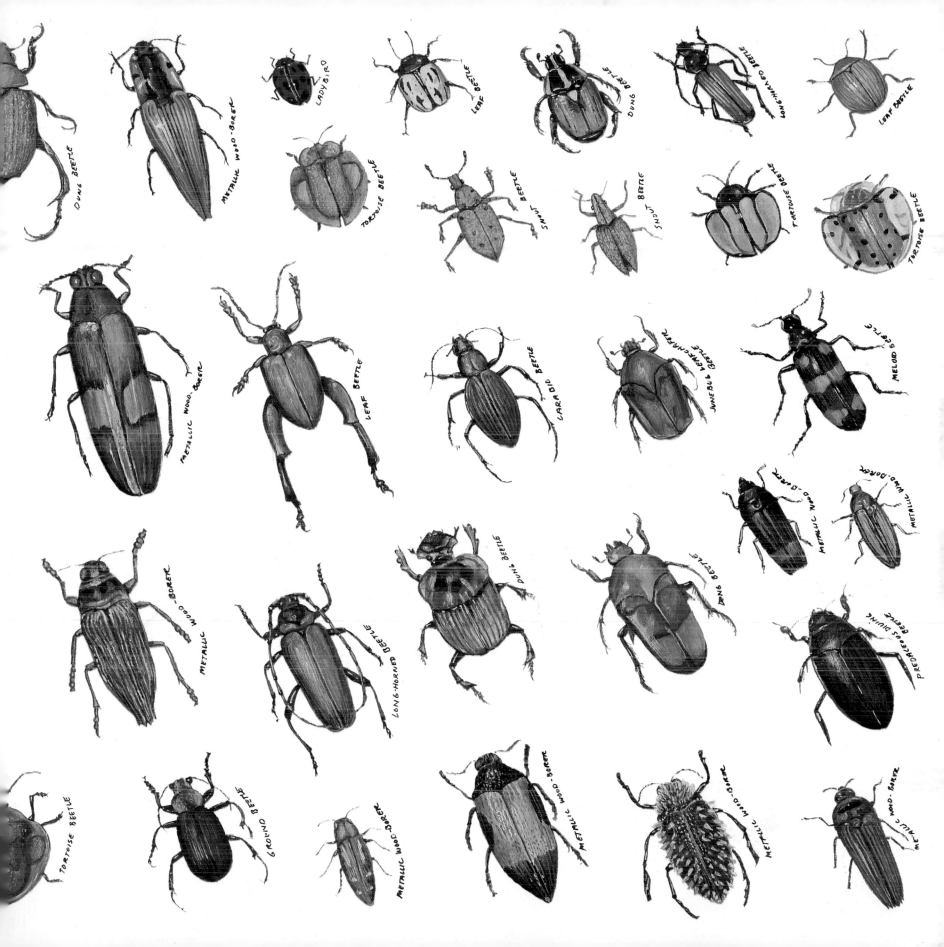

KIRIBATI 60c *Rodolia pumila*

KIRIBATI 75c *Rodolia cardinalis*

No. 7306

Old German postcard

Beetle antennae

threadlike

beadlike

sawtoothed

comblike

clubbed gradual

clubbed abrupt

lamellate

BEATALL HATS

While most beetles are somber shades of brown and black, many display dazzling colors, iridescent hues, and spectacular patterns of stripes and dots.

There are over 350,000 known species of beetles, compared with only 8,600 species of birds and between 4,000–5,000 species of mammals.

Lamellicornia Beetle

Beetle Basics

A central figure in the creation myth of the native American Cochiti people is a small, black beetle with an enormous task: to position all the stars in the heavens. According to the tale, the insect at first worked diligently but soon became careless. Rather than arranging the stars uniformly throughout the firmament, the beetle clustered many too closely together, creating the Milky Way. The shamed and dejected beetle then hid its face in the dirt, and continues to do so even today.

Beetle Tracks in The Sand

Perhaps even more fantastic than the beetle's rise in mythology are the simple facts of its existence on Earth.

One out of every five species of insect is a beetle.

Click Beetle

Click beetle falls

lies on its back for a minute

Then, with a loud click it flips into the air and lands right side up.

Beetles thrive everywhere except in the ocean and at the north and south poles. No other insect has adapted to this planet so successfully.

elongate-slender nearly parallel-sided

elongate-slender

Beetle Body Shapes

elongate-oval

elongate-robust

broadly oval

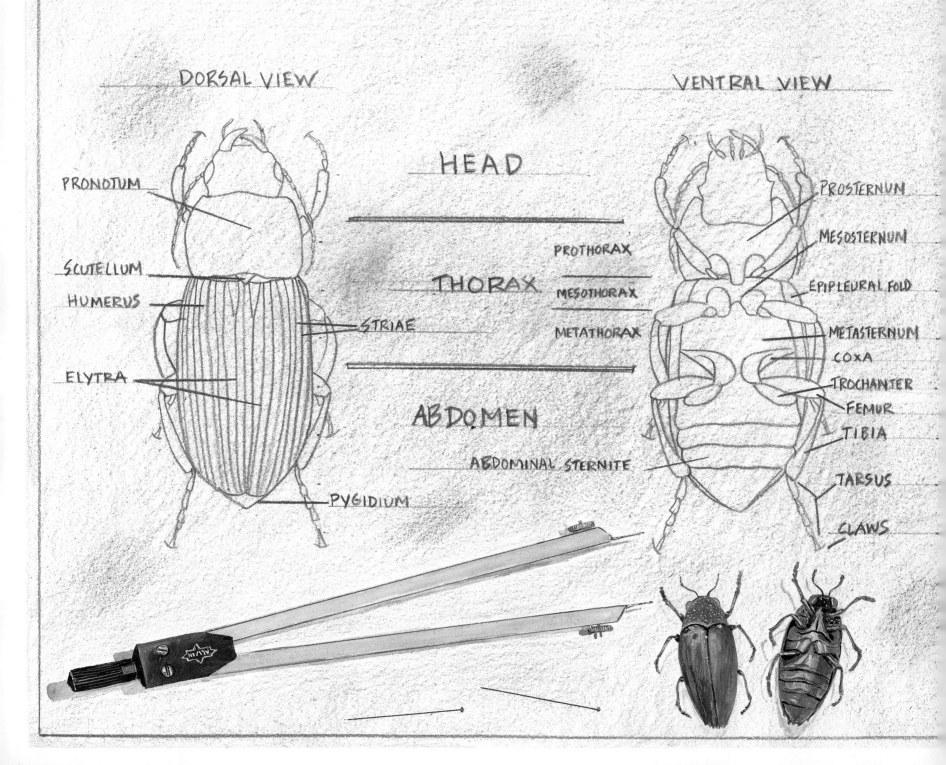

BODY PLAN OF AN ADULT BEETLE SCALE: 2"= 1"

DORSAL VIEW

PRONOTUM

SCUTELLUM

HUMERUS

ELYTRA

PYGIDIUM

HEAD

THORAX

PROTHORAX

MESOTHORAX

METATHORAX

STRIAE

ABDOMEN

ABDOMINAL STERNITE

VENTRAL VIEW

PROSTERNUM

MESOSTERNUM

EPIPLEURAL FOLD

METASTERNUM

COXA

TROCHANTER

FEMUR

TIBIA

TARSUS

CLAWS

STRENGTH IN STRUCTURE

INSECTS HAVE A GREATER VARIETY OF FORM AND FUNCTION THAN ANY OTHER CLASS OF ANIMALS, BUT THEIR BASIC STRUCTURE IS UNIFORM.

THE BODY OF THE ADULT INSECT IS DIVIDED INTO THREE MAIN SECTIONS: THE HEAD, THE THORAX, AND THE ABDOMEN. THE HEAD, OUTFITTED WITH EYES, ANTENNAE, AND MOUTH PARTS, IS RESPONSIBLE FOR FEEDING AND ORIENTATION. THE THORAX, WITH ITS MASSIVE MUSCULATURE, IS AN EFFICIENT LOCOMOTION MACHINE. THE ABDOMEN CONTAINS THE DIGESTIVE AND REPRODUCTIVE ORGANS, TOGETHER WITH A LONG, TUBULAR HEART AND MOST OF THE SPIRACLES, SMALL HOLES LEADING TO THE BREATHING NETWORK OF TRACHEAL TUBES. ATTACHED TO THE BODY'S THREE SEGMENTS ARE THREE PAIRS OF LEGS AND THE WINGS.

ALL OF THESE BUG BODY BITS ARE MADE OF VARIOUS TYPES OF CHITIN, A COMPOSITE OF SUGARS, STARCHES, AND PROTEINS. THE CUTICLE IS MADE LARGELY OF CHITIN, A THIN LAYER OF CELLS COVERING THE ENTIRE SURFACE OF THE INSECT. THE OUTERMOST LAYER OF THE CUTICLE IS HARDENED INTO THE RIGID, WATER-PROOF EXOSKELETON.

STURDY BUT LIGHTWEIGHT, THE EXO-SKELETON PROVIDES EXCELLENT PROTECTION FOR TINY, COLD-BLOODED BODIES. ITS FRAMEWORK OF HOLLOW TUBES OFFERS GREATER STRENGTH THAN THE INTERNAL HUMAN SKELETON OF SOLID BONES.

THE MONUMENTAL DRAWBACK TO THIS OTHERWISE INGENIOUS DESIGN EXPLAINS WHY INSECTS ARE SO SMALL. BECAUSE THE EXOSKELETON DOES NOT GROW ALONG WITH THE CREATURE INSIDE IT, IT MUST BE SHED, OR MOLTED, IF THE INSECT IS TO INCREASE IN SIZE. THE AVERAGE INSECT MOLTS SIX TIMES BEFORE REACHING ITS ADULT SIZE, AND EACH TIME, BEFORE THE CUTICLE CAN HARDEN AGAIN, THE GROWING ARTHROPOD IS VULNERABLE TO THE ELEMENTS AND TO PREDATORS.

Ouch!

Spines, spikes,
quills, stingers
prongs, and pokers
broadcast a
universal insect
message: Keep off!

Thorn Bug
ACTUAL SIZE
1/4"

Time-proven camouflage tactics also include mimicry — the art of looking nasty when you are really quite harmless. Swollen abdomens and tiny wings make mild-mannered aegerid moths seem like large, hairy bees.

Until recently it was believed that viceroy butterflies were just another troupe of well-clad impersonators who bedecked themselves in a distinctive, boldly patterned warning coloration similar to that of monarch butterflies, who are poisonous because of their milkweed diet. Current studies reveal that both are equally unpleasant tasting, to the chagrin of inexperienced american blue jays on the prowl for a snack.

monarch

Viceroy

Dung Beetles

The 'Sacred Beetle' FROM FABRE'S BOOK OF INSECTS

Dung Doctors and Beetle Carats

The tumblebug, a scarab beetle, is a warm-climate dung roller that does something exceptional: it carefully packs and rolls huge quantities of manure into balls and buries them. Underground, the beetle will either consume the manure or lay an egg in the middle of the ball. When a beetle larva hatches, it will eat its way out. In this way the dung beetle removes potentially harmful bacteria from the environment and minimizes water pollution.

Rolling its ball from east to west, the dung beetle evoked the metaphor of the sun as a dung ball. To the ancient Egyptians, the beetle represented Ra, the sun god, the source of all existence. In tribute, they created the scarab, a life-giving amulet in the shape of a beetle, which conferred daily well-being and protective against evil.

The iridescent cryptic patterns on the scarab beetle's back often glow with a green, velvety softness, a hard red metallic sheen, or an unmatched blue luminescence. These living gems have become literal jewels to the people of the Waugi Valley in the interior highlands of New Guinea. Stringing the insects side by side between two strands of plant fiber, they wear them as headbands or as headdress decorations.

LADYBIRD, LADYBIRD, FLY AWAY, DO!

Ladybirds

THE LADYBIRD IS SAID TO HAVE GOTTEN ITS NAME DURING THE MIDDLE AGES IN EUROPE, WHEN A PLAGUE OF APHIDS DEVOURED THE GREAT VINEYARDS. THE POPULACE WAS ABOUT TO GIVE UP WHEN A SWARM OF SCARLET, DOTTED BEETLES CONSUMED THE PESTS. IN THANKS FOR SERVICES RENDERED, THE PEOPLE MENTIONED "OUR LADY BUGS" — NAMED FOR MARY, MOTHER OF CHRIST — IN THEIR PRAYERS.

THE SAME PRETTY COLORING THAT ATTRACTS HUMANS TO THESE LITTLE BEETLES ACTUALLY KEEPS OTHER CREATURES AWAY. RED IS A DANGER SIGN TO PREDATORS, OFTEN INDICATING THAT AN INSECT IS HIGHLY UNPALATABLE. LADYBIRDS ARE POISONOUS, ALTHOUGH NOT TO HUMANS, AND HUNGRY BIRDS AND INSECTS ARE WARNED AT A GLANCE.

FEED UPON DEW, AND WHEN YOU ARE THROUGH,

FLY TO THE MOUNTAIN TO FEED UPON DEW.

*L*ADYBIRDS ARE PREDATORY. THE HUNT, HOWEVER, IS HARDLY A HIGH-SPEED CHASE. LADYBIRDS SIMPLY STROLL AFTER THEIR PREY, WHICH INCLUDE NOT ONLY APHIDS BUT OTHER PLANT-EATING INSECTS THAT MOVE EVEN SLOWER THAN THEY, AND LEAF-DWELLING SCALE INSECTS THAT DO NOT MOVE AT ALL.

*M*EALTIME OFTEN STRETCHES INTO AN ALL-DAY AFFAIR FOR THE RAPACIOUS LADYBIRD, SO BY SUNSET IT HAS CONSUMED ITS WEIGHT IN FOOD.

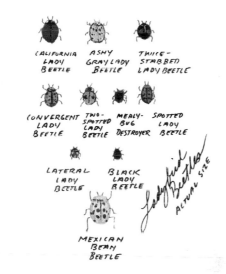

CALIFORNIA LADY BEETLE · ASHY GRAY LADY BEETLE · TWICE-STABBED LADY BEETLE
CONVERGENT LADY BEETLE · TWO-SPOTTED LADY BEETLE · MEALY-BUG DESTROYER · SPOTTED LADY BEETLE
LATERAL LADY BEETLE · BLACK LADY BEETLE
MEXICAN BEAN BEETLE
Ladybird Beetles ACTUAL SIZE

*C*ONTRARY TO THE OLD WIVES' TALE, A TALLY OF A LADYBIRD'S POLKA DOTS WILL NOT REVEAL ITS AGE AND ONLY DENOTES THE PARTICULAR SPECIES. ALL LADYBIRDS LIVE FOR ONE YEAR.

*T*ODAY LADYBIRDS ARE USED AS A SIX-LEGGED ALTERNATIVE TO CHEMICAL PESTICIDES. A VALUABLE COMMODITY IN THE GROWING MAIL-ORDER BUG INDUSTRY, THEY ARE LITERALLY COLLECTED BY THE GALLON AND, WITH OTHER GARDEN-FRIENDLY INSECTS, SHIPPED TO PEST-PRONE ORCHARDS, FIELDS, AND BACKYARDS. LOCAL NURSERIES OFTEN SELL LADYBIRDS BY THE QUART, WHICH GENERALLY CONTAINS ABOUT FIFTEEN HUNDRED BUGS. RECOMMENDED USE: TEN TO TWENTY-FIVE BUGS PER PLANT.

Ladybird tree ornament

LADYBIRD, LADYBIRD, FLY HOME AGAIN, DO!
TRADITIONAL CHINESE NURSERY RHYME

Big Beetles

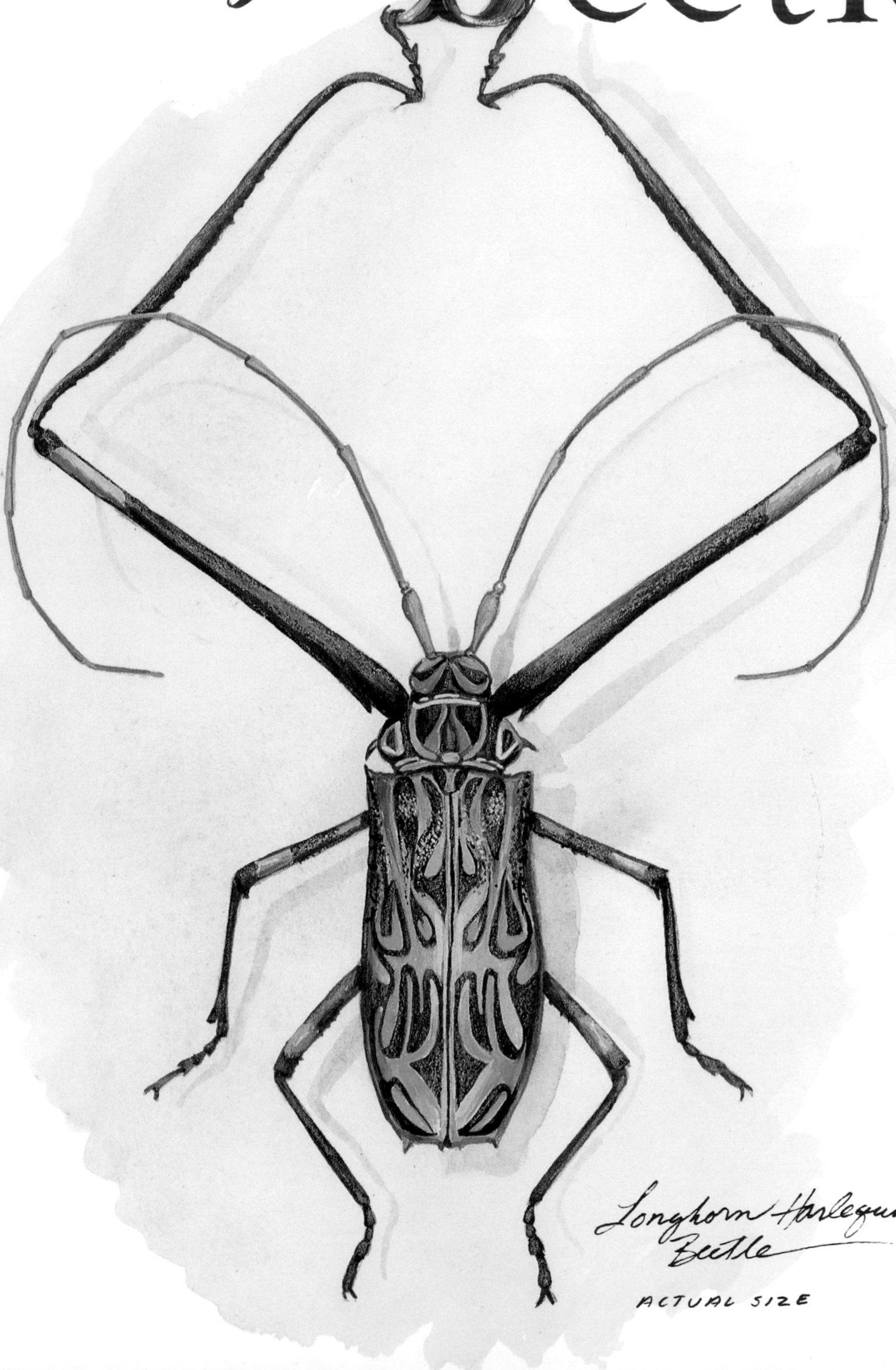

The longhorn harlequin beetle thrives in South America. Its theatrical wing-case markings are imitated on the shields of Amazonian Indians. Extending up to three inches, the long "horns" of these beetles are in fact long antennae.

Longhorn Harlequin Beetle

ACTUAL SIZE

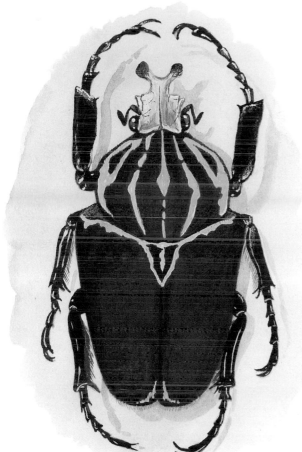

Goliath Beetle
ACTUAL SIZE

GOLIATH BEETLES HOLD THE HEAVYWEIGHT TITLE IN THE BATTLE OF THE BIG BUGS, WEIGHING IN AT HAMSTERLIKE PROPORTIONS. THOUGH THEY PROJECT AN OMINOUS IMAGE, THEY ARE ACTUALLY HARMLESS. IN THE ITURI RAIN FORESTS OF AFRICA, CHILDREN OF THE PYGMY PEOPLES KEEP THEM AS PETS. GROWN-UPS PREFER THEM ROASTED OVER A CAMPFIRE AND EAT THE NEWLY HATCHED LARVAE AS A SUMPTUOUS SNACK.

REPUBLIQUE DU BURUNDI

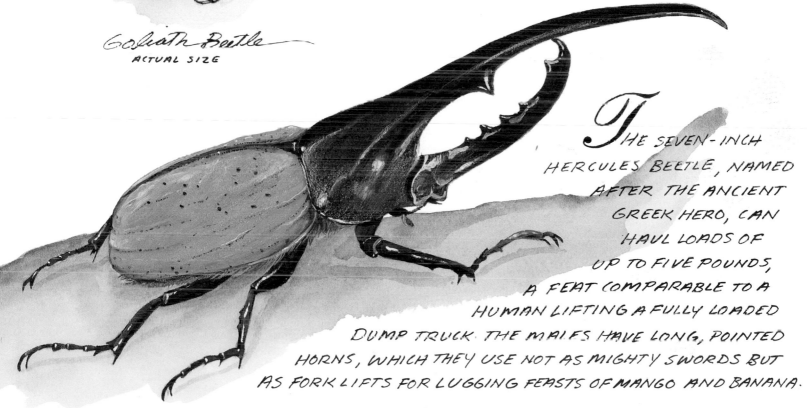

Hercules Beetle — ACTUAL SIZE

THE SEVEN-INCH HERCULES BEETLE, NAMED AFTER THE ANCIENT GREEK HERO, CAN HAUL LOADS OF UP TO FIVE POUNDS, A FEAT COMPARABLE TO A HUMAN LIFTING A FULLY LOADED DUMP TRUCK. THE MALES HAVE LONG, POINTED HORNS, WHICH THEY USE NOT AS MIGHTY SWORDS BUT AS FORKLIFTS FOR LUGGING FEASTS OF MANGO AND BANANA.

WETLANDS

Diving Beetles
1 ⅝"

WETLANDS FORM AN ECOLOGICAL BRIDGE BETWEEN LAND AND WATER. WHILE SOME CREATURES LIVE EXCLUSIVELY ON THE LAND, OTHERS ABIDE SOLELY IN THE WATER, AND SOME ARE EQUALLY AT HOME IN BOTH. THE LARVAE OF MANY TYPES OF INSECTS, SUCH AS THE DRAGONFLIES, DEVELOP IN WATER AND THEN EMERGE INTO THE WORLD ABOVE AS ADULTS.

INSECTS WHO HAVE ADAPTED TO A WATERY LIFESTYLE EMPLOY VARIOUS APPENDAGES SUCH AS OARS, PADDLES, AND GRASPERS TO HELP THEM NAVIGATE THROUGH DAILY LIFE AND ANCHOR IN SAFE HARBOR.

THE BREATHING APPARATUS OF WETLAND INSECTS ALLOWS THEM TO EXTRACT AIR FROM WATER. THE MANY CLEVER VARIATIONS THEY HAVE DEVELOPED SUGGEST THAT THEY ORIGINALLY EVOLVED ON LAND, NOT IN THE SEA, BEFORE COLONIZING FRESHWATER HABITATS.

MANY OF THE TRULY AQUATIC INSECTS LIVE ALMOST ENTIRELY ON THE WATER'S SURFACE AND THUS HAVE NO NEED FOR SPECIAL RESPIRATORY EQUIPMENT. SOME DO HAVE GILLS, BUT THEY ARE UNLIKE THE BLOOD GILLS OF THEIR REMOTE ARTHROPOD RELATIONS, THE CRUSTACEANS. MOST INSECT GILLS ARE A MODIFICATION OF THE HOSELIKE TRACHEAL SYSTEM, WHICH DELIVERS AIR THROUGHOUT THE BODY ALMOST LIKE A CENTRAL HEATING SYSTEM.

MOSQUITOES AND WATER SCORPIONS SNORKEL ABOUT, COLLECTING AIR THROUGH TUBELIKE STRUCTURES THAT PROTRUDE FROM THEIR ABDOMENS AND EXTEND ABOVE THE SURFACE OF THE MUDDY DETRITUS IN WHICH THEY FEED.

DIVING BEETLES ARE FIERCE PREDATORS. THEY STORE AIR UNDER THEIR WINGS IN A BUBBLE AS THEY PLUNGE IN PURSUIT OF THEIR PREY.

BREATHTAKING!

IMAGINE SCUBA DIVING WITHOUT HAVING TO RETURN TO THE SURFACE FOR ANOTHER TANK. INSECTS LIKE THE NAUCORID BUG ENJOY THIS CONVENIENCE, HAVING DEVELOPED PLASTRON RESPIRATION. THEY CAN REMAIN SUBMERGED FOR A LIFETIME, AS LONG AS THEY RESIDE IN WATER WITH A RELATIVELY HIGH CONCENTRATION OF OXYGEN. THE TINY, DENSELY PACKED, WATER-REPELLENT HAIRS THAT COVER THEIR BODIES TRAP A LAYER OF AIR THAT NEVER NEEDS REPLACEMENT.

DRYLANDS

Surprisingly, MORE THAN ONE-THIRD OF THE WORLD'S SURFACE IS SO ARID THAT IT QUALIFIES AS DESERT OR SEMIDESERT. MORE WATER EVAPORATES THERE THAN FALLS AS RAIN.

At FIRST GLANCE, DESERTS MAY SEEM BARREN OF INSECT LIFE, BUT THE PRESENCE OF INSECTIVOROUS BIRDS AND LIZARDS ANNOUNCES AN ABUNDANCE OF WELL-CAMOUFLAGED INSECTS.

Black WIDOW SPIDERS INHABIT THE DRY RANGES OF NEVADA AS WELL AS THE FOOTHILLS AND CENTRAL VALLEY OF CALIFORNIA, FINDING MINUTE BUT SUFFICIENT QUANTITIES OF WATER IN CREVICES AMONG VOLCANIC ROCKS. OTHER PREDATORY ARTHROPODS NEED NO WATER BEYOND THAT WHICH IS STORED IN THE BODIES OF THEIR PREY.

Dung Beetles rolling ball of dung
enlarged

Eremiaphila, a member of the mantid family, hunts freely over the open ground in the subdeserts of Morocco's Atlas Mountains. Its mottled, light coloration not only protects it from predators but also helps reflect sunlight in an environment that offers little shade.

Foraging among the sparse, woody vegetation of wadis (gullies) or oases, the Agapanthea beetle, like many desert insects, relies on deceptive coloration and form, a camouflage that mimics the thorny desert plants.

Desert arachnids such as spiders and scorpions frequently burrow into the sand to avoid the extremes of either heat or cold. A large number of these species are unexpectedly dark or black in color. This odd adaptation is thought to reradiate heat rather than absorb it.

One glorious exception to the camouflage crowd is the lustrous gold-green Buprestid beetle, which may be seen basking on tamarind trees at twilight. During the day its metallic wing cases reflect heat.

Darkling Beetle
enlarged

Metallic Buprestid
Beetle
enlarged

Butterfly

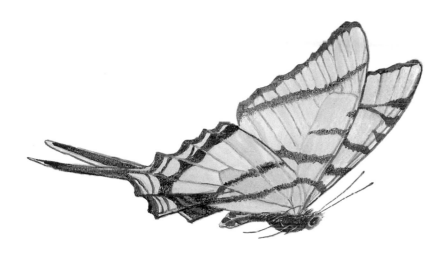

WHAT IS A BUTTERFLY? AT BEST

HE'S BUT A CATERPILLAR DRESSED.

BENJAMIN FRANKLIN 1706-1790

ORANGE OAKLEAF BUTTERFLY - NYMPHALIDAE

HAIRSTREAK LYCAENIDAE BUTTERFLY

PAPILIONIDAE BUTTERFLY

ELEPHANT HAWK MOTH

LYCAENIDAE BUTTERFLY

LYCAENIDAE BU

POSTMAN - NYMPHALIDAE BUTTERFLY

SATURNID MOTH

PEACH BLOSSOM MOTH THYATIRIDAE

LYCAENIDAE BUTTERFLY

NEMEOBIIDAE BUTTERFLY

HAIRSTREAK BUTTERFLY LYCAENIDAE

LYCAENIDAE BUTTERFLY

BIRDWING BUTTERFLY - PAPILIONIDAE

DOG'S-HEAD BUTTERFLY

PEACOCK BUTTERFLY - NYMPHALIDAE

LYCAENIDAE BUTTERFLY

HAIRSTREAK BUTTERFLY

LYCAENIDAE

LYCAENIDAE BUTTERFLY

NYMPHALIDAE BUTTERFLY

LYCAENIDAE BUTTERFLY

HELICONIIDAE BUTTERFLY

NYMPHALIDAE - BUTTERFLY

PIERIDAE - BUTTERFLY

NYMPHALIDAE BUTTERFLY

ERASMIA SANGUIFLUA MOTH

ORIENTAL LEAF BUTTERFLY - NYMPHALIDAE

ADONIS BLUE BUTTERFLY - LYCAENIDAE

LYCAENIDAE BUTTERFLY

LYCAENIDAE BUTTERFLY

FLY

SATYRIDAE BUTTERFLY

NEMEOBIIDAE BUTTERFLY

ITHOMIIDAE BUTTERFLY

PANTHEROIDES PARDALIS

SATYRIDAE BUTTERFLY

NYMPHALIDAE BUTTERFLY

AFRICAN GIANT SWALLOWTAIL BUTTERFLY - PAPILIONIDAE

NYMPHALIDAE BUTTERFLY

ARCTIIDAE MOTH

ESSEX EMERALD MOTH - GEOMETRIDAE

LYCAENIDAE BUTTERFLY

PIERIDAE BUTTERFLY

LYCAENIDAE BUTTERFLY

NEMEOBIIDAE BUTTERFLY

SPHINGIDAE MOTH

LYCAENIDAE BUTTERFLY

LYCAENIDAE BUTTERFLY

METAMORPHOSIS, CHANGE IN FORM, DEFINES THE LIFE CYCLE OF MANY INSECTS. THE COMPLEX ROUTE TO MATURITY CAN INVOLVE A SERIES OF SMALLER CHANGES AND THEN A DRAMATIC TRANSFIGURATION IN ONE FELL SWOOP INTO A COMPLETELY DIFFERENT ADULT FORM. ALTERNATIVELY,

etamorphosis

TRANSFORMATION CAN OCCUR GRADUALLY OVER A SERIES OF ENLARGEMENTS THAT OCCUR AT INTERVALS VARYING FROM SPECIES TO SPECIES. THE BASIC BODY PLAN ALTERS SLIGHTLY WITH EACH MOLT, CULMINATING IN THE FULL EMERGENCE OF WINGS.

*T*HE EIGHT-FOLD PATH TO INSECT SELF-REALIZATION

1. THE EGG HATCHES AND THE NEWBORN INSECT, THE LARVA, EMERGES.

2. THE SOFT-BODIED CATERPILLAR, GRUB, OR MAGGOT REFLEXIVELY SEARCHES FOR SAFETY WITH ITS SIMPLE EYES.

3. AS ITS SPINES OR OUTER SURFACES HARDEN, THE INSECT EATS ITS EGGSHELL FOR A FIRST MEAL, THEN FEEDS VORACIOUSLY THEREAFTER.

4. THE INSECT PREPARES TO PUPATE AND SHEDS ITS LARVAL SKIN.

5. THE PUPA—AN INSECT IN A "RESTING STAGE" BETWEEN FORMS—INDUSTRIOUSLY REORGANIZES ITS ENTIRE PHYSICAL STRUCTURE, LITERALLY DISSOLVING OLD MUSCLES AND LEGS AND REPLACING THEM WITH NEW ONES.

6. THE PUPAL SKIN SPLITS AND THE YOUNG ADULT SLOWLY WORKS ITSELF FREE, HEAD FIRST.

7. AS THE WING CASES HARDEN, THE INSECT EXTENDS ITS WINGS TO ALLOW THEM TO DRY.

8. THE INSECT TAKES ITS FIRST FLIGHT, DEVELOPING ITS MATURE ADULT COLORATION WITHIN MINUTES OR DAYS, DEPENDING ON THE SPECIES.

Swallowtail Butterfly on Fennel   MARIA SIBYLLA MERIAN

ADVICE FROM A CATERPILLAR

caterpillar

"WHO ARE YOU?" SAID THE CATERPILLAR.
ALICE REPLIED, RATHER SHYLY "I - I
HARDLY KNOW, SIR. BEING SO MANY
DIFFERENT SIZES IN A DAY IS VERY
CONFUSING." "IT ISN'T," SAID THE
CATERPILLAR. "WELL, PERHAPS YOU
HAVEN'T FOUND IT SO YET," SAID
ALICE; "BUT WHEN YOU HAVE TO
TURN INTO A CHRYSALIS - YOU WILL
SOME DAY, YOU KNOW - AND THEN
AFTER THAT INTO A BUTTERFLY, I
SHOULD THINK YOU'LL FEEL IT A
LITTLE QUEER, WON'T YOU?"
"NOT A BIT," SAID THE
CATERPILLAR.

LEWIS CARROLL 1865

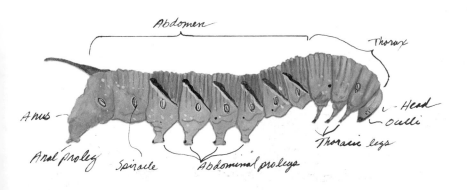

Abdomen

Thorax

Head
ocelli

Anus

Thoracic legs

Anal proleg

Spiracle

Abdominal prolegs

DO NOT STEP ON CATERPILLARS

Woolly Bear ACTUAL SIZE

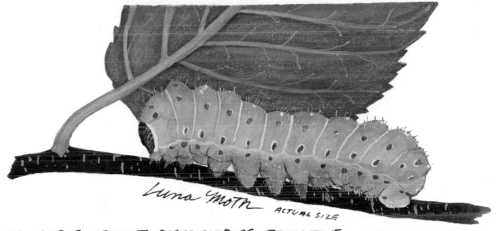

Luna Moth ACTUAL SIZE

Caterpillars have been likened to, and sometimes dismissed as, primitive feeding tubes with feet. In just two weeks of continuous eating after they hatch, monarch butterfly caterpillars reach 2,700 times their original weight. If a six-pound human baby did the same thing, it would weigh eight tons twelve days after birth.

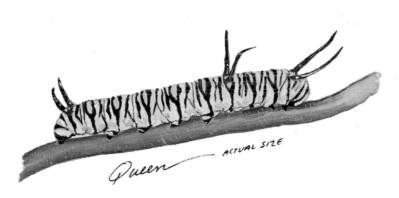

Queen ACTUAL SIZE

Monarch ACTUAL SIZE

Caterpillars are in fact complex animals, carrying within their cells everything necessary to create adult butterflies and moths. As they inch their way through larval life, they must protect themselves against countless predators in an eat-or-be-eaten world. Carnival colors advertise their poisonous dispositions, and some add spikes, hair, and other tactile warning signs to put off critters who might relish a juicy snack.

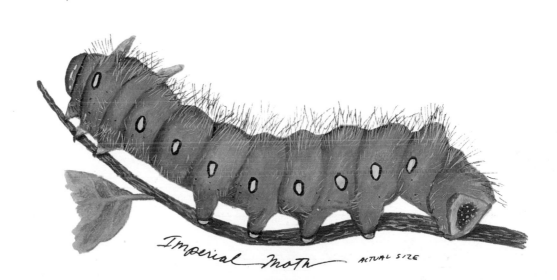

Imperial Moth ACTUAL SIZE

*L*EPIDOPTERA *B*ASICS:
*M*OTHS AND *B*UTTERFLIES

Butterfly (label)

Moth (label)

WINSOR & NEWTON
DESIGNERS'
GOUACHE
ALIZARIN
CRIMSON
14ml ℮
0.47 US Fl OZ

*V*IEWED THROUGH A STRONG MAGNIFYING LENS, THE WINGS OF THE MEMBERS OF THE INSECT ORDER LEPIDOPTERA PRESENT IMPRESSIONIST MASTERPIECES. ONLY 24 THOUSAND OF THE 140 THOUSAND SPECIES OF INSECTS WITH SCALY WINGS ARE BUTTERFLIES; THE REST ARE MOTHS. SOME AFICIONADOS JEST THAT ALL LEPIDOPTERA ARE MOTHS AND THAT BUTTERFLIES ARE MERELY SPECIAL MOTHS.

*G*ENERALLY SLIM-BODIED DAY FLIERS COLORED WINGS (WHICH THEY FOLD DAINTILY HAVE ANTENNAE THAT END IN LITTLE KNOBBED ILLUSTRIOUS IMAGO, OR ADULT BUTTERFLY, FROM A CHRYSALIS SPUN BY ITS CATERPILLAR

BUTTERFLY SCALES (label)

WITH GAILY PATTERNED AND WHEN ALIGHTING), BUTTERFLIES FINIALS. THE EMERGES ALTER EGO.

*N*ATURE KEEPS HUMAN OBSERVERS ON THEIR TOES, OFFERING MOTHS AS COLORFUL AS BUTTERFLIES, SUCH AS THE PALE GREEN LUNAS AND THE BIG, SHOWY CECROPIAS. SKIPPERS, MEANWHILE, ARE LARGE-BODIED, FURRY BUTTERFLIES.

MEMOIRS of a PAINTED LADY

Study of Painted Lady Butterfly Wings

From "Episodes of Insect Life" 1867

AFTER COMPLETING THE APPROPRIATE NUMBER OF MOLTS FOR THEIR SPECIES, EVERY LEPIDOPTERAN CATERPILLAR STOPS FEEDING AND PREPARES FOR METAMORPHOSIS. THE RADICAL TRANSFORMATION FROM CATERPILLAR TO IMAGO TAKES PLACE DURING THE PUPAL PHASE, INSIDE A COCOON OR CHRYSALIS MADE OF SILK SECRETIONS FROM THE CREATURE'S LABIAL GLANDS.

TO PROTECT ITSELF DURING THE IMMOBILE, VULNERABLE PUPAL STAGE, THE CATERPILLAR INSTINCTIVELY SPINS ITS TEMPORARY HOME IN ROCK CREVICES, AMID DENSE VEGETATION, UNDER THE BARK OF TREES, OR BENEATH MOSS. OFTEN RESEMBLING A DIMINUTIVE MUMMY, THE COCOON OR CHRYSALIS VARIES IN SHAPE, STRUCTURE, AND COLOR FROM SPECIES TO SPECIES.

DEPENDING ON LOCAL CONDITIONS, THE PUPAL PHASE MAY LAST ONLY TWO WEEKS, AS IN SOME FAMILIES OR MICROLEPIDOPTERA, OR MORE THAN TWO YEARS, AS FOR COSSID MOTHS. HAWK MOTH LARVAE PUPATE SIX INCHES BENEATH THE SOIL SURFACE, VIRTUALLY ENTOMBED DURING PERIODS OF DROUGHT WHEN THE GROUND BECOMES ROCK HARD. THEY WAIT TO EMERGE WHEN THEY SENSE THAT CONDITIONS ARE MORE PROPITIOUS.

ACTUAL SIZE

ATLAS MOTH

Moth. Scales

Snake-head pattern on forewing protects moth from predators.

Unscaled shiny areas reflect light to confuse predators.

MOTHS STEREOTYPICALLY SPORT EARTHY COLOR SCHEMES, LARGE FURRY BODIES, AND PLUMED, FEATHERY ANTENNAE. THEY FLY AT NIGHT, ALIGHTING WITH OPEN WINGS, AND MATURE FROM JUVENILE TO ADULT WITHIN COCOONS.

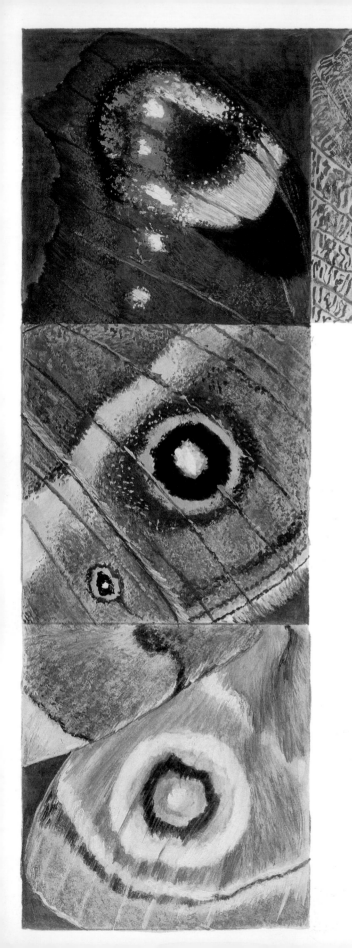

Eyespots

*I*T MAY SEEM THAT LARGE, LUSCIOUS
MOTH AND BUTTERFLY EYESPOTS WOULD ATTRACT MORE
ATTENTION THAN DESIRED IN A WORLD FULL OF PREDATORS.
BUT THESE INGENIOUS WING DESIGNS ALLOW FOR ONE OF
NATURE'S MOST EYE-CATCHING MEANS OF ESCAPE.

$\mathcal{M}$ANY MOTH AND BUTTERFLY SPECIES, SUCH AS THE PEARLY EYE BUTTERFLY AND THE POLYPHEMUS MOTH, NAMED FOR THE ONE-EYED GIANT OF GREEK MYTH, ARE IDENTIFIED BY FLAMBOYANT EYESPOT MARKINGS.

$\mathcal{S}$OME DOUBLE-SPOTTED MOTHS CONCEAL THEIR LUMINOUS HIND WING DESIGNS UNDER THE FOREWING. SHOULD A CURIOUS BEAK APPROACH, THE INSECT SUDDENLY FLASHES THE EYESPOTS AND THE WOULD-BE ATTACKER FINDS ITSELF STARING INTO A GLEAMING PAIR OF WIDE-SET GOGGLE-EYES. ALTHOUGH THE DECEPTION IS SHORT-LIVED, THE FEW SECONDS IT BUYS ARE JUST ENOUGH FOR THE BUG TO MAKE ITS GETAWAY.

$\mathcal{O}$THER SPECIES ARE LESS SECRETIVE WITH THEIR EYESPOTS. OFTEN A SERIES OF CONSPICUOUS ORBS OUTLINES THE WING, OFFERING COLORFUL TARGETS PURPOSEFULLY POSITIONED AWAY FROM VITAL ORGANS. THE WINGS OF BUTTERFLY SURVIVORS OF BIRD ATTACKS OFTEN SHOW BEAK MARKS FROM PREVIOUS NEAR MISSES.

Butterflies: Temperate Climes

Butterfly Babes — 1903

𝓔MBODYING THE SPIRIT OF SUMMER, BUTTERFLIES ANNOUNCE THE BEGINNING AND END OF THE FLOWER SEASON. THEIR NAME MAY HAVE COME FROM THE BUTTERY YELLOW BRIMSTONE SPECIES, ONE OF THE FIRST BUTTERFLIES TO APPEAR IN EUROPE EACH SUMMER.

European Brimstone
ACTUAL SIZE

Elysian Fields

Meadow-dwelling butterflies feed on grasses when they are caterpillars and on field flowers when adults.

The Aphrodite Butterfly, adorned in faux tortoise hues, enjoys sipping the nectar of violets in the open woodlands of North America.

A tawny sun worshiper, the Wall Butterfly basks on the ancient walls of Europe, North Africa, and Asia.

The radiant Adonis Blue Butterfly is now protected by French law from urban encroachment on its grassland habitat.

Hailing from the mountains of India and Thailand, the Bhutan Glory sports large eyespots and prominent tails that distract hungry birds but only make them more desirable to human butterfly collectors.

The Apollo Butterfly, snowy white with terra cotta dots, flies to Olympian heights in some of the highest mountains of Europe and Asia.

Wall Butterfly
ACTUAL SIZE

Aphrodite Butterfly
ACTUAL SIZE

Adonis Blue Butterfly
ACTUAL SIZE

Apollo Butterfly
ACTUAL SIZE

Bhutan Glory Butterfly
ACTUAL SIZE

Exotic Butterflies

Tropical Climes

IN THE CHIAROSCURO OF DENSE EQUATORIAL RAIN FORESTS, THE OUTLANDISH COLORS OF CERTAIN BUTTERFLIES STAND OUT LESS THAN ONE MIGHT IMAGINE, BUT ARE STILL DISTINCTIVE ENOUGH TO WARN OTHER ANIMALS AWAY FROM INEDIBLE PREY.

THE RARE PURPLE-AND-BLACK ROYAL ASSYRIAN BUTTERFLY IS SEEN ONLY BY THE LUCKY FEW NEAR ROCKY OUTCROPS, QUARRIES, OR ROADSIDES IN MALAYSIA AND INDONESIA.

PREDATORS BEDAZZLED BY THE GORGEOUS AZURE BLUE MORPHO BUTTERFLY OF SOUTH AMERICA ARE LEFT PERPLEXED AS IT SEEMS TO VANISH BEFORE THEIR VERY EYES. THE BRILLIANT BLUE WINGS HAVE A BROWN UNDERSIDE, SO WHEN THE BUTTERFLY ALIGHTS, WINGS UP, POOF! IT BECOMES JUST ANOTHER LEAF.

Royal Assyrian Butterfly
ACTUAL SIZE

Morpho   UPPER SIDE ACTUAL SIZE   UNDERSIDE

APTLY NAMED,
THE MOTHER OF PEARL
BUTTERFLY OF AFRICA
CATCHES THE LIGHT
ON IRIDESCENT WINGS.
ITS PEARLY COLORING
MAKES IT LOOK LIKE LEAF
LITTER WHEN IT SETTLES ON
THE FOREST FLOOR.

Mother of Pearl Butterfly ACTUAL SIZE

THE BIRDWING SWALLOWTAIL
FROM PAPUA NEW GUINEA HAS
METALLIC GREEN WINGS MARKED
WITH BLACK GRAPHICS, JOINED TO
A SCHOOL-BUS-YELLOW FUSELAGE
OF A BODY. THE GOLDEN
FRINGE WORN BY
MALES UNDER THEIR
HIND WINGS RADIATE
A SCENT IRRESISTIBLE
TO FEMALES DURING
COURTSHIP.
UNFORTUNATELY,
COLLECTORS HAVE ALSO
FOUND THEM HARD
TO RESIST, AND THEY
ARE NOW A PROTECTED
SPECIES.

Costume design for Adeline Genée in
the revival of "A Dream of Butterflies and Roses"
from watercolour by C. Wilhelm (1858-1925)

RAIN FOREST

A confetti of blue Morphea and other gaudily attired butterflies sambas through dense foliage. A caravan of ants pauses in the shade while sojourning in the rich tropical heat. The forest canopy hosts the aerial pandemonium of beetles who, eyes aglitter, stalk prey among the vine-clad trees.

Scientists who surveyed one tree in a rain forest canopy found over six hundred different species of beetles living there. But despite such robust fecundity, the rain forest is extremely fragile. All its species are extraordinarily interdependent, more than in any other ecosystem.

The luxuriance of the rain forest depends on the careful recycling of nutrients. The soil, while old and deep, is of very poor quality, but each year more than four tons of leaf litter falls on every acre of the forest floor. The woody tissues are gradually broken down by termites and the softer organic matter by mites. Other insects and the fungal mycorrhiza release the nutrients, which are taken up by plant roots.

Rajah Brooke's Birdwing Butterfly
ACTUAL SIZE

In this perpetually warm, damp climate, the world's largest plants are pollinated by some of the world's largest insects. The rain forest of Papua New Guinea is home to stick insects that can grow to the gargantuan proportions of a foot long. Birdwing swallowtail butterflies have wingspans of more than one foot.

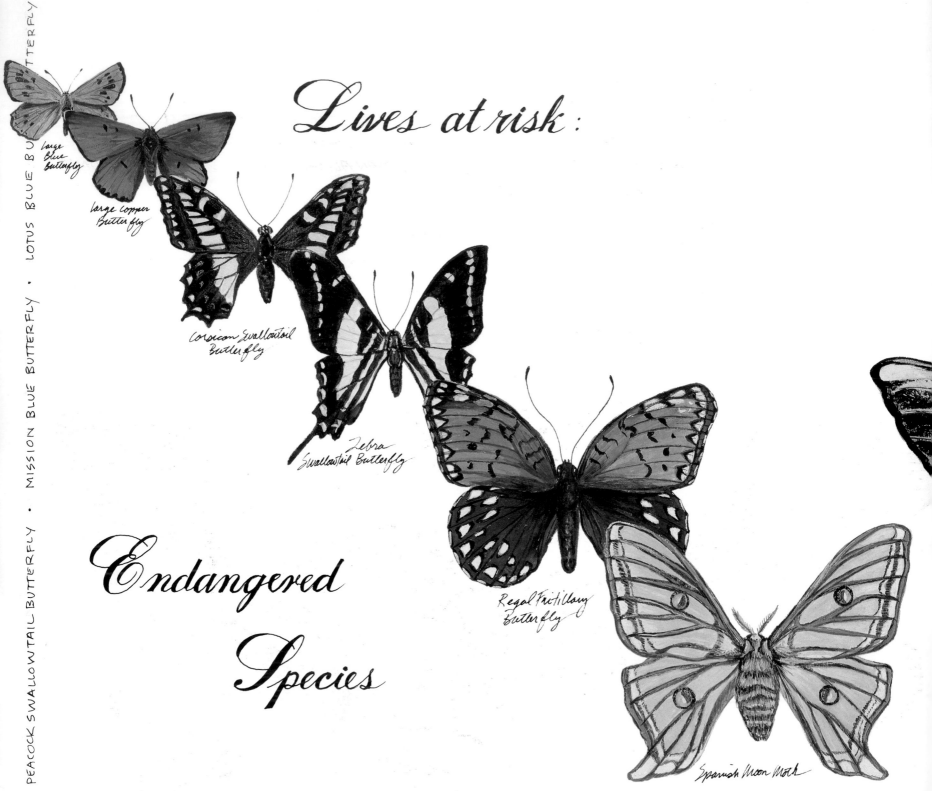

Lives at risk:

Endangered
Species

Large Blue Butterfly

Large Copper Butterfly

Corsican Swallowtail Butterfly

Zebra Swallowtail Butterfly

Regal Fritillary Butterfly

Spanish Moon Moth

LARGE BLUE BUTTERFLY · LOTUS BLUE BUTTERFLY · MISSION BLUE BUTTERFLY · LUZON PEACOCK SWALLOWTAIL BUTTERFLY

*L*IKE THE PROVERBIAL CANARY IN A COAL MINE, INSECTS ARE SENSITIVE GAUGES OF ENVIRONMENTAL CONDITIONS. TODAY THE WORLD'S MOST ADAPTABLE CREATURES ARE STRUGGLING TO COPE WITH THE IMPACT OF HUMAN ACTIVITY ON THE WORLD. SHOULDN'T THIS SERVE AS A POWERFUL WARNING TO THE REST OF US?

*U*NCONTROLLED INDUSTRIAL AND URBAN DEVELOPMENT, NOT TO MENTION PESTICIDE USE, KILLS INSECTS IN DROVES. MANY SPECIES ARE EITHER THREATENED, ENDANGERED, OR, LAMENTABLY, EXTINCT.

*T*ROUBLE FOR THEM IS TROUBLE FOR US ALL.

Queen Alexandra's Birdwing Butterfly

Homerus Swallowtail Butterfly

pecial effects

As they slowly glide close to the ground, hovering to feed, the satyrid and ithomii butterflies of Costa Rica are all but invisible with their crystalline wings. Many larval insect forms are translucent, if not transparent, blessed with the ultimate in camouflage.

Environmental changes can permanently alter the color of a camouflaged insect species. One moth in England is a case study of the process called industrial melanism. Originally a dappled beige, this species became charcoal tinged as the coal dust from mines and heating systems filled the air. Petroleum products gradually replaced coal, clearing the atmosphere sufficiently to allow the moths to revert to their original color.

Invisible ink

Some white, yellow, and red flower pigments fluoresce in ultraviolet light but seem to have no color in daylight. With these hues flower petals send secret messages to nectar-seeking insects, who can readily see them.

The metallic colors of beetles are produced by the onionlike layering of cuticle over underlying pigment. Light diffracts through these lamellae, or layers, which are separated by fluid, yielding iridescent effects. If a beetle becomes dehydrated, its colors will shift from green-gold to violet and finally to brown within less than one minute.

Fireflies are not flies at all but bioluminescent beetles. They have generated for millenia what people have only managed to produce very recently: cold light. Glowing insects make heatless light by oxidizing luciferin with the enzyme luciferase, within a specialized part of their abdomen called the lantern.

Child's Play

In Papua New Guinea the aquamarine Queen Alexander Bird Wing butterfly grows to a wingspan of up to one foot. Children carefully tie strings around the insects' thoraxes and joyously fly them like kites. African children fly large beetles in the same manner. The insects' buzzing wings produce the droning sound and appearance of bush biplanes.

Create summer magic in your garden — plant a garden full of flowers that will attract frolicsome butterflies. The Xerces Society, an organization concerned with the well-being of invertebrates, including arthropods, recommends thirty different types of readily available flowering plants.

Sunflower

Spike Gayfeather

Goldenrod

Japanese Privet

Glossy Abelia

Pincushion Flower

Cosmos

Frikart Aster

Red Valerian

Orange Milkweed

Daisy

Yellow Sage

Heliotrope

Day Lily

Summer Phlox

Purple Coneflower

Mint

Bee Balm

Zinnia

Only let your friendly robin catch butterflies in your butterfly garden.

JOE-PYE WEED

ENGLISH LAVENDER

BLACK-EYED SUSAN

FERNLEAF YARROW

JAPANESE HONEYSUCKLE

SUMMER LILAC

ROSEMARY

FRENCH MARIGOLD

SHOWY STONECROP

FLOWERING TOBACCO

PETUNIA

Moths

Most moths feed on flower nectar with long proboscises, but many large species do not feed at all as adults. The Indian moon moth lives entirely off of food stored in its body as a caterpillar.

Darwin's hawk moth
actual size

Darwin's hawk moth, from Madagascar, may have the world's longest tongue, which uncoils to the fantastic length of twelve inches. When naturalist Charles Darwin observed a Madagascan orchid with a base twelve inches long, he conjectured that there must be a local moth with a proboscis long enough to pollinate it. Years later, the discovery of the hawk moth proved Darwin's theory correct.

Indian Moon Moth
ACTUAL SIZE

𝒜 PIRATE AND A THIEF

𝒯HE DEATH'S HEAD HAWK MOTH
OF ASIA, AFRICA, AND EUROPE HAS A
CHUNKY BODY WITH A JOLLY ROGER SKULL
PATTERN ON ITS BACK. IT SQUEAKS IF IT IS
DISTURBED WHILE INDULGING IN STOLEN HONEY.

𝒯HE CATERPILLAR OF THE SWALLOWTAIL MOTH OF
ASIA AND EUROPE GETS WHERE IT'S GOING IN MUCH THE
SAME WAY AS ITS NORTH AMERICAN COUSIN. ITS
SCRUNCHING, LOOPING MOTION EARNS IT THE NAME
INCHWORM OR MEASURING WORM.

𝒯HE NORTH AMERICAN ROBIN MOTH HAS
THE FEATHERY ANTENNAE TYPICAL OF THE SATURNID
FAMILY OF MOTHS. THE FLUFFIER THE ANTENNA,
THE GREATER THE SURFACE AREA THAT CAN
PICK UP SCENT AND OTHER CHEMICAL
SIGNALS THAT GUIDE NIGHT
FLYERS MORE SURELY
THAN SIGHT.

*Death's Head
Hawk Moth*
ACTUAL SIZE

Exotic Moths

Sloan's Urainiid Moth
actual size

Butterflies have been described as flying flowers, but moths are peerless in their variation of color, pattern, and wing form.

Noctuids have irregular wing patterns that disguise their shape as well as their color.

The black-and-white caterpillar of the European Alder Moth looks like bird droppings. As it grows, its white marks are replaced with more aggressive orange stripes. Trick or treat!

The elaborate Rastafarian-colored Sloan's Urainiid Moth of Jamaica feeds on poisonous plants, thereby making its body fluids poisonous to other animals.

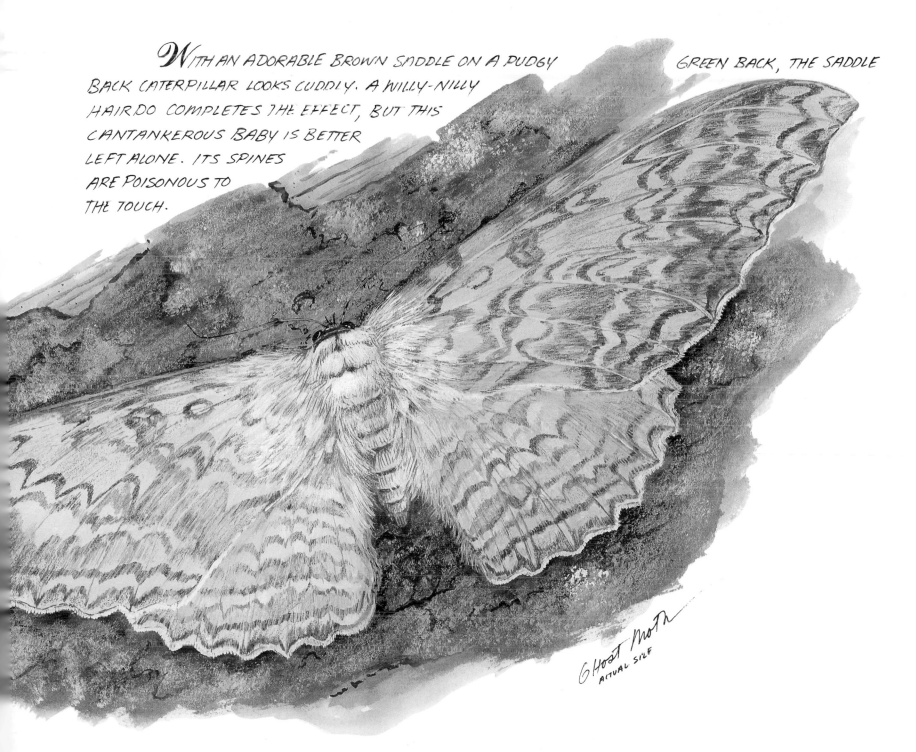

The GHOST MOTH OF CENTRAL AND SOUTH AMERICA IS THE SIZE OF A DINNER PLATE, A STAGGERING TWELVE INCHES ACROSS. WAVY LINES LIKE THE DESIGNS ON MARBLED PAPER HELP CAMOUFLAGE THIS GIANT AMONG TREE TRUNKS.

With AN ADORABLE BROWN SADDLE ON A PUDGY GREEN BACK, THE SADDLE BACK CATERPILLAR LOOKS CUDDLY. A WILLY-NILLY HAIRDO COMPLETES THE EFFECT, BUT THIS CANTANKEROUS BABY IS BETTER LEFT ALONE. ITS SPINES ARE POISONOUS TO THE TOUCH.

Ghost Moth
ACTUAL SIZE

SILK (ENGLISH) SIRKET (MONGOLIAN) SOIE (FRENCH)

Pastel-hued Silkworm cocoons

BUG BY-PRODUCTS:

Silk

DURING ITS LARVAL CAREER, BOMBYX MORI, A FUZZY WHITE TEDDY BEAR OF A MOTH, IS THE FAMOUS SILKWORM. ITS HUGE SALIVARY GLANDS SECRETE A FLUID WHICH, WHEN IT COMES INTO CONTACT WITH AIR, HARDENS AND BECOMES SILK. THE SILKWORM FORMS A COCOON WITH THIS THREAD AND MATURES INTO A MOTH IN ENVIABLE LUXURY.

SILK IS THE STRONGEST KNOWN FIBER. A SILK CABLE CAN SUSTAIN HEAVIER WEIGHTS THAN A METAL CABLE OF COMPARABLE DIMENSIONS.

CLINGING WITH AN EPHEMERAL LIGHTNESS, SILK CARESSES THOSE WHO WEAR IT WITH THE TACTILE EQUIVALENT OF MOONGLOW. THESE QUALITIES HAVE MADE SILK THE MOST SOUGHT-AFTER, JEALOUSLY GUARDED, AND FURIOUSLY DEFENDED OF FIBERS.

A NEWLY HATCHED FEMALE SILKWORM MOTH ON TOP OF HER EMPTY COCOON.

SETA (ITALIAN) SEIDE (GERMAN)

SERI (JAPANESE) SERIK (ARABIC) SERICUM (LATIN)

History credits Lady Hsi-Ling-Shi, wife of Emperor Huang-ti, with the discovery of silk in 2640 B.C. As she sipped tea in her garden one day, the cocoon of a pupating silkworm fell into her steaming cup. Reaching in to pluck out the little oblong, Hsi-Ling-Shi was surprised to find a mass of shimmery fibers. The sericin that makes silk cocoon fibers stick together had melted in the hot tea and the threads were released.

Merchants of old brought silk to the west along the great silk road, a trade route that extended more than six thousand miles from China to the northeast coast of the Mediterranean Sea. For many years silk was manufactured only in China, and the penalty for exporting silkworm eggs or cocoons from China was death. Then in 555 A.D. the great Justinian I, Emperor of the Eastern Roman Empire, commissioned two Nestorian monks to smuggle bamboo staffs full of eggs out of China. Westerners finally learned the secrets of making silk.

A great deal of labor, energy, and money goes into sericulture—the raising of silk worms. 1,700 cocoons yield but one silk dress; the nourishment of 1,100 caterpillars requires about 125 pounds of mulberry leaves.

Mulberry silkworm building a silk cocoon

GRANDVILLE

'A SILK MILL' GRANDVILLE 1803-1847

TUSSAH SILK WORMS

SILKE (SWEDISH) SEDA (SPANISH)

Arachnids

Whip spider

And along came a spider, and sat down beside her.

Arachnomania! Arachnophobia! Fossils tell us that spiders have been here, complete with silk-spinning apparatus, for about 380 million years. Their evolution is marked by several predatory highlights, including the development of venomous fangs. Above all else, spiders are remarkable for their use of silk to catch prey, ability to communicate by plucking, to transfer sperm, to protect their spiderlings, and to create silken balloons on which to fly away.

The class Arachnida includes spiders and relatives such as scorpions, creatures with no antennae, no wings, no compound eyes, a cephalothorax instead of a separate head and thorax, and an extra set of legs.

Tarantula

Fly away Spiderlings

*T*HIRTY-SIX THOUSAND SPECIES OF SPIDERS HAVE BEEN DESCRIBED BY ENTOMOLOGISTS, WHO ESTIMATE THAT THIS IS PROBABLY ONLY HALF THE NUMBER IN EXISTENCE. EACH SPECIES OF SPIDER HAS A DIFFERENT VENOM, A FACT WHICH IS CURRENTLY OF GREAT INTEREST TO MEDICAL RESEARCHERS. SPIDER VENOM IS NOW BEING USED IN NEUROLOGICAL STUDIES AS A BLOCKER ACROSS NERVE SYNAPSES.

*S*PIDERS ARE A DIVERSE GROUP OF PROBLEM-SOLVING JACKS-OF-ALL-TRADES. THEY HUNT, TRAP, AND RAID THE WEBS OF OTHER SPECIES, THEY GLUE PREY TO ANY SURFACE WITH ADHESIVE SPITBALLS, AND THEY CAN MAKE A GETAWAY BY SWINGING OFF, TARZAN-STYLE, ON A SILKEN THREAD OR BY TURNING INTO A LIVING WHEEL.

*D*ESPITE THEIR REPUTATION AS LONG-LEGGED BEASTIES, VERY FEW SPECIES ARE CAPABLE OF HARMING HUMANS. ONE BRITISH ARACHNOLOGIST ESTIMATED THAT SPIDERS IN BRITAIN ANNUALLY CONSUME MORE INSECTS, POUND PER POUND, THAN THE COMBINED WEIGHT OF THE COUNTRY'S HUMAN POPULATION. WITHOUT SPIDERS, THERE MIGHT BE LITTLE LEFT FOR ANYONE ELSE TO EAT. PERHAPS A LITTLE GRATITUDE IS IN ORDER.

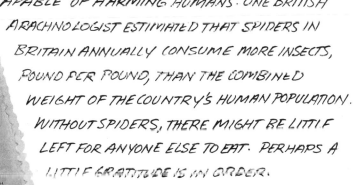

Garden Spider

WEBS

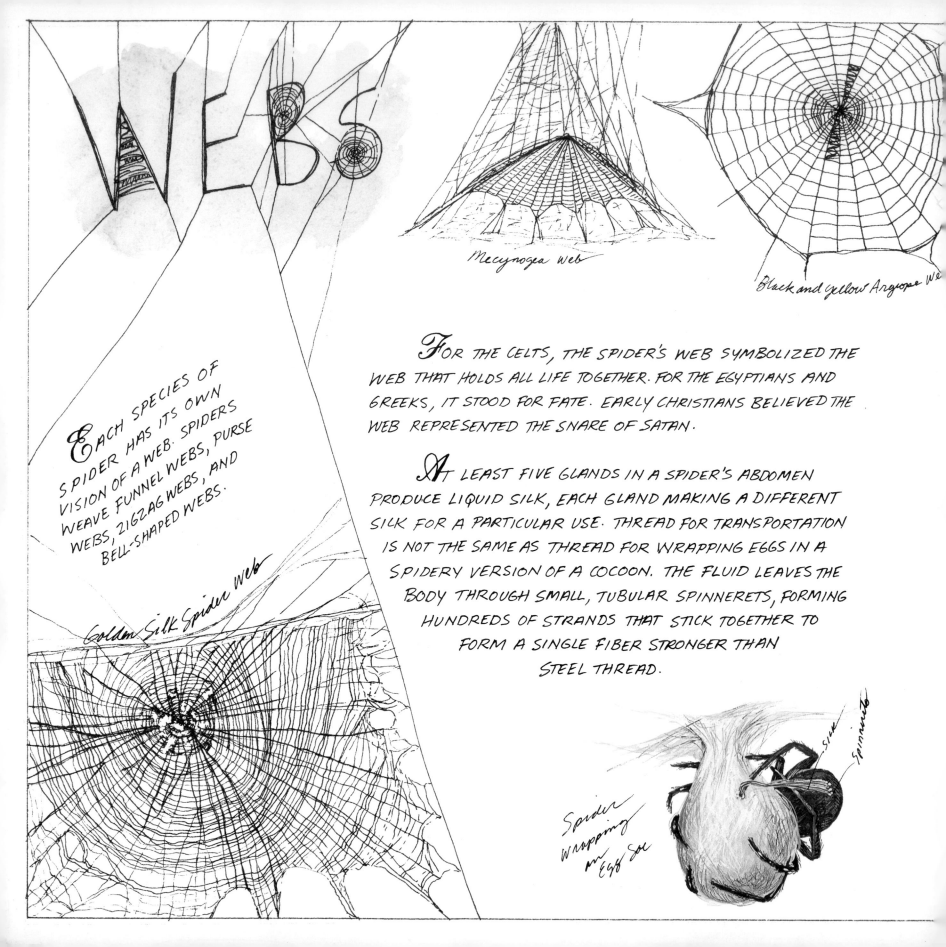

Mecynogea Web

Black and Yellow Argiope We

Each species of spider has its own vision of a web. Spiders weave funnel webs, purse webs, zigzag webs, and bell-shaped webs.

Golden Silk Spider Web

For the Celts, the spider's web symbolized the web that holds all life together. For the Egyptians and Greeks, it stood for fate. Early Christians believed the web represented the snare of Satan.

At least five glands in a spider's abdomen produce liquid silk, each gland making a different silk for a particular use. Thread for transportation is not the same as thread for wrapping eggs in a spidery version of a cocoon. The fluid leaves the body through small, tubular spinnerets, forming hundreds of strands that stick together to form a single fiber stronger than steel thread.

silk
spinnerets

Spider wrapping an Egg Sac

MAKING AN ORB WEB IN 12 EASY STEPS

ORB WEAVERS CREATE ROUND WEBS. GENERALLY NOCTURNAL, THEY REPAIR OR REPLACE THEIR WEBS NIGHTLY. DURING THE DAY THEY CAN OCCASIONALLY BE FOUND DOZING IN SILKEN HAMMOCKS INTO WHICH THEY HAVE WOVEN SPECIAL CAMOUFLAGE DESIGNS THAT MAKE THEIR BODIES DIFFICULT TO SEE.

Motif

LASTLY HIS SHINIE WINGS AS SILVER BRIGHT,
PAINTED WITH THOUSAND COLORS PASSING FARRE
ALL PAINTERS' SKILL HE DID ABOUT HIM DIGHT---

EDMUND SPENSER 1591

EVERY HUMAN ART FORM OFFERS DESCRIPTIONS OF THE PHYSICAL BEAUTY OF INSECTS, AT ONCE LITERAL, RESPLENDANT, AND MYSTERIOUS. THESE REPRESENTATIONS OFTEN IMBUE INSECTS WITH ALLEGORICAL AND SYMBOLIC MEANING. TRANSMIGRATION OF THE SOUL, REBIRTH, AND REINCARNATION HAVE ALL BEEN INTERPRETED THROUGH THE MEDIUM OF THE INSECT WORLD.

20th Century Italian Mosaic Button

18th Century French Button

18th Century French Button

Art Nouveau 19th Century Button

20th Century Italian Mosaic Button

20TH Century Italian Mosaic Button

18TH Century French Button

18TH Century French Button

18TH Century Irish Button

Comb of Tortoise Shell with Opal inlaid by Mucha 1901

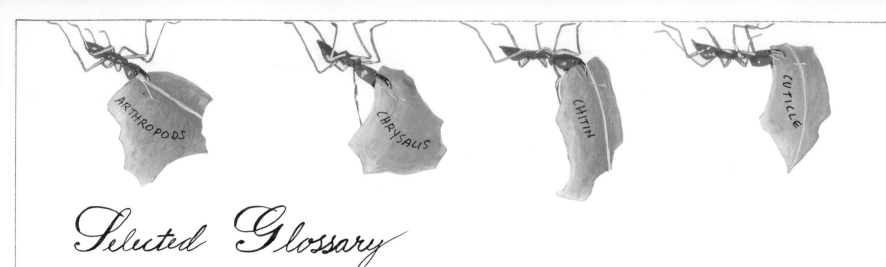

Selected Glossary

ARTHROPODS – PHYLUM OF ANIMALS WITH JOINTED BODY AND LEGS, AND A CHITINOUS SHELL. INCLUDES CRUSTACEANS, MILLIPEDES, CENTIPEDES, INSECTS, AND ARACHNIDS.

CHRYSALIS – THE COCOON OR PROTECTIVE SILK SACK WHICH ENCASES A CATERPILLAR WHILE IT CHANGES INTO A BUTTERFLY OR MOTH.

CHITIN – COMPOSITE OF SUGARS, STARCHES, AND PROTEINS, OF WHICH ARTHROPOD BODY PARTS ARE MADE.

COMPOUND EYES – EYES WITH INDIVIDUAL LIGHT-PROCESSING UNITS (CALLED OMMATIDIA) EACH CONSISTING OF A CRYSTALLINE CONE TOPPED BY A HEXAGONAL CORNEAL LENS. DIFFERENT SPECIES MAY HAVE AS FEW AS A DOZEN OR MORE THAN TWENTY THOUSAND LENSES PER EYE.

CUTICLE – MADE OF CHITIN, THIS IS A THIN LAYER OF CELLS COVERING AND PROTECTING THE ENTIRE SURFACE OF THE INSECT.

ENTOMOLOGY – THE STUDY OF INSECTS.

EXOSKELETON – A FRAMEWORK OF HOLLOW TUBES WHICH OFFERS THE INSECT BODY GREATER STRENGTH THAN THE INTERNAL HUMAN SKELETON OF SOLID BONES.

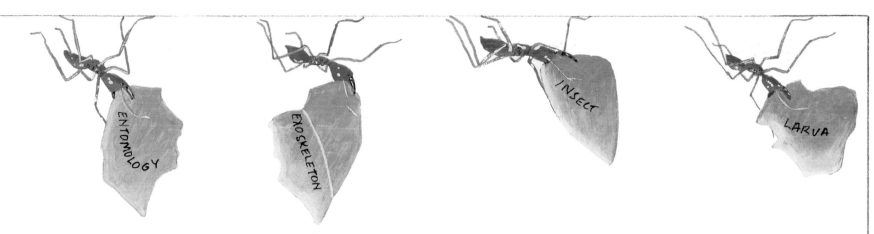

INSECT – A SMALL ANIMAL WITH SIX JOINTED LEGS AND A BODY DIVIDED INTO THREE MAIN PARTS: HEAD, THORAX, AND ABDOMEN. MOST INSECTS ALSO HAVE WINGS.

LARVA – THE IMMATURE, WINGLESS FORM OF MANY INSECTS WHICH HATCHES FROM THE EGG. DURING THE LARVAL STAGE, THE INSECT GROWS, PASSING THROUGH SEVERAL MOLTS UNTIL IT FINALLY IS TRANSFORMED INTO A PUPA.

METAMORPHOSIS – THE CHANGE IN FORM SOME INSECTS GO THROUGH IN ORDER TO REACH A MATURE SHAPE.

OCELLI – SIMPLE INSECT EYES WHICH CONSIST OF A DOME-SHAPED CORNEAL LENS, AND A LIGHT-SENSITIVE LAYER OF NERVES.

PUPA – THE INTERMEDIATE INSECT STAGE DURING WHICH THE INSECT FORMS A CHRYSALIS AROUND ITSELF AND MUTATES FROM ITS LARVAL FORM INTO ITS ADULT FORM.

SERICIN – THE "GLUE" PRODUCED BY THE SILKWORM WHICH MAKES THE SILK FIBERS STICK TOGETHER TO FORM A COCOON.

SETAE – BRISTLE-LIKE HAIRS OFTEN LOCATED ON INSECTS' LEGS, WHICH CONTAIN TOUCH-SENSITIVE NERVE ENDINGS THAT ARE STIMULATED WHEN AIR CURRENTS, WATER MOVEMENTS, OR ANY OTHER VIBRATIONS STIR THEM.

STRIDULATION – THE RUBBING TOGETHER OF VARIOUS BODY PARTS TO CREATE SOUND.

TAXONOMY – THE SYSTEMATIC CLASSIFICATION AND NAMING OF SPECIES.

TYMPANUM – THE INSECT VERSION OF AN EAR.

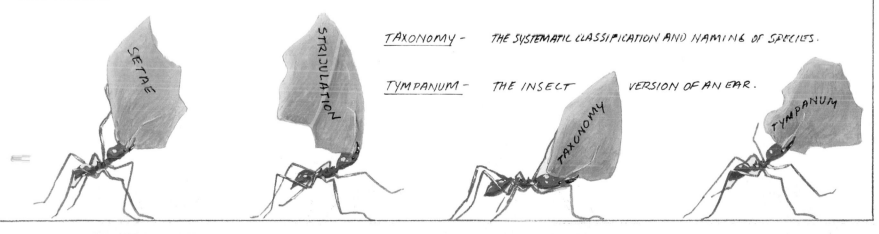

$\mathcal{I}$ REMAIN GRATEFUL AND HUMBLED BY SUCH SPLENDID AND INSPIRATIONAL VARIETY. I LONG TO BETTER UNDERSTAND THE COMPLEXITY AND FRAGILITY OF THE INSECTS ENTOMOLOGICAL PARADISE. MY DEEPEST GRATITUDE ALSO EXTENDS TO THE FOLLOWING INDIVIDUALS OR ORGANIZATIONS WHO MAKE THESE BOOKS A JOY TO CREATE.

TO KRISTIN JOYCE, MY CREATIVE PARTNER ON THESE PROJECTS, WHO NURTURES OUR FRIENDSHIP AS SHE CONTINUES TO CHALLENGE MY SKILLS AS AN ARTIST AND AS A NATURALIST. OUR LIVES ARE BLESSED AND CHANGED BY THESE EXPERIENCES. YOU ARE THE CURIOUS CREATURE I OBSERVE BUZZING ABOUT, CREATING THE REMARKABLE BUSINESS OF SWANS ISLAND BOOKS--EVEN WHILE IN REPOSE!

TO SHELLEI ADDISON, ANOTHER ASTONISHING TALENT, WHO IS BOTH AN AUTHOR AND THE OWNER OF A GREAT EDITORIAL ARTS BUSINESS, FLYING FISH BOOKS. YOU BREATHE GLORIOUS LIFE INTO THE TEXT WITH YOUR METICULOUS WORDS. AND TO CONSTANCE JONES FOR HER CRITICAL EDITING.

TO DON GUY, KRISTIN'S HUSBAND, FOR THE GREAT SPIRIT AND LOVE HE SHOWS US, AND FOR THE CONTRIBUTION OF HIS MANY, MANY RESOURCE BOOKS THAT ARE VITAL TO THESE PROJECTS.

TO PROFESSOR CAUSSANEL OF THE MUSÉE D'HISTOIRE NATURALE IN PARIS, AND MADAME RASSA, OF ORANGE, FOR THEIR HELP IN ARRANGING A REMARKABLE VISIT TO HARMAS IN PROVENCE, THE FORMER HOME AND CURRENTLY RENOWNED MUSEUM AND GARDENS OF THE LATE FRENCH ENTOMOLOGIST EXTRAORDINAIRE, J.H. FABRE.

TO THE CALIFORNIA ACADEMY OF SCIENCES FOR THE PRIVILEGE OF ONCE AGAIN RAMBLING THROUGH THEIR AMAZING BIODIVERSITY RESOURCES. SPECIAL THANKS TO NORMAN D. PENNY, P.H.D., SENIOR COLLECTIONS MANAGER FOR THEIR ENTOMOLOGY DEPARTMENT.

TO OUR FORMER PUBLISHER, THE DELIGHTFUL JENNY BARRY OF COLLINS PUBLISHERS SAN FRANCISCO, AND TO HER GREAT STAFF.

TO OUR EXCITING, NEW HOME WITH SMITHMARK PUBLISHERS AND TO THE CONTAGIOUS ENTHUSIASM OF OUR NEW PUBLISHER, MARTA HALLETT AND HER WONDERFUL EXECUTIVE EDITOR, ELIZABETH SULLIVAN.

TO THE XERCES SOCIETY FOR THEIR WILLINGNESS TO READ THE MANUSCRIPT AND FIND ANY 'BUGS' IN IT.

WITH LOVE, ALWAYS TO MY THREE CHILDREN, WENDY, SUNNY AND JONATHAN, FOR THEIR CEASELESS HELP AND ENCOURAGEMENT THROUGHOUT THE LONG DAYS AND NIGHTS OF PAINTING. A SPECIAL THANK YOU TO SUNNY FOR HER CREATIVE EYE.

Brush-footed
Butterfly wings
(*Limenitis bredowii*)

underside

Marigold
Yellow

Sky Blue
w/ Brilliant
Violet
+ White

Vandyke
Brown

Ivory
Black

Ivory
Black
w/ Olive Green

upperside

Wood Duck

Butterfly

tongue

Bee

Bumble Bee

Burnt
Sienna

Cadmium
Yellow
w/ Yellow
Ochre

Ivory Black

Vandyke
Brown

Spectrum
Violet

Foxglove

Bee Balm

Spectrum
Violet

Sap Green
w/ Yel. Ochre

Bengal
Rose

Red Ochre
w/ Bengal
Rose

Olive
Green

WINSOR & NEWTON
DESIGNERS
GOUACHE
YELLOW
OCHRE

Printed in Hong Kong by
Hong Kong Graphic and Printing Ltd.